Criminal Justice Act 199
LEGAL PO.
Commentary & Annotated

GW00870830

Criminal Justice Act 1991

LEGAL POINTS

Commentary & Annotated Guide for Practitioners

Editorial contributors

Andrew Ashworth
Professor of Criminal Law and Criminal Justice, King's College, University of London. Editor of the Criminal Law Review

Paul Cavadino
Clerk to the Parliamentary All-Party Penal Affairs Group and Principal Information Officer, NACRO

Bryan Gibson
Clerk to the North-west Hampshire Justices and a former co-editor of Justice of the Peace. Author of Unit Fines (Waterside Press, 1990)

John Harding
Chair of the Association of Chief Officers of Probation Young Offenders Committee. Chief Probation Officer for Hampshire

Andrew Rutherford
Director of the Institute of Criminal Justice, University of Southampton. Chairman of the Howard League. Author of Prisons and the Process of Justice (Heinemann, 1984) and Growing Out of Crime (Penguin, 1986)

Peter Seago JP
Head of Department, Centre for Criminal Justice Studies, University of Leeds

Lorna Whyte
Principal Officer, Courts and Adolescent Services, Hammersmith and Fulham Social Services Department, and with a special interest in Discrimination in the Justice System

Criminal Justice Act 1991

LEGAL POINTS

Commentary & Annotated Guide for Practitioners

WATERSIDE PRESS

Criminal Justice Act 1991

LEGAL POINTS

Commentary & Annotated Guide for Practitioners

Published 1992 by
WATERSIDE PRESS
Domum Road
Winchester SO23 9NN

ISBN Paperback 1 872870 04 X

One of three books on the Criminal Justice Act 1991 produced by an editorial team for Waterside Press. The other books in the series are:

Introduction to the Criminal Justice Act 1991

ISBN 1 872870 02 3

and

The Youth Court ISBN 1 872870 031

Printing & binding Copyman, Jewry Street, Winchester SO23 8RZ

Foreword

This is one of three books on the Criminal Justice Act 1991 written by an editorial team with wide experience of the issues and a diversity of perspectives. The aims have been: to present all the main aspects of the new law (as it affects sentencing) in a form which meets the needs of both the seasoned practitioner and the general reader; to do this with reference to the background to the Act and the thinking which underpins it; and to cast light on how the Act works as a whole, via regular themes and interdependent parts.

One common link between the contributors is that they each take a positive view of the Act and of its potential to effect reform. The legislation calls, at the very least, for a reappraisal of existing ideas and approaches to sentencing, and at certain points for much more by way of change. Understood and applied as intended, the Act may be seen, with hindsight, as the single most important criminal justice measure this century. An attempt is made in each of the three texts to emphasise points of similarity with, and of divergence from, existing law and practice. The books, which complement one another, are as follows:

Introduction to the CRIMINAL JUSTICE ACT 1991 This is a basic guide to the new law for general readers. The book contains an outline of the Act, including sections on General Principles, Custodial Sentences, Community Sentences, Unit Fines and Anti-discrimination. There are also *summaries* of the provisions concerning the Youth Court and of Parole and Early Release of Prisoners (the first of these dealt with more fully in the separate work below). In relation to unit fines, the book draws freely on experiences in the pilot areas since 1988 and contains information which is essential to implementation of the new system.

The Youth Court This work is designed to meet the needs of all those involved in the new court. The items covered include jurisdiction, powers and procedures. There is a chapter on remands, including changes scheduled to come into force over the next few years. The book examines developments which have taken place concerning juveniles and young adults in recent years, and places the youth court in context. Summaries of existing sentencing rulings appear in *Chapter 5A, Custody. Statutory Provisions* are reproduced at the end of certain chapters where these provisions relate to 10 to 17 year olds. The Act's more general provisions are mentioned in the text of each chapter and can be found reproduced in full in *Legal Points.*

Criminal Justice Act 1991 LEGAL POINTS Commentary & Annotated Guide for Practitioners This book adopts a style similar to that of the standard legal work *Criminal Jurisdiction of Magistrates*. Each chapter contains a technical legal commentary followed by annotated *Statutory Provisions*. Legal provisions which refer exclusively to, or are more closely associated with, people below the age of 18 are mentioned in the text of *Legal Points* and dealt with in greater detail in *The Youth Court* (including, for convenience, the new children's evidence provisions). Sentencing rulings on cases dealt with under the Criminal Justice Act 1982 are summarised as background information in *Chapters 2, Seriousness* and *3, Protection of the Public*.

Method
In the first instance, chapters were written by individual contributors and according to areas of special expertise. The majority of the contributions were then read by two or three further contributors (in some instances by all) and revised in the light of comments, suggestions and additions. Each manuscript was then adapted to a common style.

Acknowledgements
The work did not begin and end with the seven contributors. Special thanks are also due to: Gordon Barclay (Home Office Statistical Branch, who supplied the graphs and charts which appear in two of the books), Sue Rex, Vikki Harris, John Griffin, Robert Stevens, Jane Oswell and many others who have assisted in the production or provided important information.

Commencement of the Act
At the time of going to press, the main body of the Act is scheduled for implementation in October 1992.

There have been two commencement orders: the Criminal Justice Act 1991 (Commencement No 1) Order 1991 SI 2208 and the Criminal Justice Act 1991 (Commencement No 2 and Transitional Provisions) Order 1991 SI 2706. Relevant information is given in the texts as appropriate (and in *Legal Points* and *The Youth Court* in the *Notes to Statutory Provisions*). The main transitional provisions are contained in schedule 12 to the Act which is reproduced in *Chapter 12* of *Legal Points*.

Bryan Gibson, Coordinating Editor
20 January 1992.

Criminal Justice Act 1991

LEGAL POINTS

Commentary & Annotated Guide for Practitioners

CONTENTS

Chapter

Each chapter contains a *Commentary* followed by selected *Statutory Provisions* in chronological order, first of Acts of Parliament and then of any Rules or Regulations. Sections or paragraphs are accompanied by explanatory *Notes* as appropriate. *Chapter 2* contains selected rulings on the meaning of 'seriousness' under s1(4) Criminal Justice Act 1982.

WATERSIDE PRESS

Criminal Justice Act 1991

LEGAL POINTS

Commentary & Annotated Guide for Practitioners

Abbreviations used in this work

CYPA 1933 Children and Young Persons Act 1933

CJA 1967 Criminal Justice Act 1967

CYPA 1969 Children and Young Persons Act 1969

PCCA 1973 Powers of Criminal Courts Act 1973

MCA 1980 Magistrates' Courts Act 1980

CJA 1982 Criminal Justice Act 1982

MHA 1983 Mental Health Act 1983

CJA 1988 Criminal Justice Act 1988

CJA 91 or 'the Act' Criminal Justice Act 1991

Statutory Provisions Certain provisions of the Criminal Justice Act 1991 are mentioned in several chapters. They are located as follows: s1 (restrictions on custodial sentences): *Chapter 4*; s2 (length of custodial sentences): *Chapter 4*; s3 (procedural requirements for custodial sentences): *Chapter 8*; s6 *et al* (restrictions on community sentences): *Chapter 5*; s18 *et al* (fixing fines by reference to units): *Chapter 6*; s25 (committal for sentence - see s38 MCA 1980): *Chapter 4*; s28 (savings for mitigation, etc): *Chapter 1*; s29 (effect of previous convictions, etc) *Chapter 1*; s31 (definitions): extracts in individual chapters as appropriate.

Chapter 1

Introduction

The Criminal Justice Act 1991 contains 102 sections and 13 schedules. The impact is considerable and the changes fundamental and wide ranging. The Act is unique as a criminal justice measure in introducing legal provisions linked by regular themes and a common philosophy. The individual sentencing provisions are more readily understood when viewed against this background and the totality of the changes. The Act works best when viewed as a whole and familiarity with *all* its main provisions enhances understanding about each. The chapters which follow have been written with this in mind.

The New Sentencing Framework
The central feature of the CJA 91 is a new sentencing framework contained in Part I. There are two dimensions: first, the Act establishes criteria for the use of custody, community sentences and fines, together with some new, or altered, sentencing powers; second, it links these options via comparable procedures, approaches and terminology. The framework comprises:

Custody
Standard criteria are applied to custodial sentences, irrespective of the age of the offender or the legal power under which the sentence is passed. The main provisions are s1 to s5 CJA 91, discussed in *Chapter 4, Custody*. The use of custody will depend on the *seriousness* of the offence (*Chapter 2*) or the need to *protect the public* from serious harm from the offender (*Chapter 3*): s1(2)(a) and (b), *ibid*. Custody may also be used where the offender refuses to consent to a community sentence which requires that consent: s1(3), *ibid*. 'Custodial sentence' means: imprisonment where the offender is 21 years of age or over; or, if 15 to 20, detention in a young offender institution, or under s53 CYPA 1933, or custody for life under s8(2) CJA 82: s31(1) CJA 91. No restrictions attach where the sentence is 'fixed by law' (ie a life sentence for murder): s1(1) CJA 91. Partly suspended sentences are abolished: s5(2)(b); as are extended sentences of imprisonment: s5(2)(a). Ordinary suspended sentences of imprisonment continue: s22 PCCA 1973, as amended by s5(1) CJA 91. As under existing law, suspended sentences are *not* available for offenders below the age of 21 years.

Community sentences
The Act introduces 'community *sentences*'. These comprise one or more of a range of six 'community *orders*' (note the terminology). These orders can be used individually, or in combination (with one exception in relation to

combination orders, *post*), and in conjunction with financial penalties. The main provisions are s6 to s13 CJA 91. The new range of community orders, depending on age, is as follows:

Age 16 years upwards: **probation**: s2, 3 PCCA 73, as substituted by s8, 9 CJA 91; **community service**: s14, 15 PCCA 73, as amended by s10 CJA 91; **combination order**: s11 CJA 91* ; **curfew order**: s12 CJA 91*. *Age 10 to 17 years inclusive*: **supervision order**: s7(7), s12 CYPA 1969 (largely unaffected by the CJA 91 except for new enforcement procedures and the fact that this new age range is introduced by s68 and sched 8 CJA 91). *Age 14 to 20 years inclusive*: **attendance centre order**: s17, 18 CJA 82, as amended by s67 CJA 91.

The new orders are marked with an asterisk. A 'combination order' combines probation and community service (in consequence of which probation orders and community service orders cannot, themselves, be combined with one another: s6(3) CJA 91). According to the Home Office *General Guide to the Criminal Justice Act 1991* (Home Office, 1991), the combination order '... is aimed particularly at persistent property offenders, who might now be given custody'. The other new order, the 'curfew', can be supplemented by a condition of electronic monitoring when this facility becomes available: s13 CJA 91. Community sentences are intended as *Restrictions on liberty*: this chapter *post*. Whilst such sentences feature between custody and financial penalties in terms of their general severity, ie the extent to which they restrict liberty, individual community orders, or mixes of orders, do not form any tariff or hierarchy. They can only be used if commensurate with seriousness: s6(1), although the precise restrictions on liberty, ie the which order or orders are used will depend on balancing the seriousness of the *offence* and what is suitable for the *offender*: s6(2), *ibid*. These matters are discussed in *Chapter 5, Community Sentences*.

Financial penalties
The Act introduces a new system of unit fines based on the experiences of four pilot projects since 1988. Unit fines will apply in magistrates' courts to offenders who are *individuals*, ie as opposed to *corporations*. The principal provisions are contained in s17 to s23 CJA 91. A separate scheme for attaching income support is introduced by s24, *ibid*. These items are dealt with in *Chapter 6, Unit Fines*. The unit method represents a significant change in the way fines are imposed. It involves setting fines in accordance with the formula in s18(2) CJA 91 which can be simplified as follows:

units of seriousness x disposable weekly income.

Units are determined on a scale rising from one to a maximum of 50 units according to the seriousness of the individual offence and its 'level' on the standard scale s37(2) Criminal Justice Act 1982. The number of units must be commensurate with the seriousness of the offence. Disposable weekly income is discerned via a prescribed means enquiry form by the application of assessment rules set out in the Magistrates' Courts (Unit Fines) Rules 1992 (in draft). The Crown Court will continue to use 'cash fines' (but see the note on this in *Chapter 6*). Cash fines will also be used in the magistrates' court for corporations, local authorities etc, and in relation to (a relatively few) offences where statute provides for unusually high maximum fines on summary conviction, eg under s9 or s10 Video Recordings Act 1984 (£20,000). The principle is introduced that 'cash fines' must be *increased* or *decreased* to take account of means (so far as known to the court): s19(2) CJA 91; something implicit with unit fines: s18(2).

Discharges
The Act does *not* make any substantive changes to the legal provisions applicable to absolute discharges or conditional discharges. However, sched 1 CJA 91 inserts new provisions in the PCCA 73 to bring the relevant law into line with that in the rest of the CJA 91: see s1A to 1C PCCA 1973 reproduced in *Chapter 12*.

General principles
The Act does not alter existing sentencing principles except insofar as these are in conflict with the new thinking, such as deterrent sentencing which is inconsistent with the commensurate approach, *semble* (see the discussion on *Punishment and Proportionality* in *Chapter 2* of *Introduction to the Criminal Justice Act 1991*). Otherwise, these general considerations remain but are not the subject matter of this work, eg: discount for a guilty plea; the effect of age or maturity on sentence (but see *The Youth Court*); the effect of the sentence on others such as family (which can be relevant: see, eg *Franklyn* (1981) 3 Cr App R (S) 65); or conduct of the offender unconnected with the offence itself (see *Reid* (1982) 4 Cr App R (S) 280 (rescuing children)); or collateral effects (*Grant* (1990) 12 Cr App R (S) 441 (community service used where custody would have ended employment), *Rees* (1982) 4 Cr App R (S) 71 (custody would have resulted in discharge from the army)). The new framework introduces one important general approach:

Aggravating and mitigating factors
In practice, courts must identify *aggravating* and *mitigating* factors in each case. The court is required to consider *all* such information about the circumstances of an offence, including any aggravating or mitigating factors, as is available to it: s3(3) (custody), s7(1) (community sentences), s18(3) (unit fines). This must include a *Pre-sentence Report* in those situations detailed in *Chapter 8*. An important general provision is s28 CJA 91 which deals with mitigation and states as follows: '(1) Nothing ... shall prevent a court from mitigating an offender's sentence by taking account of any such matters as, in the opinion of the court, are relevant in mitigation of sentence. (2) Without prejudice to the generality of subsection (1) above, nothing ... shall prevent a

court - (a) from mitigating any penalty included in an offender's sentence by taking account of any other penalty included in that sentence; or (b) in a case of an offender who is convicted of one or more other offences, from mitigating his sentence by applying any rule of law as to the totality of sentences'. This is the first time that a provision concerning mitigation or the 'totality principle' (see s28(2)(b), *ibid*) has appeared in a sentencing statute (although, in fact, both principles exist at common law). Section 28(3) applies the mitigation principle to the unit fines system by stating that 'Any mitigation ... shall be effected by determining ... a smaller number of units than would otherwise have been determined'. Mitigation may be on the basis of any matters which, in the opinion of the court, '... are relevant in mitigation of sentence'. This would include matters affecting the seriousness of the *offence* or matters relevant to the *offender*. The latter can always affect the final disposal. It is debatable whether matters concerning the offender can in fact affect the seriousness of the offence (cf *R v Doncaster Justices, ex p Boulding* (1991), *The Independent*, October 30). Some early comment on the Act suggested that the custodial provisions might prove counter-productive in that once either the new 'seriousness' test in s1(2)(a) CJA 91 is satisfied (ie '... *only* [a custodial sentence] is justified') the court has no option but to sentence to custody. Section 28 counters this view.

Mentally disordered offenders
In relation to mentally disordered offenders, s28(4) CJA 91 is quite specific as to the power to mitigate. The subsection provides that nothing shall be taken: '(a) as requiring a court to pass a custodial sentence, or any particular custodial sentence on a mentally disordered offender; or (b) as restricting any power (whether under the [Mental Health Act 1983] or otherwise) which enables a court to deal with such an offender in the manner it considers to be most appropriate in all the circumstances'.

Common themes
The second aspect of the sentencing framework lies in several common underlying themes which emerge as follows:

Proportionality in sentencing: First, and foremost, the sentence for a given offence should reflect the seriousness of the offence, sometimes called the 'just deserts' principle (see the White Paper, *Crime, Justice and Protecting the Public*, 1990, Cm 965) or 'justice model'. Proportionality is not a novel idea. The principle has been regularly applied in Court of Appeal rulings in recent years. But there are several differences between the existing approach and that under the CJA 91. The principle is employed to a greater degree than before and in a clearly structured way. The Act does not use the term 'proportionality'. The key word, which appears repeatedly throughout the CJA 91, is 'commensurate', ie the sentence should be commensurate with the seriousness of the offence: see, eg s2(2)(a) (custody); s6(2)(b) (community sentences); and s 18(2)(a) (unit fines). *Seriousness* is discussed in *Chapter 2*.

14

Protection of the public: The Act recognizes that with *violent* or *sexual* offences a purely proportionate, or commensurate, approach to sentencing may not be adequate to protect the public from serious harm from the offender. Special provision for these offences (defined in s31) *only* is a feature of the Act. A sharper distinction than hitherto is drawn generally between property offences and offences against the person. This can be seen in the reduction of the maximum penalty for theft from ten to seven years: s7 Theft Act 1968, as amended by s26 CJA 91; the inclusion of the offence of indecent assault, within the ambit of s53(2) CYPA 1933 (committal of persons under 18 to the Crown Court for trial in respect of 'grave crimes') where the offender is aged 16 or 17 even though it does not carry the 14 year maximum penalty 'in the case of an adult' normally demanded by s53(2); and in relation to more onerous conditions which can be attached to probation orders for sexual offences: sched 1A PCCA 1973, para 4 (as inserted by sched 1 CJA 91). The approach stems from widening acceptance that custodial sentences for minor property offences do more harm than good, and that, particularly for younger people, their effect can be to introduce the offender to more advanced forms of criminality. This, together with a strengthened scheme of community sentences means that many less serious *property* based crimes which might previously have led to custody may, in future, be dealt with by lesser disposals. In contrast, custodial sentences can be used for violent or sexual crimes to protect the public from future harm from the offender. It will be possible for courts to use sentences for these offences which are *longer* than is commensurate with seriousness (within the maximum penalty for the offence): s2(2)(b) CJA 91. *Protection of the Public* is discussed in *Chapter 3*.

Punishment: Just deserts connotes punishment. There is a sense in which punishment unencumbered by secondary considerations comes to the fore under the Act. Seriousness will normally determine the general level of punishment (ie whether the custody threshold has been reached: s1(2)(a) CJA 91; the community sentence threshold: s6(1), *ibid*; the number of units for a fine: s18(2)(a), *ibid*), albeit that other considerations may then come into play which may lessen the final penalty (as to mitigation see s28 CJA 91) or dictate the choice of a particular community order or mix of orders (see *Chapter 5*). Punishment, pure and simple, over and done with once the penalty has been paid, could be said to be a hallmark of the Act. This also helps to explain why previous convictions cannot increase the seriousness.

Previous record: It follows from the proportionate sentencing approach that the offender's record of previous convictions, or his or her response to previous sentences, is not directly relevant to the setting of a commensurate sentence for the present offence. One of several key provisions, s29 CJA 91 provides that: '(1) An offence shall not be regarded as more serious ... by reason of any previous convictions of the offender or any failure of his to respond to previous sentences.' However, importantly, s29 continues: '(2) Where any *aggravating factors* of an offence are disclosed by the circumstances of other offences committed by the offender, nothing ... shall prevent the court from taking those factors into account for the purpose of forming an opinion as to the seriousness of the offence.' (italics supplied). Section 29(1) is of general application to all types of sentence, as is the exception concerning aggravating factors in s29(2). Again, this approach is not inconsistent with some existing Court of Appeal rulings and dicta: see *Chapter 2*. However, the bald proposition that previous convictions cannot be taken into account may seem strange to magistrates who, until the CJA 91, have been used to committing cases to the Crown Court for a more severe sentence than the six months which they can impose, on the basis of 'character and antecedents', primarily the offender's record of previous convictions: s38 MCA 1980. To reinforce matters, the power of committal for sentence is altered in line with proportionality and protection of the public: see s38 MCA 1980 as amended by s25 CJA 91. Courts are *not* debarred from taking earlier convictions into account in relation to the 'protection of the public' criterion, either by s29 CJA 91 or any other provision.

A definite meaning to sentences: Sentences which are commensurate with seriousness, or which are increased to protect the public, ought to be more readily understood by offenders and by the public. Potentially, sentences should be less disparate judged one against another. Courts will have a duty to give reasons, *inter alia*, for decisions to use custody: s1(4) CJA 91; and when passing a sentence in respect of a violent or sexual offence which is longer than is commensurate with seriousness: s2(3), *ibid*. There is a further sense in which sentences will have a definite meaning for the courts, the public and offenders. To ensure that the administration and carrying out of sentences is rigorous and fair, including proper enforcement, the Act introduces new powers and procedures under which, for example, those who fail to carry out community orders will, in most instances, be at risk of resentencing (see, eg sched 2 CJA 91). The new unit fine scheme supplies the route to improved collection of monies (*Home Office Research and Planning Unit Paper No 59*, Moxon, Sutton and Hedderman, HMSO, 1990, at p 17) provided that the court maintains a proper focus on the the means of each individual offender at the original sentencing hearing or by making appropriate adjustments in enforcement proceedings where the Act allows this: *Chapter 6*.

Custody will have a more definite meaning due to a new system of *Parole and Early Release*, *Chapter 10*, *post*, introduced by Part II of the Act. These provisions restructure the parole scheme, abolish remission on custodial sentences and introduce new, more definite rules for early release on licence of prisoners sentenced to below 12 months and to 12 months but below four years. Many prisoners will serve longer in custody. They will also be liable to recall, or 'at risk', during the whole of the remainder of the sentence. Magistrates' courts are given power to fine released prisoners for breach of the conditions of their licence: s38(1) CJA 91; and to suspend the prisoner's licence and to order his or her recall to prison: s38(2). The parole and early release provisions are a good example of how the provisions of the CJA 91 interact. Unless there is a downwards adjustment to lengths of custodial sentences generally (made possible by the fact that strengthened community sentences may now cater for those who might previously have received short custody sentences) there could be an unplanned escalation in the prison population. This might be made worse by the new 'at risk' (of return to prison) provisions for those released on licence. The Carlisle Report (*The Parole System in England and Wales: Report of the Review Committee*, 1988, Cm 532) on which the new provisions are based said its proposed scheme '... should provide the springboard for a thorough re-assessment of present sentencing levels. We therefore recommend that the implementation of our proposals should be accompanied by a determined attempt on the part of the government and the judiciary to secure a corresponding reduction in sentencing at all levels ... [We] are quite clear that it would be an unbalanced approach and add undesirably to the overall quantum of punishment to enhance the meaning of sentences in the way we propose without at the same time working for a reduction in present tariffs, which have evolved within a quite different framework': pp 72-73.

Other steps towards giving sentences more definite meaning can found in the *National Standards* for sentences supervised by the probation service currently being devised and introduced by the Home Office. These will operate alongside *National Standards* for new style 'pre-sentence reports' (PRS), which *inter alia* will have to target seriousness and protection of the public as well as the suitability of the offender for particular sentences: see *Chapter 8*.

'Alternatives to custody' disappear: Under the CJA 91, community orders become sentences in their own right, not 'alternatives to custody'. Probation orders, for example, become 'sentences' proper for the first time: one effect of s6(1) and (4) CJA 91. The only exception to this (and an apparent anomaly, given the new way of thinking) is contained in s12D CYPA 1969 under which a court may certify that it is using a supervision order for a person under 18 *instead of* a custodial sentence: see *The Youth Court, Chapter 5B*.

Restrictions on liberty: The idea that sentences are 'restrictions on liberty' is part of the thinking which underlies the Act, not just community sentences, *supra*. Custody is an obvious form of restriction; whereas a fine restricts the offender's freedom to spend to the extent of his or her weekly disposable income under the unit method. Community orders are expressly measured for severity by the extent to which they restrict liberty in a given case. Section 6(4) CJA 91 requires that '... the restrictions on liberty imposed by the order or orders shall be ... commensurate with the seriousness of the offence ...'.

Law and policy
The essential messages of the Act are made explicit in various official

publications. These started with the White Paper *Crime, Justice and Protecting the Public, supra*, on which the Act was based, and the Green Paper, *Punishment, Custody and the Community* (1989, Cm 424). They culminate in a series of short, official guides to the Act issued by the Home Office and circulated to those directly concerned with implementation. The success or failure of the Act may well depend on the extent to which courts are prepared to exercise their judicial function against this background to the provisions. There is also the question whether various key decision makers (within the courts, probation service, social services departments, police and Crown Prosecution Service) will respond by altering existing views and practices to adjust to what, in some instances, are cultural changes. Clearly, there must be a balance between the legitimate wishes of the executive in witnessing proper delivery of the Act and the interdependent roles of criminal justice practitioners, always allowing for the special position of the judiciary. Whatever voice government has during the implementation process concerning its own view of the new framework and philosophy, judicial interpretation and discretion will ultimately determine the course of events. Equally, it would be wrong for courts to ignore certain points fundamental to the changes.

The Youth Court (and other reforms affecting young people)
A main change brought about by Part III of the Act is the replacement of the juvenile court by a new youth court, which will deal with persons below the age of 18. The significance lies as much in the structural arrangements for the new court, and the fact that it will undoubtedly attract special attention from practitioners across the criminal justice process, as in any alterations to magistrates' sentencing powers as they relate to the new 10 to 17 year (inclusive) age group. The youth court provisions are reinforced by a new onus on parental responsibility in relation to younger offenders. The Act brings about other important changes affecting young people in relation to the the law of evidence. This is revised to allow testimony to be given unsworn, and video evidence to be received in some instances. An outline of these matters is contained in *Chapter 7*. A full treatment can be found in the companion volume to this work, *The Youth Court*. The CJA 91 also introduces a new system of remand for juveniles awaiting trial or sentence. The remand of juveniles to prison under what are currently termed 'unruly certificates' is to be phased out in favour of 'remands to local authority accommodation'. There is a transitory stage until then. The remand provisions are of general application but for convenience are included in *The Youth Court* as opposed to this work (and summarised in *Chapter 9, post*).

Statutory Provisions

Criminal Justice Act 1991
Savings for mitigation and mentally disordered offenders
28.- (1) Nothing in [Part I of the CJA 91] shall prevent a court from mitigating an offender's sentence by taking into account any such matters as,

in the opinion of the court, are relevant in mitigation of sentence.

(2) Without prejudice to the generality of subsection (1) above, nothing in [Part I of the CJA 91] shall prevent a court -

(a) from mitigating any penalty included in an offender's sentence by taking into account any other penalty included in that sentence; or

(b) in a case of an offender who is convicted of one or more other offences, from mitigating his sentence by applying any rule of law as to the totality of sentences.

(3) Any mitigation of a fine the amount of which falls to be fixed under section 18 above shall be effected by determining under subsection (2)(a) of that section a smaller number of units than would otherwise have been determined.

(4) Nothing in [Part I CJA 91] shall be taken -

(a) as requiring a court to pass a custodial sentence, or any particular custodial sentence on a mentally disordered offender; or

(b) as restricting any power (whether under the [Mental Health Act 1983] or otherwise) which enables a court to deal with such an offender in the manner it considers to be most appropriate in all the circumstances.

[Section 28 Criminal Justice Act 1991]

NOTES **s28(1)** is of general application and seemingly without any limits save those of relevance in an individual case: see main text. **s28(3)** s18 contains the unit fine formula: see *Chapter 6*. **s28(4)(b)** There must be a medical report before any decision on custody can be made unless the court considers this unnecessary: s4 CJA 91, *Chapter 4*.

Effect of previous convictions etc

29.- (1) An offence shall not be regarded as more serious for the purposes of any provision of this Part by reason of any previous convictions of the offender or any failure of his to respond to previous sentences.

(2) Where any aggravating factors of an offence are disclosed by the circumstances of other offences committed by the offender, nothing in this Part shall prevent the court from taking those factors into account for the purpose of forming an opinion as to the seriousness of the offence.

[Section 29 Criminal Justice Act 1991]

NOTES **S29(1)** prevents punishment for the present offence from being increased beyond what is commensurate with seriousness, ie seriousness (and hence a commensurate sentence) cannot increase due to any previous convictions. Strictly speaking, other antecedent information is not prohibited, but eg any information which serves to undermine s29(1) should be discounted *semble*, eg a caution. The prohibition does not apply in relation to s1(2)(b) CJA 91 ('protection of the public'). Previous convictions may be one indicator of the risk of future serious harm to the public from the offender: see *Chapter 3*. **s29(2)** 'disclosed' is a key word. The circumstances of the other offences must, in effect, shed some some light on the seriousness of the present offence. **s29(1)** and **(2)** are considered in *Chapter 2, Seriousness*.

Chapter 2

Seriousness

The sentencing framework created by the CJA 91 operates primarily by reference to the 'seriousness of the offence'. Leaving aside the possibility of mitigation of sentence, *seriousness* is relevant throughout the framework as the main test for: custody: s1(2)(a) CJA 91, and length of custody: s2(2)(a), *ibid* (*Chapter 4*); as the sole test for passing a community sentence: s6(1), *ibid*, and partial test for restrictions on liberty imposed by a particular community order or mix of orders (alongside what is suitable for the offender): s6(2)(b) (*Chapter 5*); and as the sole test for the number of units in a unit fine: s18(2)(a) (*Chapter 6*). Seriousness is a question of fact for the sentencing court in the circumstances of each case. There is no finite scale. A considerable volume of case law has developed, chiefly through rulings and guideline judgements of the Court of Appeal, to assist courts in arriving at the correct decision.

Sentencing guidance
Questions concerning the *seriousness* of offences and the appropriateness of particular disposals dominate the Court of Appeal rulings. These tend to focus on two approaches: dealing with seriousness as it applies to a particular category of offence, eg theft, burglary or rape (albeit that there is ample law to the effect that the 'label' attached to a particular offence is never decisive: see, eg *Hebron and Spencer* (1989) 11 Cr App R (S) 226, *Mussell and Others* (1991) 12 Cr App R (S) 607, *Hearne and Petty* (1989) 11 Cr App R (S) 316); and/or dealing with those factors of individual offences which make them more or less serious. All earlier rulings must now be considered in the light of the new structure and thinking. The seriousness criterion in s1(2)(a) CJA 91 is completely new in relation to offenders aged 21 and over, and a more direct test than that which formerly applied to offenders below that age: see under *Comparison of old and new criteria, post*. Selected cases on the CJA 82 appear towards the end of the chapter.

The Magistrates' Association has published *Sentencing Guidelines* containing 'seriousness indicators' for particular offences, based on Court of Appeal rulings (Magistrates' Association, 1989, 1991). The *National Mode of Trial Guidelines* (Lord Chancellor's Department, 1990; *Practice Note (Mode of Trial Guidelines)* [1990] 1 WLR 1439; (1991) 92 Cr App R 142) employ seriousness as the principal indicator whether a case should be dealt with summarily or in the Crown Court. Attention is also drawn to the various guideline judgements relating to the former law not affected by the provisions of the CJA 82 Act, and which it would be beyond the scope of this work to reproduce. (The sense of many of these Court of Appeal rulings is reflected, in general terms, in the mode of trial guidelines). Among the more significant of these rulings are: *Aramah* (1982) 4 Cr App R (S) 407 (drugs); *Barrick* (1985) 7 Cr App R (S) 142 (breach of trust); *Billam* (1986) 1 WLR 349 (rape); *Stewart* (1987) 85 Cr App R 66 (social security frauds); and *Bilinski* (1987) 9 Cr App R (S) 360. An extended analysis of some of these cases, together with further authorities, can be found in *Criminal Jurisdiction of Magistrates* (Harris, edited Gibson), 11th Edition, at p 556.

Comparison with 'protection of the public'

Whilst seriousness determines the threshold for custody and for community sentences, and affects *quantum* in respect of all sentences, by comparison, *Protection of the public* from serious harm, discussed in *Chapter 3*, has a more limited role. This is confined to the threshold test for custodial sentences for violent or sexual offences *only*, or the length of such sentences. However, it must be noted that violent or sexual offences fall to be dealt with under either criterion, or both. Section 1(4) CJA 91, which requires courts to give reasons for custodial sentences contemplates that there may be situations in which the separate criteria in s1(2)(a), *ibid* (seriousness), and s1(2)(b), *ibid* (protection), are relevant to the same sentencing decision. In relation to the duty cast by s2(3) CJA 91 to give reasons for a custody sentence for a violent or sexual offence which is *longer* than is commensurate with the seriousness of the offence the court will need to measure the effect of both criteria in order to make the necessary comparison, *semble*.

Structure of the seriousness test in the CJA 91

The new seriousness test is based on statutory rules concerning the *number* of offences which can be considered 'in combination' to establish whether the custody or community sentence threshold has been reached, ie *two* offences: s1(2)(a) CJA 91 and s6(1) *ibid*, respectively. There are further rules concerning the offences which may be taken into account to determine *quantum* as opposed to the custody or community sentence threshold. In both cases the number is unlimited: s2(2)(a), *ibid* (length of custody); s6(2)(b), *ibid* (restrictions on liberty). There is a requirement that any such offences are 'associated' offences within the meaning of s31(2) CJA 91: see the *Statutory Provisions* in *Chapter 4*; broadly speaking, other offences for which the offender is sentenced at the same time, and offences taken into consideration. It is submitted that courts may wish to be cautious about imprisoning an offender partly on the basis of an offence taken into consideration of which they only have partial knowledge. As Steyn J said in *Howard* (1990) 12 Cr App R (S) 426: 'Qualitatively such an admission is different from a plea of guilty. It is not preceded by the service of an indictment, the disclosure of the prosecution case and an arraignment. In practice the judge knows a great deal about offences to which a defendant has pleaded guilty, but less about offences to be taken into consideration.' The position in relation to custodial sentences under s1(4A) CJA 82 was that each offence must be viewed individually in order to assess seriousness, no aggregation being permitted: see eg *Hassan and Khan* (1989) 11 Cr App R (S) 148; *Roberts* (1987) 9 Cr App R (S); *Thompson* (1989) 11 Cr App R (S) 245; although a rule has developed under which, once seriousness *is* established, the inhibition is removed, at least as far as concurrent sentences for other offences (not themselves meeting the seriousness criterion) are concerned: see eg *Pike* (1990) 12 Cr App R (S) 412; *Mussell, supra.* There is no compelling reason why this judicial gloss should not continue: but see the *Note* from 1991 CLR 390 on *Mussell, post.*

There is under the CJA 91 a statutory rule against taking previous convictions into account so as to increase seriousness: s29(1) CJA 91; and an inroad on this rule in relation to *aggravating factors* disclosed by the circumstances of other offences: s29(2), *ibid*: see under *Effect of a previous criminal history, post*. Sentencing under the CJA 91 will take place against the backdrop of a strengthened scheme of community sentences (subject to more rigorous enforcement powers): *Chapter 5*, a new system of unit fines: *Chapter 6*, and the *Parole and Early Release* provisions of Part II of the Act: *Chapter 10*. All these items have some bearing on the place of custody following implementation of the 1991 Act.

Pre-sentence reports and seriousness

The provisions concerning *Pre-sentence reports, Chapter 8, post*, are so drawn that reports will need to address seriousness. The *National Standards* for pre-sentence reports are being prepared on this basis. Medical reports are generally required before custody can be imposed on a person who is, or appears to be, mentally disordered: *Chapters 4* and *8*.

Effect of a previous criminal history

A notable feature of the CJA 91 and the proportionate sentencing approach is the prohibition on previous convictions being taken into account when determining the seriousness of an offence. Section 29 CJA 91 provides that '... (1) An offence shall not be regarded as more serious for the purposes of any provision of [Part I CJA 91] by reason of any previous convictions of the offender or any failure of his to respond to previous sentences'. However, the circumstances of other offences may shed light on ('disclose') aggravating factors of the present offence. Section 29(2) provides '... Where any aggravating factors of an offence are disclosed by the *circumstances* of other offences committed by the offender, nothing in [Part I CJA 91] shall prevent the court from taking those factors into account for the purpose of forming an opinion as to the seriousness of the offence' (italics supplied). 'Other offences' is not further defined in relation to s29(2), but would include previous convictions and associated offences as defined in s31(2) CJA 91. *Good* character may be general mitigation: s28(1), *ibid.*

Previous convictions

The rationale is that an offender should not be punished more than once for the same offence. Once a penalty, of whatever kind, has been paid this should be an end of that matter. This approach is not new, although existing rulings can appear equivocal in that what is expressed in terms of legal principle is not always reflected in sentences actually imposed: see eg *Galloway* (1979) 1 Cr App R (S) 311 (penalties on a persistent, alcoholic shoplifter of small items reduced to a total of two and a half years' imprisonment); *Skidmore* (1983) 5 Cr App R (S) 17 (sentences on a persistent offender for three offences of obtaining £20 by deception reduced to a total of two years' imprisonment); *Bailey* (1988) 10 Cr App R (S) 231 (sentence on a persistent offender who stole cod fillets worth £12 from a hospital freezer reduced to three months' imprisonment). In *Bailey*, the Court of Appeal held that an offender's record 'forms part of the matrix upon which he falls to be sentenced'; whilst in *Aramah* (1983) 4 Cr App R (S) 407, Lord Lane, LCJ said that '... If the history shows ... a persistent flouting of the law, imprisonment may become necessary' (small amounts of cannabis for personal use).

The new criterion will require a much sharper and more unambiguous focus on the seriousness of the current offence. It will no longer be possible for a court to regard a previous record as part of the 'matrix' on which he falls to be sentenced (except when s29(2) CJA 91 applies); whilst 'flouting' would have to be evidenced independently of previous convictions. In line with the new approach, s38 MCA 1980 is amended so that magistrates will no longer be able to commit to the Crown Court for sentence on the basis of 'character and antecedents': see under the heading *Seriousness and mode of trial, post.* Whilst previous convictions cannot increase seriousness, 'good character' remains a basis for mitigation generally.

Cautions

The statutory rule that previous convictions cannot increase seriousness must also prevent an official record which falls short of a formal conviction being taken into account. Technically, s29(1) CJA 91 does not apply to cautions, but to sanction any other rule than the one suggested would be to subvert the provision, and the commensurate sentencing approach, *semble.*

Aggravating factors

The full meaning of s29(2) CJA 91 is likely to prove elusive until the Court of Appeal comes to rule on appeals some time after the Act commences. Explanations concerning the working of the legislation given by John Patten MP, Minister of State at the Home Office, during the passage of the Bill concerned the 'systematic and professional burglar' whose offences are calculated, as part of a course of conduct, as opposed to opportunist; and the shopkeeper who regularly sells unfit food. According to Mr. Patten, courts might impose more severe sentences in these instances, the one on the shopkeeper to register his 'deliberate and sustained disregard of the law'. It would be an omission not to point to the difficulties. The examples give no real, or general, indication why some circumstances will be admissible in relation to the seriousness of another offence and some not. They come close (certainly the case of the shopkeeper) to simply restating the problem, ie there is a series of convictions. Something analogous to the 'similar facts' rule of the law of evidence appears to be required and it may be that this is the direction in which the law on s29(2) develops. Some striking similarity, eg about the way in which an earlier offence was committed might serve to increase the seriousness of the present offence. The Home Office *General Guide* to the Act instances offences linked by motivation, eg spraying of racist graffiti going to show that an assault on a member of the ethnic minorities was similarly motivated and thus more serious. This seems to be a more sound approach and one amenable to the development of principle.

In line with this approach, it is submitted that Mr. Patten is correct in suggesting that the Act would allow a more severe sentence to be imposed on the systematic burglar than on the opportunist burglar, and on the shopkeeper who deliberately disregards food hygiene regulations than on the one who sells adulterated food through oversight; but the wording of s29 requires the justification for doing so to be related more clearly to the seriousness of the present offence than is apparent from such phrases as 'part of a course of conduct' or 'sustained disregard of the law'. A burglary which is premeditated and carefully and 'professionally' planned *is* more serious than one which is opportunist; and where the circumstances of other offences help the court to see that such 'professional' planning is a feature of the present offence, s29(2) enables the court to take this into account. Similarly, an offence of selling unfit food which arises from a deliberate disregard of food hygiene regualations *is* more serious than one which arises from negligence or oversight; and, where a previous record of such offences helps the court to see that the present offence involved such a deliberate disregard, s29(2) enables it to be taken into account.

In both cases, therefore, the circumstances of other offences *shed light on* ('disclose') aggravating features of the *present* offence. This is *not* the same thing as regarding an offence as more serious simply because it is one of a series. It is submitted that a key word in s29(2) is 'disclose'. To take an analogy, when a dentist applies a 'disclosing solution' to teeth, this shows up areas in which plaque is present. The disclosing solution itself does not worsen or aggravate the plaque - it simply helps the dentist and the patient to see that it is there. In the same way, the phrasing of s29(2) indicates that the circumstances of other offences may 'disclose', or 'reveal', the existence of aggravating features of the present offence which may not otherwise be obvious.

Information concerning aggravating factors

Section 29(2) presupposes that information about the circumstances of previous offences will be available to the sentencing court (a considerable task for Crown Prosecutors, in particular). The plan appears to be that the record of previous convictions will continue to be made available to the court as before, but this does not take matters much further. There have been experiments in some areas where short factual summaries have been kept by the police to supplement the recorded conviction. Even assuming that such hurdles can be surmounted, what is the position if the offender challenges the facts of an earlier case as put forward? This is where the real difficulties may start. One solution would be something in the nature of a 'Newton' hearing: see *Newton* (1983) 77 Cr App Rep 13, [1983] Crim LR 198. On the one hand, public policy may dictate that the facts of earlier cases cannot be litigated *ad infinitum*; whilst inferences affecting sentencing and which are adverse to an offender can hardly be drawn where facts are in dispute, at least not without good cause (cf, eg *Taggart* (1979) 1 Cr App Rep (S) 144; *Milligan* [1982] Crim LR 317; *Newton, supra*). This is quite apart from any challenge which might be mounted by an offender on the basis that criminal cases do not, generally speaking, determine specific issues as opposed to the single issue of guilt or innocence (*a fortiori*, perhaps, where there has been no trial of the facts. On a plea of guilty, the facts put forward may have been minimal).

Previous responses to sentences

The commensurate approach suggests that each sentence should be viewed as a self-contained punishment. The new system of unit fines means that fines should be capable of payment, failing which enforcement of the fine is the correct approach (including the special remission powers in the case of true hardship): *Chapter 6*. In relation to community sentences, a more standard approach to breach means that an offender can be re-sentenced where there is a failure to complete any of the more demanding forms of community order: *Chapter 5*; and see the comments in relation to s1(3) CJA 91 (custody following refusal of a community sentence, or breach) in *Chapter 4*. Failure to respond to past sentences is not a basis for increasing present punishment, even under s29(2), *ibid*.

Penalty points and totting up

The penalty points and 'totting up' disqualification provisions concerning motoring matters continue to apply under the Road Traffic Act 1991. By nature, the provisions are cumulative in effect and not amenable to the proportionate sentencing approach. However, it would be wrong in principle for a court to compensate for a (perceived) low (but in fact commensurate) sentence by eg increasing the period of a disqualification. The purpose of the penalty points provisions is to ensure road safety, not punishment, *semble*.

A custody sentence for a road traffic offence must satisfy s1(2) CJA 91, of course.

Seriousness and mode of trial

A magistrates' court before which a person is charged with an 'either way' offence must first determine whether summary trial or trial at the Crown Court before a judge and jury is more suitable: s19 MCA 1980, *et al*. The magistrates retain power to commit to the Crown Court for sentence, but a new s38 MCA 1980, is substituted by s25 CJA 91 as follows: '(1) This section applies where on the summary trial of an offence triable either way ... a person who is not less than 18 is convicted of the offence. (2) If the court is of opinion - (a) that the offence or the combination of the offence and other offences associated with it was so serious that greater punishment should be inflicted for the offence than the court has power to impose; or (b) in the case of a violent or sexual offence committed by a person who is not less than 21 years old, that a sentence of imprisonment for a term longer than the court has power to impose is necessary to protect the public from serious harm from him, the court may, in accordance with section 56 of the Criminal Justice Act 1967, commit the offender in custody or on bail to the Crown Court for sentence in accordance with the provisions of section 42 of the Powers of Criminal Courts Act 1973'.

The *National Mode of Trial Guidelines*, *supra*, issued under the auspices of the Lord Chief Justice, state: 'The purpose of these guidelines is to help magistrates to decide whether or not to commit 'either way' offences for trial in the Crown Court. Their object is to provide guidance not direction. They are not intended to impinge upon a magistrate's duty to consider each case individually and on its own particular facts'. The guidelines apply to all defendants *aged 17 and above* [which, of necessity, must be read as '18 and above' once the CJA 91 is in force]. They focus primarily on the *seriousness* of the offence and thus form a convenient and authoritative distillation of factors which make particular offences more or less serious. The guidelines are reproduced at the end of this chapter.

A new section 38(4) MCA 1980 states that the provisions of s38 '... shall apply in relation to a corporation as if - (a) the corporation were an individual who is not less than 18 years old; and (b) in subsection (2) above, paragraph (b) and the words 'in custody or on bail' were omitted'. The prohibition on committing a corporation for sentence in sched 3 MCA 1980, para 5, is removed by s25(2) CJA 91.

Development of the statutory 'seriousness' criterion

The decided cases on s1(4) CJA 82 (as amended) remain pertinent due to the correlation of the criteria for imposing custodial sentences on *young offenders* contained in that provision with those in s1(2) CJA 91. Section 1(4) of the 1982 Act, as originally enacted, provided that a custodial sentence could only be imposed on a person under 21 if: '... no other method of dealing with him is appropriate because it appears to the court that he is unable or unwilling to respond to non-custodial penalties or because a custodial sentence is necessary for the *protection of the public* or because the offence was *so serious* that a non-custodial sentence *cannot be justified*' (italics supplied). The 'unwillingness' test was redrawn by s123 CJA 88 (see next section) but disappears under the CJA 91 (although there is now a separate, unfettered, basis for custody based on *refusal* to consent to a community sentence which requires that consent: s1(3) CJA 91). The 'protection' criterion of the CJA 82 is discussed in *Chapter 3*. An effect of s1(3) CJA 91 is that a custodial sentence can, *ex hypothesi*, be used, where a community sentence is refused, at a lower level of seriousness than is commensurate with custody: *Chapter 4*.

The custody test since 1988
Section 123 CJA 88 amended s1(4) CJA 82 so as to set out (in a new s1(4) and (4A) CJA 82) enhanced criteria whereby an offender under 21 years of age could only *qualify* for a custodial sentence if : (s1(4A)) '... (a) he has a *history* of failure to respond to non-custodial penalties and is unable or unwilling to respond to them [again, redundant under the CJA 91; but note s1(3), *ibid*, mentioned *supra*]; or (b) only a custodial sentence would be adequate to protect the public from *serious harm from him* [*Chapter 3*]; or (c) the offence of which he has been convicted or found guilty was *so serious* that a non-custodial sentence for it *cannot be justified*' (italics supplied). These amendments came into force in October 1988. It is important to bear the date in mind when considering reported cases.

Comparison of old and new criteria
Whilst not identical, the 'seriousness' criterion from 1988 onwards provides some indication of the kind of levels at which it may be appropriate to ask whether the new seriousness test is met. Five things, in particular, should be noted. First, s1(4) applied only to young offenders, ie those below the age of 21, who have always been allowed the benefit of their youth, inexperience or immaturity. Second, the new 'seriousness' criterion in s1(2)(a) CJA 91 is linked more directly to custody. The new test is '*only* [a custody] sentence can be justified' whereas the former test concentrated on the elimination of other disposals, ie 'a non-custodial sentence *cannot be justified*'. However, it must be noted that the test in s1(2)(a) CJA 91 is not the final word on custody. Section 28 CJA 91 permits widescale mitigation (without which courts might not find it easy to avoid the full implications of the word 'only' in s1(2)(a)). Section 28 CJA 91 is reproduced in *Chapter 1*. Third, previous convictions are no longer relevant to seriousness, *supra*: see s29(1) CJA 91, reproduced in *Chapter 1*. The law appears to have been equivocal on this point in the past, see under the heading *Effect of a previous criminal history*, *supra*. Aggravating factors disclosed by the circumstances of other offences may be relevant: s29(2), *ibid*. Fourth, the

extent to which *other* offences may be taken into account is dictated by the several provisions mentioned under *Structure of the seriousness test in the CJA 91, supra*. Fifth, the CJA 91 enables courts to impose a range of more intensive combinations of penalties, including options which were not available when earlier appeal cases were decided. This wider range of options may reduce the number of cases where *only* a custodial sentence can be justified.

Court of Appeal rulings

The following are selected summaries from Court of Appeal rulings from 1983 to 1991. They are divided into two sections, ie 1983 to 1988; then 1988 to 1991. This is because the criteria changed as a result of the CJA 88, *supra*. Further cases on s1(4) and (4A) CJA 1982 are contained in *Chapter 5A* of *The Youth Court*.

Cases on 'seriousness' under s1(4) CJA 82 from 1983 to 1988 (s1(4) CJA 82 pre-amendment)

Burglary

Moffett (1984) 6 Cr App R (S) 90. The appellant (20) had pleaded guilty to burglary of a shop, theft of a pedal cycle and theft of a jack from the boot of a car. He was said to be accustomed to glue sniffing and had previously been to detention centre, borstal, fined, and bound over. The social inquiry report recommended probation with detailed requirements. Sentence: 12 months' youth custody (as it then was). Held by the Court of Appeal: The court could not pass a sentence of youth custody unless it was satisfied that the offender would not respond to a non-custodial measure, or that a custodial sentence was necessary for the protection of the public, or that the offence was so serious that a non-custodial sentence could not be justified. The evidence showed that the first criterion (ie 'response') was not satisfied. This was not a case in which a custodial sentence was necessary for the protection of the public and the Court was not of the view that the offence was so serious that a non-custodial sentence could not be justified. The sentence was varied to a probation order.

Bates (1985) 7 Cr App R (S) 105. The appellant (under 21) had pleaded guilty to burglary. With several other youths he had entered the house of an acquaintance to steal a video recorder. They were caught in the act. No previous convictions. Sentence: one month detention centre order (as it then was). Held by the Court of Appeal: Having regard to section 1(4) CJA 1982, there was no reason why it was necessary to pass a custodial sentence. Burglary was a *serious* offence, even though in the circumstances of this particular case a custodial sentence was not called for. The appropriate sentence would have been a community service order. As the appellant had already served some time in a detention centre, the sentence was varied to a conditional discharge.

Grimes (1985) 7 Cr App R (S) 137. The appellant (18) had pleaded guilty to two offences of burglary. He broke into a school, in company with another, and stole equipment valued at £508, most of which was recovered. He also broke into an unoccupied house and stole some bathroom furniture which was later recovered. No previous convictions. Held by the Court of Appeal: While the offences were not trivial, they were not at the upper end of the scale of criminality as far as dishonesty was concerned. The Court had to have in mind the provisions of s1(4) CJA 82. It seemed that the sentencer was not in a position to impose a custodial sentence. A custodial sentence was not necessary for the protection of the public and the offences were not in the view of the Court sufficiently *serious* to justify the imposition of a custodial order. The sentence should have been a community service order.

Roberts (1987) 9 Cr App R (S) 152. The appellant (18) had pleaded guilty to three counts of burglary and asked for 12 other offences (six burglaries and six attempted burglaries) to be taken into consideration. He broke into several buildings, including dwelling houses, but selected only unoccupied houses and never burgled by night. Most of the offences were committed within a period of two months. No previous convictions. A social inquiry report described him as a 'normally well-adjusted young man who had gone off the rails' and recommended a non-custodial disposal. Held by the Court of Appeal: Section 1(4) CJA 1982 provided that a youth custody sentence might not be imposed on a person under 21 unless the case fell into one of of three categories ... The third criterion (the offence was so *serious* that a non-custodial penalty could not be justified) must be applied to each offence individually rather than to the aggregated gravity of all the offences.

The relevant question was 'Was any of the burglaries committed by the appellant at dwelling houses known to be unoccupied so serious that a non-custodial sentence could not be justified?'. Burglary was always a serious offence, and burglary of a dwelling house doubly so, but the Court could not assent to the proposition that the gravity of any one of the burglaries committed by the appellant was such as to make it impossible to say that a non-custodial sentence could not be justified.

Theft
Bradbourn (1985) 7 Cr App R (S) 180. The appellant (20) had pleaded guilty to theft. She was a sales assistant in a shop in which unexplained losses had occurred. Security officers made test purchases using marked notes and coins. The appellant served one of the security officers on a purchase for £2.15: she rang up 15p on the till and put £2 in her handbag. A marked note and a marked coin were found in her handbag. She had no previous convictions. Held by the Court of Appeal: The Court could not see what basis there was for saying that the appellant was unable or unwilling to respond to non-custodial penalties, or that a custodial sentence was necessary for the protection of the public. In the circumstances of the present case, stealing £2 from the till of a shop was not so *serious* that a non-custodial sentence could not be justified. The appellant had spent one month in custody: the sentence would be quashed. A conditional discharge was substituted.

Munday (1985) 7 Cr App R (S) 216. The appellant (17) pleaded guilty to six counts of theft. He and a girl committed several thefts from shops in the course of a single afternoon. Most of the property stolen was clothing, to a value of about £168. The appellant had one previous conviction for theft and had been fined £40. Sentence: six months' youth custody. Held by the Court of Appeal: The protection of the public was not in issue, and the offences were not *so serious* that a non-custodial sentence could not be justified. Although the appellant had been fined a few months earlier for another offence of theft, that was a slender basis for saying that he was unable or unwilling to respond to non-custodial penalties. The sentence was quashed and a fine was substituted.

Scorey (1988) 9 Cr App R (S) 536. The appellant (19) pleaded guilty to three counts of theft. Together with others, he had taken part in three raids on a car depot where new cars were awaiting delivery, where a total of 115 radio cassette players worth £23,000 were stolen. On the first occasion, 32 radio cassette players worth £6,400 were taken; on the second occasion, 28 sets worth £5,600; and on the third, 55 sets valued at £11,000. No previous convictions. Sentence: nine months' youth custody. Held by the Court of Appeal: The raids were very skilfully carried out and planned well in advance. Each raid, taken in isolation, was a serious matter and fell within the *seriousness* criteria in the CJA 82.

Taking motor vehicles without consent
Emery (1985) RTR 415. The appellant (20) had pleaded guilty to taking a conveyance without authority and reckless driving. He saw a parked motor cycle and he and his co-accused decided to take it. They were seen by police riding it and a chase ensued during which the appellant went through two sets of traffic lights at red, exceeded the speed limit and drove on the wrong side of the road, causing two vehicles to brake suddenly. Finally the motor cycle mounted a pavement, the two men fell off, were chased by the police and apprehended. No previous convictions. Sentence: consecutive terms totalling six months' youth custody. Held by the Court of Appeal: Although the taking of the motor vehicle was premeditated and the reckless driving bad and continued over a period of time, nevertheless for a young man of previous good character the appropriate sentence was a community service order. The sentence was quashed in favour of such an order.

Jeary (1987) 9 Cr App R (S) 491. The appellant (18) had pleaded guilty to two counts of taking a conveyance and asked for two other offences to be considered. He and a number of other youths took cars, using keys in the possession of one of them, and drove them around a city at high speed, colliding with each other several times. Eventually, the two cars collided head on and one was damaged beyond repair. The youths then drove off in the surviving car, which mounted a verge and collided with a tree. The appellant later stated that the cars had been taken for a 'bit of fun'. He had one previous conviction: he had been ordered to attend an attendance centre and fined. Sentence: detention centre orders totalling four months. Held by the Court of Appeal: The sentence had clearly been imposed on the basis of the third criterion mentioned in s1(4) CJA 82, ie that the offence was 'so *serious* that a non-custodial penalty cannot be justified'. These were serious offences involving taking vehicles and deliberately destroying them, and the sentences were fully justified.

Criminal damage
Ferreira and Belic (1988) 10 Cr App R (S) 343. One appellant pleaded guilty to criminal damage and the other to having articles with intent to damage property. The appellants were found early one morning at a London Underground depot at

which carriages had been damaged with paint sprays. One appellant admitted being present when the carriages were sprayed, the other had cans of paintspray in a rucksack which he admitted intending to use for painting graffiti. Sentence: in one case a four month detention centre order; in the other, where the appellant had previously been conditionally discharged for a similar offence, six months' youth custody. Held by the Court of Appeal: this was the kind of case for which, in the judgement of the Court, a community service order was designed. Such an order, for 120 hours, was substituted in each case. [Note, in any event, the effect of s29(1) CJA 91 on the second defendant's situation: previous convictions cannot now increase seriousness (although the appellant may have lost any credit for good character)].

Robbery
Balogun unreported (18 November 1983). The defendant (17) attacked an educationally subnormal youth of the same age as they walked home after both had been paid their wages. After hitting him in the face, he stole £5. Sentence: three months detention. Held by the Court of Appeal: It was accepted that the defendant was a bully but the Court considered the offences not to be 'so *serious*' as to warrant custody. The sentence was replaced by a probation order.

Willis and Willis (1984) 6 Cr App R (S) 68. The appellants (16 and one 'slightly older') pleaded guilty to robbery and having an imitation firearm with intent. They had gone with a third boy to a shop and demanded money at the point of an air rifle. The shopkeeper gave them £40. Both were of previous good character. Sentence: 12 months' and two years' youth custody, respectively. Held by the Court of Appeal: A court could not impose a custodial sentence unless it was satisfied that the offender would not respond to a non-custodial measure, or that a custodial sentence was necessary for the protection of the public, or that the offence was so serious that a non-custodial sentence could not be justified. The third factor, that the offence was 'so *serious*', was applicable. The 12 months' sentence was upheld but the two year sentence reduced to 12 months.

Assault
McDermot (1984) 6 Cr App R (S) 377. The appellant (18) and of previous good character, pleaded guilty to unlawful wounding. He had attacked the proprietor of a fish bar by hitting him over the head with a piece of wood, causing a two and a half inch laceration to the scalp. It was said that the attack was in revenge for an assault by the victim on the appellant some weeks previously, in which the appellant claimed to have been stabbed in the back. Sentence: twelve months youth custody. Held by the Court of Appeal: A period of community service could and should have been considered by the judge as an alternative to a custodial sentence. Taking into account all the circumstances, including the fact that the appellant was serving an apprenticeship which was still open to him, the sentence would be varied to a community service order. ['Alternatives to custody' disappear under the CJA 91 in favour of 'commensurate' sentences].

Jeoffroy and others (1985) 7 Cr App R (S) 135. The appellants (under 21) with no previous convictions, had pleaded guilty to assault occasioning actual bodily harm. Following an incident at a dance, they went with a group of about five others in two cars. They attacked a boy who was unknown to them who was walking down the street with his girlfriend: the victim was kicked and suffered injuries to his eye, face, chest and stomach. The injuries were not serious: he was initially discharged from hospital within an hour and was thought to have made a complete recovery. The appellants were either attending courses or in employment. They were all recommended for community service. Sentence: three months' detention. <u>Held by the Court of Appeal</u>: The only criterion of s 1(4) CJA 82 applicable to the case was that the offence was 'so *serious*'. The Court took the view that the offence demanded an immediate custodial sentence.

Arson

Massheder (1985) 5 Cr App R (S) 442. The appellant (15) had pleaded guilty to arson (ie criminal damage by fire). He had been concerned with others with lighting a fire in a lift shaft. The fire was deliberately started using some form of fire lighting liquid and over £5,000 damage was done. There were a number of boys present and another boy aged 17 was the main culprit. Sentence: 18 months' detention under s53 CYPA 1933 ('grave crimes'). <u>Held by the Court of Appeal</u>: The appellant was guilty of a 'very *serious* offence', but he was not the prime mover. He was very young, and the Court could substitute for the sentence imposed a two year supervision order. [Note that arson is capable of being 'serious harm' for the purposes of the 'protection of the public' criterion: s31(3) CJA 91: see also *Dewberry and Stone* (1985) 7 Cr App R (S) 202 in *The Youth Court*].

Wilcock (1988) 10 Cr App R (S) 113. The appellant (18) had pleaded guilty to arson, being reckless as to whether damage would be caused. He had been employed in a warehouse. When still aged 16, he caused a fire which destroyed the contents of a warehouse and caused substantial structural damage. A woman working in the factory was trapped by fumes: she was rescued just in time. The cost of the damage was estimated at about £8.8 million. The fire had apparently been started by the appellant playing with matches in a 'no smoking' area. He had one previous conviction of an irrelevant nature and was treated as of good character. Sentence: 30 months' youth custody. <u>Held by the Court of Appeal</u>: It was clear that the reason the judge had passed a youth custody sentence was that the offence was 'so *serious*'. The Court acknowledged and followed the principle that the real seriousness of the offence of arson lay in the intent with which it was committed rather than the amount of damage which it caused; but the amount of damage caused could not be ignored and was a factor which the judge was entitled to bear in mind when considering what was the appropriate sentence. The judge was entitled to have regard to the fact that the offence had endangered life. It was a case of *serious* recklessness at the appellant's place of work. The sentence was upheld. [See the note to *Massheder, supra*]

Cases on 'seriousness' under s1(4) CJA 82 from 1988 to 1991 (s1(4A) CJA 82, ie following amendment by s123 CJA 88, *supra*)

Hassan and Khan (1989) 11 Cr App R (S) 148. The appellants (under 21) pleaded guilty to three burglaries and asked for a further nine charges to be taken into consideration. They broke into several schools and a college, in some cases more than once, and stole property such as video recorders and computers, worth £3,000. Neither had previous convictions. Sentence: 18 months' detention in a young offender institution in each case. Held by the Court of Appeal: Section 123 CJA 88 had significantly increased the restrictions on the imposition of custodial sentences on young offenders. The wording of the third criterion, ie that the offence was 'so serious that a non-custodial sentence for it cannot be justified', had been amended in a way which reinforced the decision of the court in *Roberts* (1987) (summarised *supra*) where it had been held that the relevant question, in the case of an offender who committed a large number of offences of modest individual gravity, was whether *any one* of the offences was so serious that a non-custodial sentence could not be justified. It was clear from the words 'for it' in the 1988 legislation that the decision in *Roberts* must be enforced. The proper disposal would have been a community service order together with a compensation order. [The CJA 91 allows any *two* associated offences to be considered in combination: s1(2)(a), *ibid*].

Poyner (1989) 11 Cr App R (S) 173. The appellant (20) had pleaded guilty to affray. He was one of a group of men who attacked another man who was walking in the early hours of the morning. The victim was knocked down, kicked about the head and forced to hand over his watch and some money. The appellant denied that he was involved in the robbery but admitted punching the victim. He had five previous convictions for various offences including assault occasioning actual bodily harm and threatening behaviour. Sentences had included an attendance centre order, two community service orders (he had been fined for breach of one) and a total of 12 months' youth custody. Sentence: six months' detention in a young offender institution. Held by the Court of Appeal: There was some history of failure to respond to non-custodial penalties, but the court might have been faced with the problem of whether there was inability or unwillingness to respond to them in the future, in the light of the recommendation in the social inquiry report. This recommended a probation order, on the basis that the appellant was trying to stabilise his life. However, the offence was so *serious* that a non-custodial sentence for it could not be justified. [See also *Jacobs and Kinsella* (1989) 11 Cr App R (S) 171, *Camp* (1989) 11 Cr App R (S) 196, *Hebron and Spencer* (1989) 11 Cr App R (S) 226, summarised in *Chapter 3*].

Thompson (1989) 11 Cr App R (S) 245. The appellant (19) pleaded guilty to two counts of handling stolen property, two of obtaining by deception and one of attempting to obtain by deception. Twenty similar offences were taken into consideration. She had committed several frauds using stolen cheques and credit cards. She claimed that stolen cheque books and cards had been given to her by a youth with whom she had shared the proceeds. She was effectively of good character. Sentence: six months' detention in a young offender institution. Held by the Court of Appeal: Sentencers should bear in mind the principle enunciated in *Roberts* (1987), *supra*, which was binding on those called to interpret s1(4) CJA 82. They must not pass sentences on the basis that the aggregate of a number of offences transmuted them into so serious a matter that the court was justified in passing a custodial sentence. It could not be said that any one of the offences, looked at individually, justified the description of being 'so *serious* that a non-custodial sentence for it cannot be justified'. A custodial sentence was not merely inappropriate but outwith the powers of the court. The sentence was quashed and a probation order was substituted.

Eddy and Monks (1989) 11 Cr App R (S) 370. Monks was under 21. Both appellants were involved in a series of systematic burglaries of commercial premises. A high powered car would be taken and concealed, the premises would be attacked, and the burglars would then withdraw to see whether the police would respond to any alarm: if not, they would proceed with the burglary. Neither appellant was involved in all the burglaries. Monks pleaded guilty to involvement in a burglary of a newsagents in which property worth £11,500 was stolen, and in a second burglary of commercial premises in which property worth £9,500 was stolen. He asked for a further similar burglary to be considered, and taking or being carried in a conveyance on two occasions. He had one previous conviction for which he was fined. Sentence: 18 months' detention. Held by the Court of Appeal: The only ground on which the sentence could be justified under s1(4A) CJA 82 was under the 'so *serious*' head. It was not open to courts to pass a sentence of detention in a young offender institution on an offender convicted of a number of offences on the basis that the aggregate transmuted them into so serious a matter that the court was justified in passing a custodial sentence. In the present case the court concluded that each of Monks' burglaries taken in isolation was 'so *serious*'. However, the sentence was reduced to nine months. [The CJA 91 allows any *two* associated offences to be considered in combination: s1(2)(a), *ibid*].

Wilson (1989) 11 Cr App R (S) 344. The appellant (20) pleaded guilty to unlawful wounding. He became involved in a fight with another man outside a nightclub where they had been drinking. The appellant knocked the other man to the ground and continued to punch him in the face as he lay on the ground. The victim suffered a fractured cheekbone, two black eyes, a cut lip and internal haemorrhage to one eye, although the damage to the eye was not permanent. The appellant had no previous convictions. Sentence: nine months' detention in a young offender institution. Held by the Court of Appeal: The appellant had committed an offence for which, if he had been an adult, a sentence of imprisonment would have been imposed, and the offence was so serious that a non-custodial penalty for it could not be justified. However, the appellant had served six weeks in custody and the sentence was reduced to a term which would result in his immediate release. [The reference to 'imprisonment in the case of an adult' is to one of the former qualifying grounds under s1(4) CJA 82, as amended].

Rhoades (1989) 11 Cr App R (S) 538. The appellant (20) pleaded guilty to two counts of common assault and various traffic offences. He had several previous convictions, including violent disorder, and one previous custodial sentence. He had spent an evening drinking with two friends. He was stopped by police officers in uniform driving a marked police car, who asked him to submit to a breath test: the appellant refused to do so and was arrested. In the course of being taken to the police car, the appellant struggled and one officer was kicked and another struck with a fist. The appellant also sustained some injuries. The prosecution accepted that the apppellant had not aimed blows deliberately at the officers. Sentence: six months' detention in a young offender institution concurrent on each count of common assault, plus 18 months' disqualification from driving. Held by the Court of Appeal: The appellant did not qualify for a custodial sentence under either paragraph (a) or (b) of s1(4A) CJA 1982 (ie 'unwillingness'; 'protection of the public'). The offences of common assault had to be considered in the light of their surrounding circumstances. Each involved an assault, committed on a police officer in the execution of his duty and each was 'so *serious* that a non-custodial sentence for it cannot be justified'.

Davison (1989) 11 Cr App R (S) 570. The appellant (17) pleaded guilty to eight offences of burglary and asked for three similar offences to be considered. He had burgled commercial premises by night, stealing cash and confectionery. A total of about £500 was stolen, and about £500 worth of damage was done. Previous convictions: one for burglary, placed on probation after deferment (the probation order was made after the commission of the burglaries in the present case, but the offence was committed previously); one theft from a shop, conditional discharge. Sentence: three months' detention in a young offender institution. Held by the Court of Appeal: The appellant could not qualify for a custodial sentence under criteria (a) or (b) in s 1(4A) CJA 82 (ie 'unwillingness'; 'protection of the public'). He could only qualify under criterion (c), ie 'so *serious*' , if all 11 offences could be taken together. In *Roberts* (1987), *supra*, it had been held that the original form of the criterion had to be applied to each offence individually. In the new wording of the criterion, the words 'for it' had been added. The new form of the criterion had been considered in *Hassan and Khan* (1989), *supra*, where it was held that the decision in *Roberts* should be followed. the Court had come to a similar conclusion in *Thompson* (1989), *supra*. In the Court's view the law was correctly stated in *Hassan and Khan*. Where an offender did not qualify for a custodial sentence under (a) or (b), it was not possible to aggregate offences under (c) where each did not qualify on its own. The totality of offending could be considered under criterion (b) where the concern was to protect the public from serious harm from the offender [now restricted to violent and sexual offences: s1(2)(b) CJA 91]. The sentence of three months' detention would be quashed: no separate penalty would be imposed in view of the existing probation order.

Howard (1989) 11 Cr App R (S) 583. The appellant (under 21) pleaded guilty *inter alia* to one count of blackmail. He had demanded money from a man, who immediately reported the matter to the police and did not pay over any money. The sentencer said that the offence of blackmail was too *serious* to permit a non-custodial sentence. Sentence: 15 months' detention in a young offender institution. Held by the Court of Appeal: The Court could not agree with the view that the offence of blackmail was 'so *serious*'. The sentence was quashed and replaced by a probation order.

Scott (1990) 12 Cr App R (S) 23. The appellant (20) had pleaded guilty to an offence of attempted theft and nine offences of theft. She was employed as a check-out assistant at a supermarket where she allowed customers to take goods out without paying, or sometimes paying a nominal sum. She had gained almost nothing herself except that one of the thieves gave her a couple of jumpers and a baking set which had been stolen. It was impossible to give any accurate estimate of the amount of the loss suffered by the store: the appellant guessed that it was about £4,000. The appellant, who had no previous convictions, was a single mother, living alone with a two month old baby. Sentence: six months' detention in a young offender institution. Held by the Court of Appeal: The appellant's reason for committing the thefts was not easy to determine. It was probably partly an effort to buy popularity and partly the momentum of events once the behaviour started. The case was not so *serious* that a non-custodial sentence could not be justified. That was so taking the various offences to which she had pleaded guilty as a composite whole and not individually. But the wording of s1(4A) CJA 82 was such that the court was only entitled to consider the gravity of each individual offence: on that technical ground also it was plain that the judge's sentence was wrong.The sentence was quashed and a two year probation order was substituted.

Osborne (1990) 12 Cr App R (S) 55. The appellant (20) with no previous convictions, pleaded guilty to reckless driving and driving with excess alcohol in his breath. He had drunk about four pints of lager over a period of two hours and then set off to drive home. He drove into a housing estate at a high speed and lost control of the car which mounted the pavement, glanced off a lamp post and hit a hedge before eventually hitting another lamp post which broke off. When the police arrived he was chased at speeds of 60 and 70 mph before stopping and attempting to hide. He was later found to have a breath alcohol level of nearly twice the legal limit. Sentence: nine months' detention in a young offender institution. Held by the Court of Appeal: The sentencer had been right in saying that this offence was so *serious* that a non-custodial sentence for it could not be justified. However, the sentence was reduced to three months.

Parry (1990) 12 Cr App R (S) 69. The appellant (18) pleaded guilty to a single count of burglary. With another young offender, he broke into a house while the occupants were out in the daytime. Rooms on three floors were entered, searched and ransacked and a variety of different items stolen including a video recorder, a camera and accessories, jewellery and coins, stamp collections, a television set, a hi-fi tuner and tapedeck, and some Australian currency. The appellant had four previous convictions for various offences and had received financial penalties and an attendance centre order. Sentence: 18 months' detention in a young offender institiution. Held by the Court of Appeal: This was a particularly *serious* dwelling house burglary, albeit committed by day when the occupants were out. The offence was of so *serious* a character that a non-custodial sentence for it could not be justified. However, the sentence was reduced to nine months.

Keane (1990) 12 Cr App R (S) 132. The appellant (18) was convicted of a robbery, a burglary, three attempted burglaries and possessing cocaine. The robbery, committed with another man, involved accosting a 17 year old on a bus and taking his personal stereo and headphones while the other man held the victim's arms The burglary, committed when aged 16, involved breaking into a house and stealing property worth £1,000, none of which was recovered. The attempted burglaries involved three unsuccessful breakings into flats. The drugs offence concerned 600 milligrammes of cocaine worth around £50. He had one previous conviction for handling stolen property for which he had been conditionally discharged. Sentence: a total of three years' detention in a young offender institution. Held by the Court of Appeal: The offender did not have a history of 'failure to respond' and there was no risk to the public of serious harm from him. The court had to consider whether the offences, taken individually, were 'so *serious*'. The court considered that the criterion was not met by any of the offences. A probation order was substituted.

Littler and Dooley (1990) 12 Cr App R (S) 143. The appellants (both 18) pleaded guilty to one count of burglary. Together with an accomplice, aged 22, they broke into a house while the owner was away. Property, including a microwave oven and two television sets, two music centres and jewellery worth £1,660 was stolen. Littler had no previous convictions. Dooley had two findings of guilt for burglary and one for theft and being carried in a stolen vehicle. He had received a conditional discharge and an attendance centre order. Sentence: Littler, 12 months' detention in a young offender institution; Dooley 15 months' detention. Held by the Court of Appeal: The sentencer appeared to have considered that s1(4A)(a), 'failure to respond' applied to Dooley [consider now the effect of s1(3) CJA 91]. The Court disagreed, since he had complied with earlier orders in a satisfactory manner. The sentencer also appeared to consider that the offence was 'so *serious*'. The Court considered that he was wrong in this. Community service orders were substituted.

See *McCarroll* (1990) 12 Cr App R (S) 147 in *Chapter* 3 which deals with seriousness and protection of the public.

Tonks (1990) 12 Cr App R (S) 282. The appellant (19) with no previous convictions for sexual offences, pleaded guilty to unlawful sexual intercourse with a girl under the age of 13. Five other offences involving the same girl were taken into consideration. The appellant, then aged 18, met a girl aged 12 and began to go out with her. After some time, the girl's stepfather, and his own father, warned him that she was too young to go out with him. After they had known each other for about a month, sexual intercourse took place on five occasions and the girl became pregnant. Sentence: 18 months' detention in a young offender institution. Held by the Court of Appeal: There were some important mitigating factors. There was evidence that the appellant was emotionally immature for his age. There was some genuine affection between the two. He was candid with the police, pleaded guilty immediately and showed remorse. On the other hand, the association continued despite warnings and he acted in a grossly irresponsible manner in allowing the girl, little more than a child to become pregnant. A custodial sentence was inevitable, but the court reduced it to nine months.

Smith and Gilhooley (1990) 12 Cr App R (S) 172. The appellants (two young women aged 19) with no previous convictions, were convicted of assault occasioning actual bodily harm. They encountered two other young women in the same street late at night and there was a confrontation leading to a fight. When the fight broke up, one of the other women ran off and the appellants chased her, and kicked and punched her. The victim was found to have a fractured nose, a fracture of the floor of the left orbit, and multiple bruises and abrasions. The appellants were both affected by drink. Sentence: six months in a young offender institution. Held by the Court of Appeal: The Court was not satisfied that the offence was 'so *serious*'. The appropriate disposal was a community service order with £400 compensation each.

Wilson (1990) 12 Cr App R (S) 284. The appellant (18) with no previous convictions, pleaded guilty to one count of opening a postal packet and two of theft. He had worked for the Post Office for about three months and admitted opening postal packets and stealing two telephones, two track suits, a jumper and a medallion. All the property was recovered. Sentence: three months' detention in a young offender institution. Held by the Court of Appeal: The offences, considered individually, were not 'so *serious*'. In the judgement of the Court, a sentence, for example, of community service or indeed of probation could have been justified in relation to any one of the three offences. A conditional discharge was substituted.

Furnell (1990) 12 Cr App R (S) 306. The appellant (20) was convicted of assault occasioning actual bodily harm. He was one of several young people behaving in an unruly manner in the street, running, shouting, and cutting flowers from gardens of houses with a pair of shears. A householder, believing that they had damaged his car, went into the street to remonstrate with them, and a scuffle broke out between him and a member of the group. The householder broke off from the scuffle and had gone about 100 yards when he was struck on the head. The blow knocked him to the ground and caused a laceration one and a half centimetres long in the back of his head. He suffered concussion, nausea and visual blurring. The blow was delivered by the appellant using the pair of shears. Sentence: six months' detention in a young offender institution. Held by the Court of Appeal: The circumstances, involving street violence, the use of a weapon and the delivery of a blow to the back of the head, justified the sentencer in concluding that the offence was 'so *serious*'. However, six months was excessive. Three months was appropriate.

Beddoes (1990) 12 Cr App R (S) 363. The appellant (20) pleaded guilty to one count of violent disorder and one of handling stolen goods. He was involved in a fight involving 15 young men who attacked a group of soldiers outside a public house. The soldiers were attacked with snooker cues and glasses were thrown. Two people were taken to hospital. The handling offence consisted of £30, part of a larger sum, stolen in a burglary. The appellant had two previous convictions for criminal damage, each resulting in a fine. Sentence: nine months' detention in a young offender institution for violent disorder, with one month concurrent for handling. Held by the Court of Appeal: So far as violent disorder was concerned, the appellant qualified for a custodial sentence having regard to the *seriousness* of the offence; but the Court reduced the sentence to six months. The offence of handling was not 'so *serious*' and neither did the 'failure to respond' criterion apply. The one month sentence was quashed.

Hunter (1991) Crim LR 146. The appellant (20) pleaded guilty to two counts of criminal damage and three of assault occasioning actual bodily harm. He had been living with a woman who terminated the relationship following a series of incidents. He subsequently damaged a van belonging to her employers and caused damage inside her parents' home. He then attacked the woman, dragging her by the hair and punching her many times; he then attacked the woman's father who intervened, kicking him as he lay on the ground after falling; and finally the appellant attacked another man who intervened, kicking him unconscious as he lay on the floor. The woman had returned to the appellant since and indicated that they were reconciled. The appellant had numerous previous convictions for which he had received one conditional discharge, three custodial sentences, a bind over and a fine. Sentence: consecutive terms of three, four, six, four and four months' detention in a young offender institution (total 21 months). Held by the

Court of Appeal: The two later assaults, which involved 'horrifying personal violence', were 'so *serious*', as was one of the criminal damage offences, which concerned furniture and fittings to the extent of £1,384. So was the assault on the woman, but that sentence would be made concurrent. The remaining criminal damage offence did not satisfy any of the criteria in s1(4A) CJA 82.

Pike (1990) 12 Cr App R (S) 412. The appellant (19) pleaded guilty to a series of offences contained in four indictments and asked for a further 11 offences to be considered. The first indictment charged one count of theft of property worth £260 from a parked car, with three similar offences taken into consideration; the second indictment charged two burglaries of commercial premises, with property worth £780 stolen; on the third indictment he admitted handling stolen property taken from a parked car and attempting to obtain by deception by selling it. The fourth indictment charged burglary of a jeweller's shop and theft of jewellery from a shop, with eight other burglaries of shops taken into consideration: these offences involved property worth in excess of £20,000. The appellant had two previous convictions for minor offences, for which he was fined and conditionally discharged. Sentence: two years detention in a young offender institution. Held by the Court of Appeal: It was conceded by counsel that the offences in the fourth indictment satisfied the 'so *serious*' criterion. The Court reduced the sentence for those offences to 15 months in view of the appellant's previous history, and accepted the contention that the other offences were not 'so *serious*'. However, it concluded that where, when looking at the offences in isolation, the inhibition on custodial sentencing was removed, the Crown Court was not thereafter inhibited from imposing a concurrent sentence on the lesser matters (though it reduced the length of each).

See Grant (1990) 12 Cr App R (S) 441 which resulted in a community service order, mentioned in *Chapter 5*.

Parsley (1990) 12 Cr App R (S) 498. The appellant (19) pleaded guilty to one count of theft and five counts of burglary divided between three indictments. Together with three others he stole 13 T-shirts from a shop and threatened the assistant when challenged; he stole a holdall from a shop window by climbing over a partition; and he committed four burglaries of dwellings while the owners were away. The premises were ransacked and property worth nearly £10,000 was stolen. The appellant asked for nine further burglaries and one attempted burglary to be taken into consideration: these offences involved property worth about £10,000. He had one previous conviction for theft, resulting in a probation order. Sentence: a total of 27 months' detention in a young offender institution. Held by the Court of Appeal: Burglary of someone's home was a very *serious* offence, whether the burglary was by night or day, whether the property was occupied or not, and whether much or little was stolen. The seriousness of the offence was in the invasion of a person's home and privacy, and the distress and fears it left behind. The Court did not consider that the four thefts satisfied the 'so *serious*' criterion, but the four offences of burglary of dwelling houses did. The sentence was upheld.

Mussell and Others (1991) 12 Cr App R (S) 607. The four appellants (under 21) appeared before the Crown Court for varying numbers of offences mainly of burglary and theft. They were sentenced to terms of detention in a young offender institution ranging from three to 12 months. <u>Held by the Court of Appeal</u>: When considering the 'so *serious*' criterion, a court was not permitted to take an overall view of the defendant's criminality: unless at least one offence was of sufficient seriousness, the offender did not qualify for a custodial sentence. Like any other offences, burglaries of dwelling houses varied in their seriousness. Among the features which the court was likely to consider were the extent to which the particular burglary was planned or premeditated, the numbers involved in it, whether it was committed by day or night, whether any person was or may have been at home or may have witnessed part of the burglary. Sometimes the offence was committed by day, following careful planning with the object of avoiding discovery. Within the house, the activities of the burglar were of great significance. Questions of disturbance, ransacking, vandalism, fouling and hooliganism were all relevant: so was the amount and value, both in monetary and personal terms, of any objects stolen. The effect of the burglary on the victim and family was of obvious importance. The victims of burglaries could suffer anxiety and distress which might last for years and which might far outweigh the value of the goods actually stolen.

Although always a serious offence, a dwelling house burglary was not always 'so *serious* that a non-custodial sentence for it cannot be justified'. It could not be assumed that any dwelling house burglary was an offence which automatically required a custodial sentence. Each offence had to be judged individually. The Court would not readily interfere with the conclusion of the trial judge that a particular dwelling house burglary was so serious that a non-custodial sentence for it could not be justified. In this case the sentencer had identified particular offences which he considered to be sufficiently *serious* to bring s1(4A)(c) CJA 82 into operation and the court accepted the reasoning of the sentencer. There was a crucial distinction between the stringent tests which were to be applied before any of the criteria in s1(4A), *supra*, was established, and the consequences which followed once one of those criteria had been established. Both *McCarroll* (1990) 12 Cr App R (S) 147 (*Chapter 3*), and *Marsden* (1990) 12 Cr App R (S) 274 (*The Youth Court, Chapter 5*), had focussed on the proper construction of paragraph (c) rather than on the consequences which flowed when paragraph (c) had been established. A court must not pass a custodial sentence unless it was first satisfied that the offender qualified for a custodial sentence: if after considering the appropriate tests the court considered that he did qualify, then a custodial sentence might be passed for offences which were not in themselves 'so *serious*'.

This was subject to two established principles. First, a sentencing court must be astute to ensure that when two consecutive sentences are appropriate in the case of young offenders the total sentence should not be excessive. Secondly, if a young offender qualified for a custodial sentence only because one or more of his offences were within paragraph (c), the sentencing court should ask itself whether consecutive sentences were really required, bearing in mind that but for the qualifying offence, no custodial sentence could have been imposed. The sentencer had made no reference to the possibility that the appellants might have qualified for a custodial sentence under paragraph (a) of s 1(4A) ('failure to respond'). Although the court must give close attention to the contents of a social inquiry report, the fact that there was a favourable report need not prevent the sentencer from concluding that the particular offender was unable or unwilling to respond to a non-custodial penalty. A favourable report was not conclusive on the question. The Court reduced the sentences to various terms between nine and 30 months. [*Note*: The commentary on this case in the *Criminal Law Review* 1991 CLR 390 says: 'The position now seems to be that custodial sentences may be passed for the less serious offences which would not qualify in their own right, but the sentencer should take particular care over the totality of the sentence and wherever possible make any sentences for such offences concurrent ... The reasoning of this part of the judgement depends on the concept that an offender may 'qualify for a custodial sentence': that concept will disappear when the [Criminal Justice Act 1991] is enacted.']

Morris (1991) Crim LR 563. The appellant (20) pleaded guilty to six counts of theft and asked for 41 other offences to be considered. He was employed as a cashier in a firm of builders. Over a period of two or three months he took a total of more than £1,000 from his employers by taking the money which he received from customers. The money was spent on gambling. He had two previous convictions, for burglary and taking a vehicle, and had been fined on each occasion. Sentence: five months' detention in a young offender institution. Held by the Court of Appeal: The sentencer had correctly considered each count individually for the purpose of appying s1(4A) CJA 82, but it did not seem to the Court that the thefts by the appellant from his employers of sums between £40 and £80 could be described as 'so *serious*'. The sentence was varied to a probation order.

Mode of Trial Guidelines

The *National Mode of Trial Guidelines* (Lord Chancellor's Department, 1989; *Practice Note* (*Mode of Trial Guidelines*) [1990] 1 WLR 1439, (1991) 92 Cr App R 142)), issued under the auspices of the Lord Chief Justice, state: 'The purpose of these guidelines is to help magistrates to decide whether or not to commit 'either way' offences for trial in the Crown Court. Their object is to provide guidance not direction. They are not intended to impinge upon a magistrate's duty to consider each case individually and on its own particular facts. These guidelines apply to all defendants *aged 17 and above* [of necessity, this must be read as '18 and above' once the CJA 91 is in force].

GENERAL MODE OF TRIAL CONSIDERATIONS

Section 19 of the Magistrates' Courts Act 1980 requires magistrates to have regard to the following matters in deciding whether an offence is more suitable for summary trial or trial on indictment: **1** The nature of the case. **2** Whether the circumstances make the offence one of a serious character. **3** Whether punishment which a magistrates' court would have power to inflict for it would be adequate. **4** Any other circumstances which appear to the court to make it more suitable for the offence to be tried in one way rather than the other. **5** Any representations made by the prosecutor or the defence. Certain general observations can be made: (a) The court should never make its decision on the grounds of convenience or expedition. (b) The court should assume for the purpose of deciding mode of trial that the prosecution version of the facts is correct. (c) The defendant's antecedents and personal mitigating circumstances are irrelevant for the purposes of deciding mode of trial. (d) The fact that offences are alleged to be specimens is a relevant consideration; the fact that the defendant will be asking for other offences to be taken into consideration, if convicted is not [*quare* the extent to which this survives the CJA 91, in view of the definition of associated offence: see s31(2), *ibid*]. (e) Where cases involve complex questions of law, the court should consider committal for trial. (f) Where two or more defendants are jointly charged with an offence and the court decides that the offence is more suitable for summary trial, if one defendant elects trial on indictment, the court must proceed to deal with all the defendants as examining justices in respect of that offence. A juvenile jointly charged with someone aged 17 or over ['18 or over', following the CJA 91] should only be committed for trial in the interests of justice. **(g) In general, except where otherwise stated, either way offences should be tried summarily unless the court considers that the particular case has one or more of the features set out in the following pages and that its sentencing powers are insufficient.' High value** Where reference is made in the guidelines to property or damage of 'high value' it means '... a figure equal to at least twice the amount of the limit imposed by statute on a magistrates' court when making a compensation order'. [Currently £2,000. A side effect of the raising of the maximum limit for compensation to £5,000 (sched 4 CJA 91) will be to increase the range of cases where magistrates can properly assume jurisdiction, *semble*: But note the anomaly whereby the limit for (purely) 'summary criminal damage' has not been increased beyond the existing £2,000]: see s22 MCA 1980; sched 2, *ibid*. **Presumption of summary trial** In relation to every offence dealt with in the guidelines, after the list of relevant considerations, there is a general rider as follows: 'In general, cases should be tried summarily unless the court considers that one or more of the above features is present in the case and that its sentencing powers are insufficient'. **Individual offences** [The guidelines deal with the following offences (each set out on a full page)].

Theft and fraud 1 Breach of trust by a person in a position of substantial authority, or in whom a high degree of trust is placed. 2 Theft or fraud which has been committed or disguised in a sophisticated manner. 3 Theft or fraud committed by an organised gang. 4 The victim is particularly vulnerable to theft or fraud eg the elderly or infirm. 5 The unrecovered property is of high value.

Handling 1 Dishonest handling of stolen property by a receiver who has commissioned the theft. 2 The offence has professional hallmarks. 3 The property is of high value.

Social security frauds 1 Organised frauds on a large scale. 2 The frauds are substantial and carried out over a long period of time.

Violence (s20 and s47 Offences Against the Person Act 1861) 1 The use of a weapon of a kind likely to cause serious injury. 2 A weapon is used and serious injury is caused. 3 More than minor injury caused by kicking, head butting or similar forms of assault. 4 Serious violence is caused to those whose work has to be done in contact with the public eg police officers, bus drivers, taxi drivers, publicans and shopkeepers. 5 Violence to vulnerable people eg the elderly and the infirm. The same considerations apply to domestic violence.

Public Order Act Offences 1) Cases of *violent disorder* should generally be committed for trial. 2) *Affray* 1 Organised violence or use of weapons. 2

Significant injury or substantial damage. 3 The offence has a clear racial motivation. 4 An attack upon police officers, ambulance men, firemen and the like.

Violence to and neglect of children 1 Substantial injury. 2 Repeated violence or serious neglect, even if the harm is slight. 3 Sadistic violence eg deliberate burning or scalding.

Indecent assault 1 Substantial disparity in age between victim and defendant, and the assault is more than trivial. 2 Violence and threats of violence. 3 Relationship of trust or responsibility between defendant and victim. 4 Several similar offences, and the assaults are more than trivial. 5 The victim is particularly vulnerable. 6 The serious nature of the assault.

Unlawful sexual intercourse 1 Wide disparity of age. 2 Breach of a position of trust. 3 The victim is particularly vulnerable. NOTE: Unlawful sexual intercourse with a girl under 13 is triable only on indictment.

Drugs 1) *Class A* a) Supply; possession with intent to supply. These cases should be committed for trial. b) Possession. Should be committed for trial unless the amount is small and consistent only with personal use. 2) *Class B* a) Supply; possession with intent to supply. Should be committed for trial unless there is only small scale supply for no payment. b) Possession. Should be committed for trial when the quantity is substantial.

Reckless driving 1 Alcohol or drugs contributing to recklessness. 2 Grossly excessive speed. 3 Racing. 4 Prolonged course of reckless driving. 5 Other related offences.

Criminal damage 1 Deliberate fire-raising. 2 Committed by a group. 3 Damage of a high value. 4 The offence has a clear racial motivation. *Note*: Offences set out in Schedule 2 to the Magistrates' Courts Act 1980 (which includes offences of criminal damage contrary to section 1 Criminal Damage Act 1971 which do not amount to arson) must be tried summarily if the value of the property damaged or destroyed is £2,000 or less [NB that this figure of £2,000 is *not* increased by the CJA 91].

Chapter 3

Protection of the Public

This chapter deals with the 'protection of the public from serious harm' criterion for the use of custody. Protection of the public is relevant to both the custody *threshold* and the *length* of custody: s1(2)(b) CJA 91 and s2(2)(b), *ibid*. The criterion is relevant only to *violent* or *sexual* offences. Also, unlike 'seriousness' under s1(2)(a) and 2(2)(a), *ibid* (*Chapter 2*), which is applicable generally as a measure of the appropriate level or extent of a sentence, this criterion is relevant only to *custody* decisions. It is *not* a basis for a community sentence: see s6(1) CJA 91; or fines: s18(2), *ibid*. However, 'protecting the public from harm' (a comparable but considerably reduced test) does serve as one of the criteria for the use of a probation order or a combination order (*Chapter 5*). It should be noted that violent or sexual offences fall to be dealt with under *either* of the criteria in s1(2) CJA 91. Similarly, the length of a sentence for such an offence can be judged under *either* limb of s2(2), ie on the basis of the combined seriousness of any number of offences (s2(2)(a)) or the need to protect the public (s2(2)(b)). Situations in which this criterion becomes critically relevant are thus: where seriousness alone does not justify custody but there is a risk of future serious harm from the offender; and/or where a longer sentence is necessary to protect the public than can be justified under the seriousness limb of s2(2)(a). In all other situations, the same sentence can be achieved by application of the provisions relating to seriousness alone. Courts will need to be meticulous in ensuring that their reasons under s1(4) CJA 91 precisely match the basis for the decision.

Background
Compared with the number of Court of Appeal rulings on the seriousness test in s1(4A) CJA 82, those relating to the protection of the public criterion in s1(4A) are few and far between (largely, it seems, because judicial deliberations about the old seriousness test invariably come to the fore in the judgements and arguments). The existing public protection criterion applied to *all* offences, so that, given the narrower scope of the criterion in the CJA 91 (ie it is limited to violent or sexual offences, *supra*), appeal rulings might be expected to become rarer still. However, decided cases on s1(4A) remain pertinent due to the close correlation of the protection of the public test in the CJA 82 and the CJA 91. It is often possible to conclude from an appeal ruling that protection of the public was *not* in issue: consider the wide range of offending behaviour encompassed by the summaries of rulings set out in *Chapter 2* where protection of the

public was not mentioned by the court of first instance or Court of Appeal.

Development of the test

As originally enacted, s1(4) CJA 82 provided that a custodial sentence should only be imposed on a person under 21 when, *inter alia*: '... no other method of dealing with him is appropriate because ... a custodial sentence is *necessary* for the protection of the public ... ' (italics supplied). Section 123 CJA 88 amended s1(4) so as to set out (in the new s1(4A) CJA 82) an enhanced test whereby an offender under 21 years of age could only qualify for a custodial sentence, *inter alia*, if: '... (b) only a custodial sentence would be *adequate* to protect the public from *serious harm from him...*' (italics supplied). Significantly, that criterion applied in the context of both 'adequacy' to protect the public and 'serious harm from [the offender]', albeit the meaning of serious harm or protecting the public was not further defined. The meaning of 'protecting the public from serious harm' under the CJA 91 is set out in s31(3) CJA 91 as follows: '... protecting the public from serious harm from him shall be construed as a reference to protecting members of the public from death or serious personal injury, whether physical or psychological, occasioned by further such offences committed by him.' With the addition of this definition, the 'protection of the public' ground contained in s1(2)(b) CJA 91 is similarly directed as follows: '... the court shall not pass a custodial sentence on the offender unless it is of the opinion - ... (b) where the offence is a violent or sexual offence, that only such a sentence would be adequate to protect the public from serious harm from him'. The provision applies except where the sentence is fixed by law: s1(1) CJA 91. The court must state: that it is of opinion that the criterion applies; why it is of that opinion; and explain its decision to the offender in open court and in ordinary language: s1(4) CJA 91. Additional reasons must be given for any decision to impose a *longer* sentence (than is commensurate with seriousness) under s2(2)(b) CJA 91: s2(3)(b), see *post*.

Sexual or violent offence

These categories are defined in s31(1) CJA 91. 'Violent offence' is widely defined to include any offence which leads, or is intended or likely to lead, to a death or serious personal injury. This would cover most charges of assault, riot, violent disorder and affray, and the CJA 91 specifically adds all cases of arson (ie criminal damage by fire: see s1(3) Criminal Damage Act 1971) whether or not the likelihood of, or intent to cause, personal injury can be established. 'Sexual offences' include most statutory sexual offences with the exception of those concerned with prostitution and certain consenting acts between homosexuals. The relevant part of s31(1) is reproduced in *Chapter 4*.

Protection from 'the offender'

The words 'from him' make it clear that this provision does not allow custodial sentences to be passed which are aimed at deterring others. The purpose must be to protect the public from this offender. The protection of the public from serious harm depends on the 'incapacitation' effect of the custodial sentence in keeping the offender out of circulation. It is submitted that, in view of the relative shortness of the sentences which can be imposed by magistrates' courts (ie six months, or 12 months in total where there are two or more 'either way' offences: see s133(2) MCA 1980) it is rarely likely to be appropriate for magistrates to justify a custodial sentence on this criterion.

Information

The general requirements that the court take into account '... all such information about the circumstances of the offence as is available to it': s3(2)(a) CJA 91 and concerning the obtaining of a pre-sentence report: s3(2)(b), *ibid* - see *Chapter 8*, apply. Also, and perhaps of special relevance to these types of offence, where a court is minded to impose a custodial sentence on an offender who is or appears to be mentally disordered, it must also obtain and consider a medical report: s4(1), *ibid*; unless it deems this to be unnecessary: s4(2), *ibid*. The court must also consider any other information before the court which relates to his mental condition and the likely effect of a custodial sentence on that condition: s4(3), *ibid*. Whilst there is no absolute statutory requirement of a report from a psychiatrist, such a report will usually be highly desirable because of its relevance to the question whether there is a future risk to the public, and to the extent of any risk if the offender is released into the community. Access to this kind of information may be improved where there is a local duty psychiatrist scheme (see Cavadino, *The Case for 'Duty Psychiatrist' Schemes in Magistrates' Courts*, 155 JPN 701).

Predicting future behaviour

The proportionate approach to sentencing prevents a court from looking at previous convictions in order to determine the seriousness of the present offence: s29(1) CJA 91; except where aggravating factors are disclosed: s29(2). Neither s29 CJA 91 nor any comparable provision applies to the protection of the public criterion (although, it should be noted that s29 does apply to assessing the *seriousness* of violent or sexual offences so far as the criterion in s1(2)(a) CJA 91 is concerned, *supra* and see, generally, *Chapter 2*). The court will thus be able to draw inferences from the circumstances of the present offence and the existence of any previous convictions. The offender's past record may well be an important indicator for courts in relation to the protection criterion.

Mode of trial and committal for sentence

If a magistrates' court forms the opinion, after hearing an either way case, that a 'public protection' sentence beyond its powers is necessary, it may commit to the Crown Court for sentence. The offence must be a violent or sexual one; the offender must be aged *21 or over*; and the court must be satisfied that a sentence longer than it has the power to impose is necessary for the protection of the public from serious harm from the offender: s38 MCA 1980 (as substituted by s25 CJA 91).

Sentences longer than are commensurate with seriousness

Section 2(2) CJA 91 provides that where a court passes a custodial sentence other than one fixed by law, the sentence shall be: '(a) for such term (not exceeding the permitted maximum) as in the opinion of the court is commensurate with the seriousness of the offence, or the combination of the offence and other offences associated with it; or (b) where the offence is a violent or sexual offence, for such longer period (not exceeding that maximum) as in the opinion of the court is necessary to protect the public from serious harm from the offender'. This aspect is completely new. The process is in fact cumulative. A court can only give adequate and proper reasons if it addresses both seriousness, protection of the public and the *difference* in length between a notional commensurate sentence and the actual sentence imposed to protect the public. The court is *not* limited to two offences in combination either in relation to the custody threshold in s1(2)(b) CJA 91, *supra* (ct s1(2)(a) *ibid*; or the length of sentence under any part of s2(2), *ibid*.

Existing law on protection of the public

Over the last two decades, the Court of Appeal has repeatedly emphasised the general rule that the danger posed by the offender to the community does not justify passing a sentence which is disproportionate to the offence for which it is imposed. Although there have been occasional decisions which are difficult to reconcile with this principle, for example *Kirk* (1989) 11 Cr App R (S) 453, the overwhelming majority of decisions have reaffirmned the principle succinctly summarised by Lord Bridge in *Tolley* (1978) 68 Cr App R 323: 'The principle ... is clear, that punishment should fit the crime and the fact that an offender's mental condition makes it likely that he may, if at liberty, be a danger to himself and others does not justify the use of the penal system as a kind of long stop to make good the shortcomings of social services and the mental health system.' The same principle was stated as follows by Evans J in Richardson (1990) 12 Cr App R (S) 311: 'We were therefore addressed on the option of whether the appropriate sentence in the present case should be increased beyond what would otherwise be proper by reason of the need to provide for the future protection of the public. We are satisfied that the underlying principle is ... that the punishment shall fit the crime; that it is not proper to increase custodial sentences for reasons unconnected with the crime and which would be directed solely towards increasing the period of detention.'

The only exceptions to the principle that a disproportionate sentence of imprisonment must not be imposed on grounds of dangerousness have hitherto been where it is appropriate to use either an extended sentence (abolished by s5(2)(a) CJA 91) or a life sentence. The Act contains no guidelines on the use of the new power in s2(2)(b) CJA 91, so that it will be left to the Court of Appeal to create and apply such guidelines.

A possible test

It seems likely that any guidelines will draw on elements of the current approach to imposing discretionary life sentences. It was established in *Hodgson* (1967) 52 Cr App R 113 that before a life sentence can be imposed, the following three conditions must be fulfilled: (i) the offence or offences are themselves grave enough to warrant a very long sentence; and (ii) the offender is a person of unstable character likely to commit such offences in the future; and (iii) if such offences are committed, the consequences to others may be specially injurious. The approach to interpreting conditions (ii) and (iii) may be particularly relevant to sentencing under s2(2)(b), *supra*. To satisfy condition (ii), the offender must be subject to a marked degree of mental instability (not necessarily mental illness) or a personality defect which makes him or her likely to commit grave offences in the future. In *Owen* (1980) 2 Cr App R (S) 45, Kenneth Jones J said that '... no court is entitled to take that view of a prisoner unless there is the clearest evidence before it that he does suffer from some form of mental instability'. The sentencer should warn counsel that he is considering using the power to impose a 'longer than commensurate' sentence and invite submissions on the question: see Scott (1989) 11 Cr App R (S) 249.

Birch (1989) 11 Cr App R (S) 202

This case did not directly concern the criteria in s1(4) CJA 82 but the making of a restriction order on a mentally disordered offender. As s41 Mental Health Act 1973 requires that a restriction order must be 'necessary for the protection of the public from serious harm', the judgement has potential implications for the present 'protection of the public' criterion as substituted by s123 CJA 88. The appellant pleaded guilty to manslaughter by reason of diminished responsibility. She had been married for some years to a man younger than herself. The marriage deteriorated over a period of years and the husband became involved with another woman, of whom the appellant became intensely jealous. The appellant's mental condition deteriorated and she became depressive. She obtained a shotgun and some ammunition: at some stage the barrel of the shotgun was shortened. She lured her husband by a trick to a flat where she was living and, when he was inside, she apparently fired a shot at him. The police were called and found her astride her husband who was lying on the floor with knife wounds in his chest, one of them nine centimetres deep. He had apparently been shot from a range of about three feet and had severe injuries to the thigh. He died shortly afterwards; either the gunshot wounds or the knife wounds could have caused his death.

Four medical reports were before the Crown Court. The first indicated that the appellant had a premorbid personality with histrionic traits and had suffered from depressive illness at the time of the incident. It recommended a hospital order but indicated the view that the appellant did not constitute a danger to the public or represent a serious threat of absconding. The second report concluded that the appellant was suffering from depression to the point that she was a substantial suicide risk. The third report attributed the appellant's actions to her illness, and the fourth included a statement that, if the appellant did not get into a similar situation again, a repetition was unlikely and that she was not a danger to the general public. A hospital order was made with a restriction order (ie restricting discharge from hospital) without limit of time. Reiterating that a restriction order could only be made if it was necessary to protect the public from serious harm, the Court of Appeal said the judge had power to make a restriction order even when the doctors were unanimous that the appellant was not dangerous: the assessment of risk was for the court. The harm in question need not relate to the public in general. It would suffice if a category of persons, or even a single person, were adjudged to be at risk, although the category of persons would exclude the offender himself. The potential harm must be serious and a high probability of a recurrence of minor offences would not be sufficient. A minor offence by a mentally disordered and dangerous man may properly leave him subject to a restriction. The converse might be true: a serious offence committed by someone who was adjudged to have a very low risk of reoffending may lead to an unrestricted hospital order.

On the facts, the question was simply whether, in the light of the nature of the offence, the appellant's antecedents and the risk of further offences, a restriction order was necessary for the protection of the public. This was a serious offence but the court could not find that there was material justifying the conclusion that a restriction order was necessary. The restriction order was quashed, leaving a straightforward hospital order under s37 Mental Health Act 1983.

Protection of the public and non-custodial sentences

At first sight, it might be objected that community sentences and financial penalties have nothing to offer in respect of offenders who represent a risk to the public. In relation to the truly dangerous offender this must, indeed, be so. It is hard to imagine that any court would consciously allow an offender who represents such a risk to go unrestrained. However, it should be pointed out that a statutory basis for using both probation orders and combination orders is, *inter alia*, that these orders are desirable in the interests of '... protecting the public from harm from [the offender] or preventing the commission by [the offender] of further offences': s2(1)(b) PCCA 73 (as substituted by s8 CJA 91); and s11(2)(b), *ibid*. Obviously, what is intended here is protection of the public from a lesser level of risk than that already discussed *supra* (the word used is 'harm' not 'serious harm'). Presumably, with these two community sentences, the aim is to achieve protection of the public over the longer term, through supervision, as opposed to immediate incarceration. The criteria for probation orders and combination orders are outlined in *Chapter 5*.

Statutory Provisions affecting the protection of the public criterion are contained in *Chapter 4, Custody*. Sections 28 and 29 appear in *Chapter 1*.

Chapter 4

Custodial Sentences

The CJA 91 sets out criteria and procedures for the use of custodial sentences. These provisions have their roots in s1(4) and (4A) CJA 82 (as amended by s123 CJA 88) which contained restrictions on custodial sentences for *young offenders*, ie those below 21 years of age. Subsections (4) and (4A) are repealed by s101(2) and sched 13 CJA 91. Under the CJA 91, standard restrictions on custodial sentences apply to *all* offenders, regardless of age. Custodial sentencing must be considered within the framework created by Part I CJA 91 (including strengthened community sentences: *Chapter 5*) and the 'continuum' created by Part II (*Parole and Early Release: Chapter 10*).

Sentences to which the criteria apply
The criteria apply to all custodial sentences regardless of the status of the offence or the place of trial, ie whether summary or indictable, and whether tried by magistrates or on indictment, except, in the latter case, where the penalty is fixed by law (ie life imprisonment for murder. Thus, the criteria *do* apply to *discretionary* life sentences, whatever the offence): s1(1) CJA 91. 'Custodial sentence' is defined in s31 CJA 91: in the case of a person aged 21 or over as 'a sentence of imprisonment'; and in the case of a person below 21 as 'detention in a young offender institution'; or 'under s53 CYPA 1933' (an important addition to the disposals affected by the criteria, relating to young offenders convicted in the Crown Court of 'grave crimes'); or 'a sentence of custody for life under s8(2) [CJA 82]' (persons aged over 18 only: see s63(5) CJA 91). Excluded from the definition of 'sentence of imprisonment', are committals or attachment for contempt of court: s31(1) CJA 91, eg under the Contempt of Act 1981.

Three routes to custody
There are three routes to custody: two grounds, the 'seriousness of the offence': s1(2)(a) CJA 91, or the 'protection of the public from serious harm from the offender': s1(2)(b), *ibid*; and a default provision contained in s1(3), *ibid*, ie where the offender refuses to give his or her consent to a community sentence which requires that consent.

Seriousness of the offence
The first criterion prevents a court from passing a custodial sentence unless of the opinion that the offence itself is so serious that *only* custody can be

justified. There is no absolute measure of seriousness, which is thus a question of fact in each case: but see the extended discussion in *Chapter 2* concerning this aspect. Unless the penalty, from a proportionate standpoint, is beyond the scope of a community sentence, then, subject to s1(2)(b), *ibid* (protection), or s1(3), *ibid* (refusal), it is wrong to use custody. Section 1(2)(a) CJA 91 reads: '... the court shall not pass a custodial sentence ... unless it is of the opinion - (a) that the offence, or the combination of the offence and one other offence associated with it, was so serious that only such a sentence can be justified for the offence'. 'Associated offence' is defined in s31(1) CJA 91: see *Statutory Provisions* at the end of this chapter. In forming an opinion, the court must take account of certain *Information*, see under that heading *post*. The words '*only* such a sentence can be justified' must be read in the light of s28(1) CJA 91 which permits widescale mitigation.

Two offences in combination

The seriousness criterion compels courts to view offences individually, but permits *one* other offence to be placed into the balance. The effect is that seriousness can be judged by looking to a maximum of two offences, in combination, and provided that they are 'associated offences' within the meaning of s31(2), ie: '(a) the offender is convicted of it in the proceedings in which he is convicted of the other offence, or (although convicted of it in earlier proceedings) is sentenced for it at the same time as he is sentenced for that offence; or (b) the offender admits the commission of it in proceedings in which he is sentenced for the other offence and requests the court to take it into consideration in sentencing him for that offence.'

The intention behind these provisions appears to be that where a court is dealing with an offender who has committed a large number of offences, none of which is in any way serious enough to justify a custodial sentence individually, it will not be possible for a court to aggregate the offences so as to justify custody. In contrast, where a court is faced with an offender who has committed several fairly serious offences, but none of which is quite serious enough in itself to justify custody, it will be possible to aggregate two offences where a community sentence does not represent adequate 'restriction of liberty'. 'Seriousness' is central to sentencing decisions under the whole of Part I of the Act and is treated separately, along with the historical background to s1(2)(a) CJA 91, in *Chapter 2, ante*. However, it should be noted that in relation to the former s1(4A) CJA 82 appeal rulings clearly concluded that offences should be viewed individually, and without the flexibility of a two offence rule: see eg *Hassan and Khan* (1989) 11 Cr App R (S) 148, [1989] Crim LR 593; *Davison* (1989) 11 Cr App R (S) 570.

The restriction in s1(2)(a) CJA 91 to *two* offences (ie the custody threshold test) should be contrasted with the test for the *Length of custodial sentences* (see under that heading, *post*) in s2(2)(a), *ibid*, under which *any number* of associated offences can be taken into account 'in combination'. Concerning sentence length, the Carlisle Committee indicated that some downwards re-appraisal would be necessary in the light of what are now the *Parole and Early Release* provisions of Part II CJA 1991: *Chapter 10*.

Previous convictions
In line with the move to *commensurate* sentences, previous convictions cannot be taken into account in arriving at a decision on seriousness: s29(1)(a) CJA 91; but aggravating factors of the present offence disclosed by the circumstances of other offences may be taken into account: s 29(2), *ibid*: see under the heading *Effect of previous criminal history* in *Chapter 2, ante*.

Protection of the public
The remaining criterion for a custodial sentence reflects the principle that a distinction should be drawn between offences against *property* and offences against the *person* (*Chapter 1*). It applies only to *violent* or *sexual offences* and only to custody decisions (whereas 'commensurate' sentences are a feature of the entire sentencing framework). Section 1(2)(b) CJA 91 allows custody to be used if the court is of opinion: '... where the offence is a violent or sexual offence, that only such a sentence would be adequate to protect the public from serious harm from [the offender]'.

Basic definitions
'Sexual offence' and 'violent offence' are defined in s31(1) CJA 91, as is the reference to 'protecting the public from serious harm'. These key definitions are as follows: *violent offence* - '... an offence which leads, or is intended or likely to lead, to a person's death or to physical injury to a person, and includes an offence which is required to be charged as arson [ie criminal damage by fire: see s1(3) Criminal Damage Act 1971] (whether or not it would otherwise fall within this definition)'; *sexual offence* - '... means an offence under the Sexual Offences Act 1956, the Indecency with Children Act 1960, the Sexual Offences Act 1967, section 54 of the Criminal Law Act 1977 or the Protection of Children Act 1978, other than (a) an offence under section 12 or 13 of the Sexual Offences Act 1956 which would not be an offence but for section 2 of the Sexual Offences Act 1967; (b) an offence under section 30, 31 or 33 to 36 of the said Act of 1956; and (c) an offence under section 4 or 5 of the said Act of 1967'. Broadly speaking, the list includes most statutory sexual offences except those concerned with prostitution and certain consenting acts between homosexuals.

Serious harm
The meaning of 'protecting the public from *serious harm*' is defined in s31(3) CJA 91 as meaning: '... protecting members of the public from death or serious injury, whether physical or psychological, occasioned by further such offences committed by [the offender]'.

Application of the criterion
Protection of the public is the subject matter of *Chapter 3*, where the background to the criterion in s1(2)(b) CJA 91 is also explored. Several points should be noted. First, the provision is *prospective* in nature, looking to future risk. In contrast, s1(2)(a) CJA 91 requires a court to look to *past* conduct when viewing seriousness (there may be other, forward looking, *offender* based factors which affect the ultimate sentence, but the seriousness test itself concerns past behaviour). It is *not* the present offence which must cause serious harm. An offender can receive a custodial sentence within s1(2)(b) notwithstanding that the present offence is neither serious enough to qualify for custody under s1(2)(a) nor one which causes serious harm itself. It is also implicit in s1(4)(a) CJA 91 (which requires a court to give *reasons* for a custodial sentence) that what may justify such a sentence is an amalgam of seriousness under s1(2)(a) and the need for protection under s1(2)(b).

The *two* offence approach of s1(2)(a) CJA 91 in relation to seriousness is inappropriate to s1(2)(b); or to s2(3), *ibid, post* (length of sentence). Neither does s29 CJA 91 (inadmissibility of previous convictions) apply to s1(2)(b). It can be urged that the main purpose of the criterion is to enable courts to pass custodial sentences on sexual or violent offenders who pose risks evidenced by a previous history of similar offences which indicates that they are a continuing danger to the public. The potential relevance of medical reports under s4 CJA 91 to this criterion cannot be overstated.

Refusal to accept a community sentence
The third basis for custody is provided for by s1(3) CJA 91 which states that: '... Nothing ... shall prevent the court from passing a custodial sentence on the offender if he refuses to give his consent to a community sentence which is proposed by the court and requires that consent.' This replaces the less direct power in s1(4A)(a) CJA 82 under which it was permissible to use custody where the offender 'has a history of failure to respond to non-custodial penalties and is unable or unwilling to respond to them'. The existence of s1(3) CJA 91 means that custodial sentences can, *ex hypothesi*, be used at a lower level of seriousness than is commensurate with that of the offence under s1(2)(a), *ibid*, or where the need for public protection is not sufficiently high to justify the use of s1(2)(b), *ibid*. However, this result is not automatic. It may be that another community sentence could be tried. On failure, without reasonable excuse, to comply with a community sentence which initially required consent, the court may not only re-sentence but '... may assume, in the case of an offender who has wilfully and persistently failed to comply ... that he has refused to give his consent to a community sentence which has been proposed by the court and requires that consent': sched 2 CJA 91, para 3(2)(b) (magistrates' court);

para 4(2)(b) Crown Court. The effect is that s1(3) CJA 91 will then apply.

Length of custodial sentences
The statutory test for the *length* of a custodial sentence is contained in s2 CJA 91. The section provides that where a court passes a custodial sentence, other than one fixed by law (ie a mandatory life sentence): '... the custodial sentence shall be - (a) for such term (not exceeding the permitted maximum) as in the opinion of the court is commensurate with the seriousness of the offence, or the combination of the offence and other offences associated with it; or (b) where the offence is a violent or sexual offence, for such longer term (not exceeding the permitted maximum) as in the opinion of the court is necessary to protect the public from serious harm from the offender': s2(1), (2), *ibid*. [Note that there is a similar structure for community sentences, ie a basic test whether a community sentence is justified, focusing on seriousness and restricted to *two* offences: s6(1) CJA 91; and a further test for the order or orders to be used (ie the precise restrictions on liberty) based on a mixture of seriousness and suitability for the offender: s6(2), *ibid*, see *Chapter 5*]. Unless the penalty, from a proportionate standpoint, is beyond the scope of a community sentence, then, subject to s1(2)(b), *ibid* (protection), or s1(3), *ibid* (refusal), it is wrong to use custody.

Committal for sentence
Mode of trial (s19 MCA 1980, *et al*) and associated provisions are amended by sched 8 CJA 91 so that they apply only to persons aged *18 and over*. The power to commit for sentence is altered by means of a substituted s38 MCA 1980 which expressly refers to 'persons not less than 18 years old': see s25 CJA 91. Where, in the case of an either way offence dealt with summarily, it transpires that an offence, or the combination of the offence and other offences associated with it, is more serious than is commensurate with the six months' imprisonment which magistrates have power to impose, they may commit to the Crown Court for sentence: s38(2)(a) MCA 1980. No limit is placed on the number of associated offences which may be taken into account 'in combination'.

Offences taken into consideration ('t.i.c.') are 'associated offences' (s31(2) CJA 91) and may thus justify committal for sentence, as was the case before the CJA 91: cf, eg *Vallet* [1951] 1 All ER 231 (albeit that the emphasis will shift to the effect which such offences have when the new statutory formula in s1(2), *ibid*, is applied to a given case). 'Character and antecedents' cease to be a basis for committal and ought to be no longer relevant, *a fortiori* where this means *previous convictions*: s29(1) CJA 91. But s29(2), *ibid*, applies (aggravating factors); and it might conceivably be argued that seriousness and character overlap to some extent: cf *R v Doncaster Justices, ex p Boulding* (1991), *The Independent*, October 30 (discussed at 155 JPN 745); but *quaere* whether such arguments can survive the new commensurate approach to sentencing.

The power to commit for sentence can also be exercised where there is a need for the public to be protected from serious harm from the offender for longer than six months, but only, in this instance, where the offender is *21 years of age or over*: s38(2)(b) MCA 1980, as substituted. The new s38 CJA 91 is in line with the proportionate sentencing approach of the Act. Mode of trial decisions, ie decisions by magistrates as to whether summary trial or trial in the Crown Court is more appropriate, are unavoidably affected by s38 and this is mentioned in *Chapters 2* and *3*, *ante*, in relation to seriousness and protection of the public respectively. [Corporations can now be committed for sentence (though obviously not for custodial sentences). Schedule 3 MCA 1980, para 5, which previously prevented this, is abolished by s25(2) CJA 91].

Information and procedures

The court is required to consider certain matters before reaching a decision about custody or the length of custody. These are: '... (a) all such information about the circumstances of the *offence* (including any *aggravating* or *mitigating* factors) as is available to it ... and (b) ... [in relation to the protection of the public criterion *only*] may take into account any information about the *offender* which is before it': s3(3) CJA 91 (italics supplied). So far as the facts of cases are concerned, much will depend on what information the Crown Prosecution Service (or other prosecutor) places before the court, also defence advocates and other agencies (see *Pre-sentence reports, post*). This gives rise to a need for good inter-agency liaison, and solid preparation for implementation of the Act. Aggravating and mitigating factors are discussed in *Chapters 2* and *3*. Attention is again drawn to the provisions of s28 CJA 91 (general mitigation provision) and s29, *ibid* (previous convictions/aggravating factors).

Pre-sentence reports

The legal impact of the new *Pre-sentence reports* regime is discussed in *Chapter 8* (and the general background more fully in *Chapter 11* of *Introduction to the Criminal Justice Act 1991*). Pre-sentence reports have a crucial role in the information gathering and sentencing process in relation to the formation of opinions by courts concerning the statutory criteria for custody, as well as in providing information about the *offender*. Certain specific provisions apply to custodial sentences. *Before* any decision can be taken as to whether either of the criteria for custody in s1(2) CJA 91 is made out or on the length of a custodial sentence under s2(2), *ibid*, the court must obtain and consider a pre-sentence report: s3(1), *ibid*; except where the offence or any other offence associated with it is triable *only on indictment* and provided that, in the circumstances, the court is of the opinion that a pre-sentence report is unnecessary: s3(2), *ibid*. The exception applies in relation to offences triable only on indictment, a restricted category of very serious matters where custody must normally be a reasonable presumption. There is nothing to prevent a report in such cases, and this may often be a desirable course. The Crown Court *is* under a duty to obtain reports in relation to other sentences: s3(2), *supra*; and in appeals against custodial sentences: s3(4) CJA 91.

Reports should deal with 'seriousness' and 'protection of the public' (as appropriate) as well as the personal circumstances of the offender. The court's duty to obtain a report '*before* forming any such opinion' as is contained in s3(1), *supra*, emphasises that there should be no provisional decision making ahead of the report being received. A high proportion of pre-sentence reports are likely to be prepared pre-trial (especially in the Crown Court). It is suggested that in other cases it would assist the timely production of reports and a sharper focus if courts were prepared to indicate those factors which are likely to be relevant to the particular sentencing decision, albeit that this may have to be in broad terms. The new regime will avoid the recommending of particular sentences in reports in favour of 'describing options' which might be suitable for the offender. There are obvious difficulties, and a potential for unnecessary tension, if probation officers and social workers are left to second guess the thinking of the court.

No custodial sentence is invalidated by the failure of a court to obtain a pre-sentence report, although any court on an appeal against such a sentence must obtain and consider a report if none was obtained by the court below: s3(4) CJA 91; similarly the appeal court must consider any reports which *were* obtained originally: *ibid*. A 'pre-sentence' report is defined in s 3(5) as a report *in writing* which '... (a) with a view to assisting the court in determining the most suitable method of dealing with an offender, is made or submitted by a probation officer or by a social worker of a local authority social services department; and (b) contains information as to such matters, presented in such manner, as may be prescribed by rules made by the Secretary of State.'

Medical reports
There are special additional requirements concerning reports in relation to mentally disordered offenders. Section 4 CJA 91 provides: '(1) Subject to subsection (2) below, in any case where section 3(1) above applies [ie the duty to obtain a pre-sentence report] and the offender *is* or *appears* to be mentally disordered, the court *shall* obtain and consider a medical report before passing a custodial sentence other than one fixed by law' (italics supplied). This subsection does *not* apply where the sentence is fixed by law (ie life for murder) or if, in the circumstances of the case, the court is of the opinion that it is *unnecessary* to obtain a medical report. Medical reports and the question *When is a report unneccessary?* are discussed in *Chapter 8*. It should be noted that the exception is of general application to all offences, in contrast to that in s3(2) CJA 91, *supra*, concerning pre-

sentence reports, which applies solely to offences triable only on indictment. There is a comparable savings provision to that in s3(4) CJA 91, *supra*, so that failure to obtain a medical report does not invalidate a sentence, but any appellate court must obtain and consider such a report: s4(4) CJA 91.

Reasons for custodial sentences

Where the court passes a custodial sentence it is placed under two duties by s1(4) CJA 91. First, it must, '... (a) ... state in open court that it is of the opinion that either or both of [the statutory criteria] apply and why it is of that opinion'. It must then '... (b) ... explain to the offender in open court and in *ordinary language* why it is passing a custodial sentence on him'. The obligation to give reasons applies to a decision to use custody following a refusal to accept a community sentence, but in an appropriately modified form, since there is no statutory criterion to identify: see s1(4)(b). The requirement to explain in ordinary language applies to *all* custody situations.

In the case of a magistrates' court (which is not a court of record) the reason stated must be specified in the warrant of commitment and entered in the court register: s1(5) CJA 91. Whilst courts should be meticulous to observe this requirement, it is suggested that the requirement goes to the form of the decision and not its substance so that it is 'directory' rather than 'mandatory'. It is unlikely that failure to observe s1(5) would invalidate the decision. It is suggested that it would not, and that reasons which existed at the time could be announced and explained at a later time in the event of a mistake resulting in their not being given originally. It might be otherwise where no proper reasons existed. Section 142 MCA 1980 (power to rectify mistakes) might be used within the 28 days envisaged by that section.

Extra reasons for longer sentences

Where a court passes a custodial sentence for a term *longer* than is commensurate with the seriousness of the offence, or the combination of the offence and other offences associated with it, the court must '... (a) state in open court that it is of opinion that [s2(2)(b) CJA 91, *supra*] applies and why it is of that opinion'. As with reasons for imposing custody, the court must also '... explain to the offender in ordinary language why the sentence is for such a term': s2(3)(b), *ibid*. An indeterminate sentence of the Crown Court is treated as a longer sentence for this purpose: s 2(4), *ibid*.

Suspended sentences

The CJA 91 retains but adjusts the suspended sentence of imprisonment by amending s22 PCCA 1973 to read as follows: '... (2) A court shall not deal with an offender by means of a suspended sentence unless it is of the opinion - (a) that the case is one in which a sentence of imprisonment would have been appropriate even without the power to suspend the sentence; and (b) that the exercise of that power can be justified by the *exceptional* circumstances of the case' (italics supplied). Section 22(2A), *ibid*, provides that 'A court which passes a suspended sentence on any person for an offence shall consider whether the circumstances of the case are such as to warrant in *addition* the imposition of a fine or the making of a compensation order' (italics supplied). The power existed before. There is now a *duty* to consider exercising it. Compensation must be given preference over a fine: s35(1) PCCA 73.

The court should thus reach a decision on custody without any regard to the fact that the power to suspend exists. It should then, and *only* then, apply the test in s22(2)(b), *supra*. There is a change to existing law aimed against too ready use of the suspended sentence, and narrowing the basis for suspension to 'exceptional circumstances'. Young offenders, ie those aged below 21, continue to be ineligible for suspended sentences. The prohibtion on making a probation order in respect of another offence for which the offender is before the court also continues: s22(3) PCCA 73. In the Crown Court, a suspended sentence supervision order can be made in respect of a single offence: s26, ibid.

Partly suspended and extended sentences
The Act abolishes extended sentences of imprisonment and the partly suspended sentence: s5(2) CJA 91.

Statutory Provisions

Powers of Criminal Courts Act 1973
Suspended sentences of imprisonment.
22.- (1) Subject to subsection (2) below, a court which passes a sentence of imprisonment for a term of not more than two years for an offence may order that the sentence shall not take effect unless, during a period specified in the order, being not less than one year or more than two years from the date of the order, the offender commits in Great Britain another offence punishable with imprisonment and thereafter a court having power to do so orders under section 23 of this Act that the original sentence shall take effect; and in this Part of this Act "operational period", in relation to a suspended sentence, means the period so specified.

(2) A court shall not deal with an offender by means of a suspended sentence unless it is of the opinion -

(a) that the case is one in which a sentence of imprisonment would have been appropriate even without the power to suspend the sentence; and

(b) that the exercise of that power can be justified by the exceptional circumstances of the case.

(2A) A court which passes a suspended sentence on any person for an offence shall consider whether the circumstances of the case are such as to warrant in addition the imposition of a fine or the making of a compensation order.

(3) A court which passes a suspended sentence on any person for an offence shall not make a probation order in his case with respect to another offence of which he is convicted by or before the court or for which he is dealt with by the court.

(4) On passing a suspended sentence the court shall explain to the offender in ordinary language his liability under section 23 of this Act if during the operational period he commits an offence punishable by imprisonment.

(5) Repealed

(6) [Effect on other enactments].

[Section 22 PCCA 1973 with s22(2), (2A) as substituted by s5(1) CJA 91].

NOTES **S22(2)(a) would have been appropriate** The court should thus reach a decision on custody without any regard to the fact that the power to suspend exists. This will involve applying the criteria and procedures in s1 to 3 CJA 91. It should then, and only then, apply the test in s22(2)(b). **S22(2)(b)** The basis for suspension once custody has been found appropriate is narrowed to 'exceptional circumstances'. **S22(2A) fine and compensation** A *duty* to consider these penalties as well as a suspended sentence is created by s22(2A). Preference must be given to compensation over a fine: s35(1) PCCA 73.

28.- 29.- Extended sentences of imprisonment for persistent offenders [Abolished by s5(2) CJA 91].

Criminal Law Act 1977 47.- Sentence of imprisonment partly served and partly suspended [Abolished by s5(2) CJA 91].

Magistrates' Courts Act 1980

Committal for sentence on summary offence triable either way

38 -. (1) This section applies where on the summary trial of an offence triable either way (not being an offence as regards which this section is excluded by section 33 above) a person who is not less than 18 is convicted of the offence.

(2) If the court is of opinion -

(a) that the offence or the combination of the offence and other offences associated with it was so serious that greater punishment should be inflicted for the offence than the court has power to impose; or

(b) in the case of a violent or sexual offence committed by a person who is not less than 21 years old, that a sentence of imprisonment for a term longer than the court has power to impose is necessary to protect the public from serious harm from him,

the court may, in accordance with section 56 of the Criminal Justice Act 1967, commit the offender in custody or on bail to the Crown Court for sentence in accordance with the provisions of section 42 of the Powers of

Criminal Courts Act 1973.

(3) Paragraphs (a) and (b) of subsection (2) above shall be construed as if they were contained in Part I of the Criminal Justice Act 1991.

(4) The preceding provisions of this section shall apply in relation to a corporation as if -

(a) the corporation were an individual who is not less than 18 years old; and

(b) in subsection (2) above, paragraph (b) and the words 'in custody or on bail' were omitted.

[Section 38 Magistrates' Courts Act 1980 as substituted by s25 CJA 91]

NOTES S38(1) **Subject to section 33 above** Section 33 MCA 1980 excludes the operation of s38 in relation to 'summary' criminal damage. **S38(3)** so that, eg s31 (definitions), *post*, applies. **S38(4)** Note that s25(2) CJA 91 also amends sched 3 MCA 1980, para 5 (provisions relating to committal to the Crown Court for sentence) so that there is no longer any bar to a corporation being committed for sentence. **See also** the note in the main text concerning the shift from 'character and antecedents' to a *commensurate* approach.

Criminal Justice Act 1991
Restrictions on imposing custodial sentences
1. - (1) This section applies where a person is convicted of an offence punishable with a custodial sentence other than one fixed by law.

(2) Subject to subsection (3) below, the court shall not pass a custodial sentence on the offender unless it is of the opinion -

(a) that the offence, or the combination of the offence and one other offence associated with it, was so serious that only such a sentence can be justified for the offence; or

(b) where the offence is a violent or sexual offence, that only such a sentence would be adequate to protect the public from serious harm from him.

(3) Nothing in subsection (2) above shall prevent the court from passing a custodial sentence on the offender if he refuses to give his consent to a community sentence which is proposed by the court and requires that consent.

(4) Where a court passes a custodial sentence, it shall be its duty -

(a) in a case not falling within subsection (3) above, to state in open court that it is of the opinion that either or both of paragraphs (a) and (b) of subsection (2) above apply and why it is of that opinion; and

(b) in any case, to explain to the offender in open court and in ordinary language why it is passing a custodial sentence on him.

(5) A magistrates' court shall cause the reason stated by it under subsection (4) above to be specified in the warrant of commitment and to be entered in the register.

[Section 1 Criminal Justice Act 1991]

NOTES S1(2)(a) '... **the offence and one other offence associated with it**' ie seriousness must be assessed by reference to these *two* offences only for the purpose of determining whether custody is the only sentence which can be justified. But note section 29(2) CJA 91, the effect of which is that aggravating factors disclosed by the circumstances of *other* offences may be taken into account in order to determine the seriousness of the two offences envisaged by section 1(2)(a). Contrast the test for *length* of sentence in section 2(2) CJA 91 which refers to an unlimited number of offences. '**Commensurate**' This indicates the underlying aim of proportionality in sentencing. '**Associated with**' Section 31(2) CJA 91, *post*, sets out the situations in which an offence is *associated* with another. '**So serious**' See the extended discussion about seriousness in *Chapter 2*. **S1(2)(b)** Note that the custody test in relation to a violent or sexual offence is not subject to the two offence rule. Neither is s29 CJA 91 (previous convictions/aggravating factors) applicable. Thus, previous convictions are admissible in relation to the prediction of future risk to the public. '**Violent offence**' is defined in s31(1) CJA 91, *post*. '**Sexual offence**' is defined in s31(1) CJA 91, *post*, by reference to a list of statutory offences. Broadly speaking, the list includes all statutory sexual offences except those concerning prostitution and certain consenting homosexual acts. **S1(3)** All community sentences capable of being imposed on adults require consent, but not attendance centre orders (under 21) or supervision orders (under 18) unless with certain added conditions: see *Chapter 5*. It would be wrong to offer a disproportionate community sentence with the aim of triggering a refusal, and thus a custodial sentence under s1(3).

Length of custodial sentences.

2.- (1) This section applies where a court passes a custodial sentence other than one fixed by law.

(2) The custodial sentence shall be -

(a) for such term (not exceeding the permitted maximum) as in the opinion of the court is commensurate with the seriousness of the offence, or the combination of the offence and other offences associated with it; or

(b) where the offence is a violent or sexual offence, for such longer term (not exceeding the permitted maximum) as in the opinion of the court is necessary to protect the public from serious harm from the offender.

(3) Where the court passes a custodial sentence for a term longer than is commensurate with the seriousness of the offence, or the combination of the offence and other offences associated with it, the court shall -

(a) state in open court that it is of opinion that subsection (2)(b) above applies and why it is of that opinion; and

(b) explain to the offender in ordinary language why the sentence is for such a term.

(4) A custodial sentence for an indeterminate period shall be regarded for the purposes of subsections (2) and (3) above as a custodial sentence for a term longer than any actual term.

[Section 2 Criminal Justice Act 1991]

NOTES S2(2)(a) In assessing *length* of a sentence, the court can have regard to *any number* of offences provided they are 'associated' (defined in s31(2) CJA 91). '**Commensurate**' This indicates the underlying aim of proportionality in sentencing. S2(2)(b) 'Violent offence' is defined in section 31(1) CJA 91, *post*. 'Sexual offence' is defined in section 31(1) CJA 91, *post*, by reference to a list of statutory offences. 'Serious harm' Defined in s31(3) CJA 91, post. S2(3) longer than Note the duty of the court to give cumulative reasons where the sentence for a violent or sexual offence is longer than is commensurate with the seriousness of the offence, ie: the basic reason for using custody, under s1(4) CJA 91; and a reason under this subsection.

Procedural requirements for custodial sentences. 3.- [Section 3 reproduced in *Chapter 8, Pre-sentence reports*]. **Additional requirements in the case of mentally disordered offenders. 4.-** [Section 4 is reproduced in *Chapter 8, Pre-sentence reports*].

Interpretation of Part I
31.- In this Part -

"custodial sentence" means -

(a) in relation to an offender of or over the age of twenty-one years, a sentence of imprisonment; and (b) in relation to an offender under that age, a sentence of detention in a young offender institution or under section 53 of the Children and Young Persons Act 1933 ("the 1933 Act"), or a sentence of custody for life under section 8(2) of the 1982 Act;

"mentally disordered", in relation to any person, means suffering from a mental disorder within the meaning of the [Mental Health Act 1983];

"pre-sentence report" has the meaning given by section 3(5) [CJA 91] [reproduced in *Chapter 8*];

"sentence of imprisonment" does not include a committal or attachment for contempt of court;

"sexual offence" means an offence under the Sexual Offences Act 1956, the Indecency with Children Act 1960, the Sexual Offences Act 1967, section 54 of the Criminal Law Act 1977 or the Protection of Children Act 1978, other than -

(a) an offence under section 12 or 13 of the Sexual Offences Act 1956 which would not be an offence but for section 2 of the Sexual Offences Act 1967;

(b) an offence under section 30, 31 or 33 to 36 of the said Act of 1956; and

(c) an offence under section 4 or 5 of the said Act of 1967;

"violent offence" means an offence which leads, or is intended or likely to lead, to a person's death or to physical injury to a person, and includes an offence which is required to be charged as arson (whether or not it would otherwise fall within this definition).

(2) For the purposes of this Part, an offence is associated with another if -

(a) the offender is convicted of it in the proceedings in which he is convicted of the other offence, or (although convicted of it in earlier proceedings) is sentenced for it at the same time as he is sentenced for that offence; or

(b) the offender admits the commission of it in the proceedings in which he is sentenced for the other offence and requests the court to take it into consideration in sentencing him for that offence.

(3) In this Part any reference, in relation to an offender convicted of a violent or sexual offence, to protecting the public from serious harm from him shall be construed as a reference to protecting members of the public from death or serious personal injury, whether physical or psychological, occasioned by further such offences committed by him.

[Section 31 Criminal Justice Act 1991 as it applies to this chapter]

Chapter 5

Community Sentences

The Criminal Justice Act 91 makes significant changes to the structure, range and terminology of community penalties. The aim is to promote 'community *sentences*' as realistic and demanding punishments in their own right so that courts will feel confident in dealing with a broader range of offences, including some quite serious ones, by means of these disposals rather than custody. The changes are contained principally in s6 to s16 CJA 91. The trend in recent years has been towards a greater use of community based orders such as probation and community service in place of custody. The Act seeks to reinforce this shift. A study of the summaries of Court of Appeal rulings in *Chapter 2, Seriousness, ante,* reveals the extent to which existing community orders are acknowledged as a proper disposal at relatively high levels of seriousness. Another example is *Grant* (1990) 12 Cr App R (S) 441 where an offence of malicious wounding resulting in two broken teeth and the need for seven stitches was described by the Court of Appeal as 'tailor made' for community service where the accused was of previous good character and stood to lose both his home and regular employment if sentenced to custody. The CJA 91 seeks to enhance the role of community sentences by requiring courts to measure the extent to which they impose 'restrictions on liberty'. There is a more rigorous approach to enforcement.

Terminology
Community disposals have become known, variously, as 'community penalties' and 'alternatives to custody'. The terms used by the CJA 91 are 'community *sentence*', the umbrella term for this form of disposal, and 'community *order*', which refers to the particular order (eg probation, community service) which is used standing alone or in conjunction with other community orders as the communty *sentence*. (Community sentences may be combined with each other and with financial penalties for the same offence. There is one exception affecting combination orders, *post*). None of the community sentences or orders in the CJA 91 are described as being 'instead of' or as 'alternatives' to custody. (There remains one, now anomalous, such reference in s12D CYPA 1969 to certain supervision orders being used instead of custody: see *Chapter 5B* of *The Youth Court*). This is to avoid the implication that, in imposing a community sentence, the court is in some way letting the offender off with lighter punishment. The constituent parts of a community sentence or order are referred to as *Restrictions on liberty*, see under this heading, *post*.

Community orders

The range of community orders which may be included in a community sentence is set out in s6(4) CJA 91 as follows: *Probation*: s2 PCCA 73 (substituted by s8, s9 CJA 91) (age 16 and over); *Community service*: s14 PCCA 73 (amended by s10 CJA 91) (16 and over); *Combination order*: s11 CJA 91, a new order combining probation and community service, as a consequence of which probation and community service cannot themselves be combined with one another: s6(3) CJA 91. (16 and over); *Curfew orders*: s12 CJA 91, a new order, which will be capable of being combined with electronic monitoring: s13, *ibid* ('tagging'), as and when this facility becomes available (16 and over); *Supervision orders*: s7(7) and s12 CYPA 91 (largely unaffected) (10 to 17 years inclusive); *Attendance centre orders*: s17 CJA 82 (as amended by s67 CJA 91) (10 to 20 years inclusive). The distinctive features of each of these orders, and the changes which the Act makes to existing orders and statutory provisions are described in later sections of this chapter (except for the supervision order, which is dealt with in *Chapter 5B* of *The Youth Court*).

Common requirements

There are certain common procedural and other requirements for the use of community sentences, set out in s6 and s7 CJA 91.

Pre-sentence reports

Under s 7(3) CJA 91 a pre-sentence report must be obtained *before* any of the following kinds of order is included in a community sentence: (a) a probation order which includes *additional* requirements authorised by sched 1A PCCA 73 (eg 'probation centre', 'participating' or 'refraining orders'); (b) a community service order; (c) a combination order; and (d) a supervision order which includes requirements imposed under s12, s12A, s12AA, s12B or s12C CYPA 1969.

'Pre-sentence report' is defined in s3(5) CJA 91 as a report *in writing* from a probation officer or social worker containing information of a kind which may be specified in rules made by the Secretary of State. The pre-sentence report (PSR) replaces the existing social inquiry report (SIR) and will be more sharply focused on the programme which the probation service or social services can provide for the offender *if* the court is minded to give a community sentence. The background, changes and legal provisions are reviewed in *Chapter 8*.

The community sentence threshold

Before passing any community sentence, the court must be satisfied that the offence is serious enough to warrant such a sentence. Section 6(1) CJA 91 provides: 'A court shall not pass on an offender a community sentence ... unless it is of the opinion that the offence, or the combination of the offence and one other offence associated with it, was serious enough to warrant such a sentence'. There is thus the same *two* offence test in relation to seriousness that there is for *Custody*, see *Chapter 4*. Similarly, too, there is no absolute standard of seriousness which will warrant a community sentence. This is a matter of fact and judgement for the court. Given the wide range and flexibility of the community orders, it is likely that courts will find that individual orders or mixes of orders can be used in a variety of situations and for offences of differing levels of seriousness. This lack of any defined hierarchy of community orders, or tariff, recognizes the scope for the construction of commensurate penalties and the effective use of restrictions on liberty in individual cases. However, if the offence is one which can adequately be dealt with by a fine or a discharge, the test in s6(1), *supra*, will not be satisfied. Note that there is no 'protection of the public' criterion in relation to community sentences (ct custody: but see the separate criteria for probation orders and combination orders, *post*, which contain a similar, though lesser, test).

General criteria for community orders
The question whether a community sentence is appropriate becomes clearer if s6(2) CJA 91 is considered. This lays down general criteria for selecting the community order or combination of orders in the sentence. There are two dimensions, set out in s6(2) as follows: '(a) the particular order or orders comprising or forming part of the sentence shall be such as in the opinion of the court is, or taken together are, the most suitable for the *offender*; and (b) the restrictions on liberty imposed by the order or orders shall be such as in the opinion of the court are commensurate with the seriousness of the *offence*, or the combination of the offence and other offences associated with it.'

The test in s6(2)(b), *supra*, concerning the extent of restrictions on liberty is comparable to that for *length* of custody in s2(2)(a) CJA 91 in that any number of offences can be taken into account at this stage. The test in s6(2)(a), *ibid*, must be applied in conjunction with any specific critera contained in independent statutory provisions affecting individual community orders, eg s2 PCCA 73 (probation); s11 CJA 91 (combination order), *post*. The tests in s6(2) combine *suitability* of a particular order for the *offender*, because, for example, the order might provide support and supervision which could assist the offender to avoid offending in the future or to make reparation, with a commensurate sentence measured against the restrictions on liberty involved.

Restrictions on liberty
This second dimension, that the restrictions on liberty contained in the community sentence should be commensurate with seriousness, goes to the heart of the new sentencing framework (with custody, the restriction is obvious; but the impact on liberty of a fine, particularly a means-related unit fine, *Chapter 6*, in the sense of curtailing choice re expenditure, cannot be underestimated). *All* community orders involve significant restrictions on liberty. Some are more demanding than others. The degree to which an offender's freedom is curtailed by a particular order may vary from individual to individual. A standard probation order, for example, might be suitable for less serious offences where the offender requires the rehabilitative skills of the probation service. A requirement to attend a probation centre or to observe a curfew order will involve a greater restriction on liberty and would therefore seem appropriate for a more serious offence. But it will be for the sentencer in each case to select the order or mix of orders which best suits the circumstances according to *both* of the criteria set out in s6(2) CJA 91.

Information
In making its selection, the court *must*, under s7(1) CJA 91, take into account

all relevant information about the circumstances of the offence, including factors which might *aggravate* or *mitigate* seriousness: see, generally, *Chapter 2, Seriousness*; and NB: the effect of s28 CJA 91 (general mitigation provision); and s29(1), (2), *ibid* (previous convictions not admissible in relation to seriousness; and aggravating factors disclosed by the circumstances of other offences). Under s7(2), the court *may* in relation to s6(2)(a) (suitability of a community order or orders for the *offender*) take into account any information about the offender which is before it. This latter requirement is, in effect, transformed into a *duty* in relation to those community orders where a pre-sentence report is a legal prerequisite to the order, supra.

Probation order

Sections 8 and 9 CJA 1991 and Part II of sched 1, *ibid*, re-enact with modifications and rearrangements the existing probation order provisions of the PCCA 1973, which deal with probation orders. (The provisions affecting discharges are separated out: see Part I of sched 1: *Chapter 12, post*). Three substantive changes are made to the existing law governing probation orders:

- The *minimum age* at which an offender may be placed on proabtion is lowered from 17 years to 16 years.
- The probation order is turned into a *sentence* of the court, rather than an order made 'instead of sentencing' the offender. This reflects the increasing use of the probation order as a penalty for persistent offenders, and for those who might otherwise be sent to prison; together with the fact that compliance with the terms of a probation order, *a fortiori* one with extra conditions, places considerable restrictions on the liberty of the offender. This new status also enables probation to be combined with a financial penalty or other community order as part of a community sentence for a single offence (except for community service: s6(3) *supra*). Section 8(2) CJA 91 repeals the effect of s13 PCCA 73 on a probation order (but not on a discharge) so that convictions resulting in probation count as *convictions* for all purposes.
- The criteria for making a probation order are more clearly defined. At present, a probation order can be made if the court considers this 'expedient' in the circumstances. Section 2(1) PCCA 73 (as substituted by s8 CJA 91) inserts the following specific criteria for making a probation order: the court must be of the opinion that: '... supervision of the offender by a probation officer is desirable in the interests of - (a) securing the rehabilitation of the offender; or (b) protecting the public from harm from him or preventing the commission by him of further offences'.

The new provisions also clarify the obligations on the offender to keep in touch with his or her supervising officer and to notify any change of address: s2(6) PCCA 73 (as substituted).

Probation order with additional requirements

Section 9 CJA 91 together with Part II of Schedule 1, *ibid*, re-enact with modifications those provisions of the PCCA 1973 dealing with additional requirements in probation orders. The requirements which may be included are set out in a substituted s3(1) and sched 1A PCCA 73. Additional requirements may be included 'during the whole or any part of the probation order' (but see the schedule) if this is in the interests of securing rehabilitation, protecting the public from harm from the offender, or preventing the commission by the offender of further offences (ie the same criteria as for the making of probation orders, *supra*). Section 3(2), *ibid*, provides that the payment of sums by way of damages for injury or compensation for loss may not be included as requirements. Thus, failure to make payments under a compensation order (*Chapter 6, post*) cannot amount to breach of probation order. The new schedule 1A PCCA 1973 sets out five types of additional requirements which may be included in a probation order. These relate to residence, activities, attendance at a probation centre, treatment for a a mental condition and treatment for drug or alcohol dependency. Provision is also made to enable longer and more intensive supervision of offenders given probation for *sexual* offences.

(i) *Residence*: The Act preserves the existing power to include requirements about where the offender should live. (ii) *Activities*: The Act also preserves, without significant change, the power of courts to require offenders who are given probation orders to participate or refrain from participating in specified activities, and to report to a specified person at a specified place for a total of up to *60 days* in the aggregate. (iii) *Probation centres*: Offender can already be required to attend a day centre run by the probation service for up to *60 days* in total. Under para 3 of Sch 1A, day centres are renamed 'probation centres', thereby better indicating their purpose and reflecting the provision of evening activities at centres. The Home Secretary's approval is required for the operation of a probation centre. The Home Office will thus be able to ensure that centres operate to *National Standards* for such establishments. (iv) *Sexual offences*: Paragraph 4 of sched 1A provides for offenders convicted of *sexual* offences to be required to participate in specified activities or to attend a probation centre without this being limited to the 60 days for other offenders, *supra*. This is to allow the probation service an opportunity to work with sex offenders over an extended period to tackle their offending, and with the aims of reducing the risk of further sexual offences and protecting the public. (v) *Treatment for mental condition*: sched 1A, para 5, continues existing powers of courts to require an offender whose mental condition requires and is susceptible to treatment, but not such as to warrant a hospital order, to submit to suitable medical treatment as a requirement of probation. (vi) *Drug and alcohol dependency*: para 6 of sched 1A provides, for the first time, for offenders who are dependent on, or who misuse *drugs* or *alcohol*, to be required to undergo treatment for their condition, where this is associated with their offending, as an additional requirement of probation. The provisions are analogous to those for offenders with a mental condition, *supra*. The offender can be required to submit for treatment only if a 'suitably qualified person' satisfies the court that the offender is dependent on or misuses drugs or alcohol, that this contributed in some way to the offence committed, and that the offender's condition requires, or may respond to treatment. The suitably qualified person may be a medical practitioner, *or* a person who, though not medically qualified, has *experience of working with people who misuse drugs or alcohol* and is able to provide suitable treatment of a high standard. This treatment may be either residential or non-residential, at an institiution or under supervision of such person as may be specified.

Community service orders

Section 10 CJA 91 makes three substantive changes to the law relating to community service orders. Under the existing s14, 15 and 17 PCCA 1973, a court may 'instead of dealing with [the offender] in any other way' require the offender to perform unpaid work in the community. The first change is the removal of the words 'instead of dealing with him in any other way'. This is to enable community service to be brought fully within the new sentencing framework of Part I CJA 91. Community service had evolved, in practice and in many areas of the country, as an 'alternative to custody' (a concept made redundant by the commensurate sentencing approach, *supra*). The offence must be imprisonable: s14(1) PCCA 73.

Secondly, the provisions relating to community service for 16 year olds are brought into line with those for offenders aged 17 and over: s14(1A) PCCA 73 (as amended by s10 CJA 91). This means that the maximum number of hours rises from 120 to 240 for 16 year olds. The provisions also reflects the fact that facilities for 16 year olds (as for older offenders) to perform community service are, so the Home Office *General Guide to the Criminal Justice Act 1991* states, now available in all parts of the country, so that there is no longer a need for a court to establish that the Home Secretary has notified them that suitable arrangements exist for offenders of this age. Finally, a new provision is added concerning the offender's duty to report to the relevant supervising officer as and when required. This will *inter alia* enable the officer to hold a disciplinary interview with an offender who has failed to comply with the order before deciding whether to initiate court proceedings for a breach.

Combination order

Section 11 CJA 91 creates a new order, the combination order, which combines elements of both probation and community service. While, in general, community orders can be combined in any permutation to make up a community sentence, the combination order is the only way in which it will be permissible to combine probation and community service: see s6(3) CJA 91. However, there is nothing to stop the combination order itself from being combined *with other community orders*, or with financial penalties where desirable (always remembering the high level of restriction on liberty that this would entail). The official Home Office view is that the combination order is intended for offenders who courts believe should make some reparation to the community, through a community service order, and who also need probation supervision to tackle problems that underlie their offending and thus reduce the risk of further offending in the future: *General Guide*.

Under s11(1) CJA 91, a combination order can be given to any offender aged *16 or over* who is convicted of an offence punishable with imprisonment. The maximum duration of the probation element will be three years; minimum 12 months. (It is intended that, whenever a combination order is made, probation supervision should continue for at least as long as the community service work is performed, and the 12 months' minimum is to allow for this, even in cases where the court gives the maximum number of community service hours which is permissible under a combination order). The limits of the community service component are 40 to 100 hours (ct the normal upper limit of 240 hours in a freestanding community service order, *supra*). Considerable debate has taken place about whether this particular order should, in practice, be reserved to the Crown Court. Such *reservation* does not represent the legal position and it could be argued that, if the new sentencing framework is to achieve much of the reappraisal and realignment of sentencing levels hoped for, the availability of this option before magistrates may be essential in relation to some more serious cases.

Curfew orders

Section 12 CJA 91 creates a new species of order, the curfew. In conjunction with this, s13, *ibid*, provides for such orders to be electronically monitored ('tagging'). The offence need not be imprisonable. The courts may make a curfew order *without* imposing an electronic monitoring requirement, but may not order electronic monitoring on its own. Curfew orders will be available for any offender aged *16 or over*. The order will require the offender to be at the place specified in the order for the period specified in it. The place will normally be the offender's residence, though it can be any place: but see s12(6), *ibid*. The maximum number of hours in a day during which a curfew can operate is *12 hours*, and the minimum is *2 hours*. The curfew may not operate for more than six months. Different lengths of time for different days, and different places, can be specified in the order, to take account of the circumstances of the offender. The maximum curfew of 12 hours in a day does not have to be specified in one block, but can be broken into several shorter periods.

Under s12(3) CJA 91, the court, in making the order, is required, so far as practicable, to avoid conflict with the offender's religious beliefs, the requirements of other community orders to which the offender is subject, and interference with the times at which the offender works or attends school or other educational establishment. A designated person must be made responsible for monitoring the offender's whereabouts during the curfew period: s12(4), *ibid*; and the court must explain the effects of the curfew order to the offender in ordinary language: s12(5), *ibid. Before* making the order, the court must obtain and consider relevant information about the places to be specified in the order, including information about the attitude of persons likely to be affected by the order, eg the offender's partner or parents: s12(6), *ibid*. It is envisaged that facilities under s13 CJA 91 for the electronic monitoring of the whereabouts of offenders given curfew orders will be made through contracts placed by the Secretary of State with private sector concerns. Under s 13, courts will not be able to impose electronic monitoring requirements unless they have been notified that such arrangements have been made for the area concerned. [The likely arrangements are that where the offender's whereabouts are to be electronically monitored, the offender will be required to wear on his or her ankle or wrist a small electronic device from which signals will be transmitted to a monitoring station, and which will alert the monitoring station if the offender leaves the premises to which the curfew order confines him. On receipt of such an alert, the monitoring station will initiate the steps necessary to check physically whether the offender has breached the terms of his or her curfew order and report the matter, so that consideration can be given to proceedings for breach of the requirements of the order.]

Supervision orders
Consistent with the policy of making the full range of adult and juvenile community orders available for both *16 and 17 year olds*, the Act makes supervision orders available for 17 year olds (thus making the full age range for this order 10 to 17 inclusive). This is one effect of s68 CJA 91. The main supervision order provisions are contained in s7(7) and s12 CYPA 69 which, the new age limits apart, stand unaffected. This leaves the anomaly of s12D CYPA 69 (supervision as an alternative to custody). However, section 66 CJA 91 and sched 7 revise and replace s15 CYPA 1969 to bring the provisions governing the variation and discharge of supervision orders broadly into line with the principles underlying sched 2 for the *Enforcement of community orders* generally: see under that heading, *post*. This also takes account of the introduction of the unit fine scheme; the increased maximum fines under the Act; and the effects of the Children Act 1989. The 1989 Act abolished care orders in criminal proceedings and added a power to add a residence requirement to a supervision order. There is some simplification of the relevant provisions.

Attendance centre orders
Section 67 CJA 91 makes several changes to the existing law concerning attendance centre orders by:

- removing the existing restriction which prevents an attendance centre order being made, in normal circumstances, on an offender who has previously received a custodial sentence. This restriction is inconsistent with the Act's commensurate approach to sentencing, ie sentences should be determined by the seriousness of the offence rather than the offender's previous record.
- bringing the maximum number of hours attendance that can be ordered for a 16 year old offender into line with that for 17 year olds (in keeping with the general policy of treating 16 and 17 year olds as a distinct group, 'near adults'). As a result, the new maxima are: *under 16*: normally 12 hours, but up to 24 hours if the court considers that 12 hours is inadequate in the circumstances of the case; *age 16 to 20*: up to 36 hours.
- bringing the procedures for enforcement of orders broadly into line with those for the enforcement of other community penalties (as set out in Schedule 2 CJA 91): s19(5A) CJA 82 as inserted by s67(6) CJA 91.

Enforcement of community orders
Section 14 and sched 2 CJA 91 set out the powers of courts to deal with breaches of requirements of community orders (except supervision orders: see s15 CYPA 69 as substituted by s66 and sched 7 CJA 91: reproduced in *The Youth Court*; and attendance centre orders: s18 and 19 CJA 82 as amended by s67(2) to (6) CJA 91), and to discharge, or vary or revoke such orders (where applicable), and to substitute other sentences which could have been imposed at the time when the order was made. These replace, with significant changes, s5,

s6, s16, s17, and sched 1 PCCA 1973. Section 16 and sched 3 CJA 91 make corresponding provision for cases where a community order is made by a court in one part of the United Kingdom but the offender resides in another.

The purpose of the new provisions governing the enforcement of community penalties is to provide a clearer, more coherent and more consistent set of arrangements. As a general rule, all types of community order will be enforceable under comparable procedures. Credit must be given for that part of a community sentence which has been completed. All this lends strength to the new system of community sentences, the new sentencing framework and the commensurate approach. Seemingly, it is part of the explanation why, under that approach, past failures in relation to community sentences cannot be taken into account in assessing seriousness: s29(1) CJA 91. It is also a reason why, with some confidence, courts should be more prepared to try community sentences whenever possible.

The new provisions also make a clear distinction between failure to comply with the requirements of a community order, and the commission of a further offence during the currency of the order. The latter is not to be regarded in itself as a breach of the terms of the new order, as is made clear by paragraph 5(1) of Schedule 2 CJA 91. Again, this reflects the view that community orders are punishments *in their own right* and are not equivalent to a conditional discharge whose terms are breached automatically if the offender commits a further offence. The new provisions give the courts full powers to deal effectively, but in different ways, with both breaches of the requirements of orders and with new offences committed during the currency of orders.

The changes summarised
The main changes introduced by Schedule 2, compared with the equivalent provisions of the PCCA 1973l, are:

- provision is made for the enforcement of combination orders. In so far as they include probation supervision, they are to be enforced as probation orders, and insofar as they include community service, they are to be enforced as community service orders: para 12.
- paragraphs 3 and 6 set out the powers which magistrates and the Crown Court respectively will have to deal with breaches of the requirements of community orders of all kinds which they have made. In all cases, a fine not exceeding £1,000 may be imposed, to be determined as a level 3 fine in accordance with the unit fine scheme: *Chapter 6*. Up to 60 hours community service may be imposed (provided this does not take the offender beyond the maximum 240 hours for which he may be liable at any one time, or beyond 100 hours in the case of a combination order). If the offender is under 21, the court may impose an attendance centre order for breach of a probation order. Finally, where the breach is a *serious* one, the court may decide to revoke the order and impose a different penalty for the original offence, as if it had just convicted the offender of it. In imposing a new penalty, the court is required, under paragraph 3(2)(a) and 4(2)(a), to take into account the extent to which the offender has so far complied with the requirements of the original order.

- if, however, the offender has *wilfully* and *persisitently* failed to comply with the requirements of a community order, the court may assume that he has refused to give his consent to the community sentence concerned: paras 3(2)(b); 4(2)(b). This exposes the offender to liability to a custodial sentence pursuant to s1(3) CJA 91: see *Chapter 4, ante.*

- Part III of sched 2 deals with the court's powers to revoke a community order. The circumstances in which an order can be revoked include (but are not restricted to) a conviction for a further offence or the fact that the offender has made good progress and is responding satisfactorily to supervision. When revoking an order, the court may deal afresh with the offence in respect of which the order was made, dealing with the offender in any manner in which it could have done if the offender had just been convicted of it (taking account of the extent to which he has complied with the requirements of the order).

Statutory provisions

Powers of Criminal Courts Act 1973

Absolute and conditional discharge

1A.- to 1C.- [Absolute and conditional discharges are not subject to any substantive changes under the CJA 91. Neither do they form part of the new sentencing framework, albeit that the possibility of a discharge must be eliminated before a sentence commensurate with seriousness, or one imposed to protect of the public, is justified, *semble*. Section 1A PCCA 73 is reproduced in *Chapter 12, Miscellaneous Items, post*].

Probation orders

2.- (1) Where a court by or before which a person of or over the age of sixteen years is convicted of an offence (not being an offence for which the sentence is fixed by law) is of opinion that the supervision of the offender by a probation officer is desirable in the interests of -

(a) securing the rehabilitation of the offender; or

(b) protecting the public from harm from him or preventing the commission by him of further offences,

the court may make a probation order, that is to say, an order requiring him to be under the supervision of a probation officer for a period specified in the order of not less than six months nor more than three years.

For the purposes of this subsection the age of a person shall be deemed to be that which it appears to the court to be after considering any available evidence.

(2) A probation order shall specify the petty sessions area in which the offender resides or will reside; and the offender shall, subject to paragraph 12 of Schedule 2 to the Criminal Justice Act 1991 (offenders who change their residence), be required to be under the supervision of a probation officer appointed for or assigned to that area.

(3) Before making a probation order, the court shall explain to the offender in ordinary language -

(a) the effect of the order (including any additional requirements proposed to be included in the order in accordance with section 3 below);

(b) the consequences which may follow under schedule 2 to the Criminal Justice Act 1991 if he fails to comply with any of the requirements of the order; and

(c) that the court has under that Schedule power to review the order on the application of either the offender or the supervising officer,

and the court shall not make the order unless he expresses willingness to comply with its requirements.

(4) The court by which a probation order is made shall forthwith give copies of the order to a probation officer assigned to the court, and he shall give a copy -

(a) to the offender;

(b) to the probation officer responsible for the offender's supervision; and

(c) to the person in charge of any institution in which the offender is required by the order to reside.

(5) The court by which such an order is made shall also, except where it itself acts for the petty sessions area specified in the order, send to the clerk to the justices for that area -

(a) a copy of the order; and

(b) such documents and information relating to the case as it considers likely to be of assistance to a court acting for that area in the exercise of its functions in relation to the order.

(6) An offender in respect of whom a probation order is made shall keep in touch with the probation officer responsible for his supervision in accordance with such instructions as may from time to time be given by that officer and shall notify him of any change of address.

(7) The Secretary of State may by order direct that subsection (1) above shall be amended by substituting, for the minimum period specified in that subsection, such period as may be specified in the order.

(8) An order under subsection (7) above may make in paragraph 13(2)(a)(ii) of Schedule 2 to the Criminal Justice Act 1991 any amendment which the Secretary of State thinks necessary in consequence of any substitution made by the order.

[Section 2 PCCA 1973 as substituted by s8 CJA 1991]

Additional requirements which may be included in such orders

3.- (1) Subject to subsection (2) below, a probation order may in addition require the offender to comply during the whole or any part of the probation period with such requirements as the court, having regard to the circumstances of the case, considers desirable in the interests of -

(a) securing the rehabilitation of the offender; or

(b) protecting the public from harm from him or preventing the commission by him of further offences.

(2) Without prejudice to the power of the court under section 35 of this Act to make a compensation order, the payment of sums by way of damages for injury or compensation for loss shall not be included among the additional requirements of a probation order.

(3) Without prejudice to the generality of subsection (1) above, the additional requirements which may be included in a probation order shall include the requirements which are authorised by Schedule 1A to this Act.

[Secton 3 PCCA 1973 as substituted by s9 CJA 91]

7.- [PCCA 1973 ceases to have effect, being re-enacted with minor modifications by s1A and s1B PCCA 73: s8(3) CJA 1991: reproduced in *Chapter 12, Definitions and Miscellaneous Items, post*]. **8.-** [PCCA 1973 ceases to have effect so far as relating to discharged offenders, being re-enacted with minor modifications by s1B and s1C PCCA 73: s 8(3) CJA 1991: see *Chapter 12*]. **9.-** [PCCA 1973 ceases to have effect along with s7, *supra*]

Effect of probation and discharge
13.- [PCCA 1973 ceases to have effect so far as it relates to offenders placed on probation: s8(2) CJA 1991; and, in relation to discharged offenders, is replaced by s1B and s1C PCCA 73: s 8(3) CJA 1991: see *Chapter 12*]

Community service orders in respect of offenders
14.- (1) Where a person of or over sixteen years is convicted of an offence punishable with imprisonment, the court by or before which he is convicted may (subject to subsection (2) below) make an order (in this Act referred to as "a community service order") requiring him to perform unpaid work in accordance with the subsequent provisions of this Act.

The reference in this subsection to an offence punishable with imprisonment shall be construed without regard to any prohibition or restriction imposed by or under any enactment on the imprisonment of young offenders.

(1A) [This subsection substitutes for paragraph (b), the words '(b) not more than 240'. The effect is to make this the maximum number of hours for all offenders aged 16 year upwards].

(2) A court shall not make a community service order in respect of any offender unless the offender consents and the court, after hearing (if the court thinks it necessary) a probation officer or social worker of a local authority social services department, is satisfied that the offender is a suitable person to perform work under such an order.

(2A) Subject to paragraphs 3 and 4 of Schedule 3 to the Criminal Justice Act 1991 (reciprocal enforcement of certain orders) a court shall not make a community service order in respect of an offender unless it is satisfied that provision for him to perform work under such an order can be made under arrangements for persons to perform work under such orders which exist in the petty sessions area in which he resides or will reside. ...

(4) [The reference to 'section 17(5) of this Act' (change of residence) becomes a reference to 'Part IV of Schedule 2 to the Criminal Justice Act 1991', *post*]

(5) [Similarly, the reference in s14(5)(b) to 'section 16' (breach of community service order) becomes a reference to 'Part II of Schedule 2 to [the 1991 Act]' and that in s14(5)(c) to 'section 17' (amendment and revocation) becomes a reference to 'Parts III and IV of [that Schedule]'.] ... ...
[Section 14 PCCA 1973 as amended by s10 CJA 1991 and sched 11, *ibid*]

Obligations of persons subject to community service orders
15.- [New s15(1)(a): '(a) keep in touch with the relevant officer in accordance with such instructions as he may from time to time be given by that officer and notify him of any change of address'. In s15(2) 'paragraph 15 of Schedule 2 to the Criminal Justice Act 1991' replaces 'section 17' (amendment etc)].
[Section 15 PCCA1973 as amended by s10 CJA 1991 and sched 11, *ibid*]

Schedule 1A [PCCA 1973] ADDITIONAL REQUIREMENTS IN PROBATION ORDERS

Requirements as to residence

1.- (1) Subject to sub-paragraphs (2) and (3) below, a probation order may include requirements as to the residence of the offender.

(2) Before making a probation order containing any such requirement, the court shall consider the home surroundings of the offender.

(3) Where a probation order requires the offender to reside in an approved hostel or any other institution, the period for which he is so required to reside shall be specified in the order.

Requirements as to activities

2.- (1) Subject to the provisions of this paragraph, a probation order may require the offender -

(a) to present himself to a person or persons specified in the order at a place or places so specified.

(b) to participate or refrain from participating in activities specified in the order -

    (i) on a day or days so specified; or

    (ii) during the probation period or such proportion of it as may be so specified.

(2) A court shall not include in a probation order a requirement such as is mentioned in sub-paragraph (1) above unless -

    (a) it has consulted a probation officer; and

    (b) it is satisfied that it is feasible to secure compliance with the requirement.

(3) A court shall not include in a probation order a requirement such as is mentioned in sub-paragraph (1)(a) above or a requirement to participate in activities if it would involve the co-operation of a person other than the offender and the probation officer responsible for his supervision, unless that other person consents to its inclusion.

(4) A requirement such as is mentioned in sub-paragraph (1)(a) above shall operate to require the offender -

(a) in accordance with instructions given by the probation officer responsible for his supervision, to present himself at a place or places for not more than 60 days in the aggregate; and

(b) while at any place, to comply with instructions given by, or under the authority of, the person in charge of that place.

(5) A place specified in an order shall have been approved by the probation committee for the area in which the premises are situated as providing facilities suitable for persons subject to probation orders.

(6) A requirement to participate in activities shall operate to require the offender -

(a) in accordance with instructions given by the probation officer responsible for his supervision, to participate in activities for not more than 60 days in the aggregate; and

(b) while participating, to comply with instructions given by, or under the authority of, the person in charge of the activities.

(7) Instructions given by a probation officer under sub-paragraph (4) or (6) above shall, so far as practicable, be such as to avoid any interference with the times, if any, at which the offender normally works or attends a school or other educational establishment.

Requirements as to attendance at probation centre

3.- (1) Subject to the provisions of this paragraph, a probation order may require the offender during the probation period to attend at a probation centre specified in the order.

(2) A court shall not include such a requirement in a probation order unless -

(a) it has consulted a probation officer; and

(b) it is satisfied -

(i) that arrangements can be made for the offender's attendance at a centre; and

(ii) that the person in charge of the centre consents to the inclusion of the requirement.

(3) A requirement under sub-paragraph (1) above shall operate to require the offender -

(a) in accordance with instructions given by the probation officer responsible for his supervision, to attend on not more than 60 days at the centre specified in the order; and

(b) while attending there to comply with instructions given by, or under the authority of, the person in charge of the centre.

(4) Instructions given by a probation officer under sub-paragraph (3) above shall, so far as practicable, be such as to avoid any interference with the times, if any, at which the offender normally works or attends a school or other educational establishment.

(5) References in this paragraph to attendance at a probation centre include references to attendance elsewhere than at the centre for the purpose of participating in activities in accordance with instructions given by, or under the authority of, the person in charge of the centre.

(6) The Secretary of State may make rules for regulating the provision and carrying on of probation centres and the attendance at such centres of persons subject to probation orders; and such rules may in particular include provision with respect to hours of attendance, the reckoning of days of attendance and the keeping of attendance records.

(7) In this paragraph 'probation centre' means premises -

(a) at which non-residential facilities are provided for use in connection with the rehabilitation of offenders; and

(b) which are for the time being approved by the Secretary of State as providing facilities suitable for persons subject to probation orders.

Extension of requirements for sexual offenders

4.- (1) If the court so directs in the case of an offender who has been convicted of a sexual offence -

(a) sub-paragraphs (4) and (6) of paragraph 2 above; and

(b) sub-paragraph (3) of paragraph 3 above,

shall each have effect as if for the reference to 60 days there were substituted a reference to such greater number of days as may be specified in the direction.

(2) In this paragraph 'sexual offence' has the same meaming as in Part I of the Criminal Justice Act 1991.

Requirements as to treatment for mental condition etc.

5.- (1) This paragraph applies where a court proposing to make a probation order is satisfied, on the evidence of a duly qualified medical practitioner approved for the purposes of section 12 Mental Health Act 1983, that the mental condition of the offender -

(a) is such as requires and may be susceptible to treatment; but

(b) is not such as to warrant the making of a hospital order or guardianship order within the meaning of that Act.

(2) The probation order may include a requirement that the offender shall submit, during the whole of the probation period or during such part of that period as may be specified in the order, to treatment by or under the direction of a duly qualified

medical practitioner with a view to the improvement of the offender's mental condition.

(3) The treatment required by any such order shall be such one of the following kinds of treatment as may be specified in the order, that is to say -

(a) treatment as a resident patient in a mental hospital;

(b) treatment as a non-resident patient at such institution or place as may be specified in the order; and

(c) treatment by or under the direction of such duly qualified medical practitioner as may be so specified;

but the nature of the treatment shall not be specified in the order except as mentioned in paragraph (a), (b) or (c) above.

(4) A court shall not by virtue of this paragraph include in a probation order a requirement that the offender shall submit to treatment for his mental condition unless it is satisfied that arrangements have been made for the treatment intended to be specified in the order (including arrangements for the reception of the offender where he is to be required to submit to treatment as a resident patient).

(5) While the offender is under treatment as a resident patient in pursuance of a requirement of the probation order, the probation officer responsible for his supervision shall carry out the supervision to such extent only as may be necessary for the purpose of revocation or amendment of the order.

(6) Where the medical practitioner by whom or under whose direction an offender is being treated for his mental condition in pursuance of a probation order is of the opinion that part of the treatment can be better or more conveniently given in or at an institution or place which -

(a) is not specified in the order; and

(b) is one in or at which the treatment of the offender will be given by or under the direction of a duly qualified medical practitioner,

he may, with the consent of the offender, make arrangements for him to be treated accordingly.

(7) Such arrangements as are mentioned in sub-paragraph (6) may provide for the offender to receive part of his treatment as a resident patient in an institution or place notwihstanding that the institution or place is not one which could have been specified for that purpose in the probation order.

(8) Where any such arrangements as are mentioned in sub-paragraph (6) above are made for the treatment of the offender -

(a) the medical practitioner by whom the arrangements are made shall give notice in writing to the probation officer responsible for the supervision of the offender, specifying the institution or place in or at which the treatment is to be carried out; and

(b) the treatment provided for by the arrangements shall be deemed to be treatment to which he is required to submit in pursuance of the probation order.

(9) Subsections (2) and (3) of section 54 of the Mental Health Act 1983 shall have effect with respect to proof for the purposes of sub-paragraph (1) above of an offender's mental condition as they have effect with respect to proof of an offender's mental condition for the purposes of section 37(2)(a) of that Act.

(10) In this paragraph 'mental hospital' means a hospital within the meaning of the Mental Health Act 1983 or mental nursing home within the meaning of the Registered Homes Act 1984, not being a special hospital within the meaning of the National Health Service Act 1977.

Requirements as to treatment for drug or alcohol dependency

6.- (1) This paragraph applies where a court proposing to make a probation order is satisfied -

(a) that the offender is dependent on drugs or alcohol;

(b) that his dependency caused or contributed to the offence in respect of which the order is proposed to be made; and

(c) that his dependency is such as requires and may be susceptible to treatment.

(2) The probation order may include a requirement that the offender shall submit, during the whole of the probation period or during such part of that period as may be specified in the order, to treatment by or under the direction of a person having the necessary qualifications or experience with a view to the reduction or elimination of the offender's dependency on drugs or alcohol.

(3) The treatment required by any such order shall be such one of the following kinds of treatment as may be specified in the order, that is to say -

(a) treatment as a resident in such institution or place as may be specified in the order;

(b) treatment as a non-resident in or at such institution or place as may be so specified; and

(c) treatment by or under the direction of such person having the necessary qualifications or experience as may be so specified;

but the nature of the treatment shall not be specified in the order except as mentioned in paragraph (a), (b) or (c) above.

(4) A court shall not by virtue of this paragraph include in a probation order a requirement that the offender shall submit to treatment for his dependency on drugs or alcohol unless it is satisfied that arrangements have been made for the treatment intended to be specified in the order (including arrangements for the reception of the offender where he is to be required to submit to treatment as a resident).

(5) While the offender is under treatment as a resident in pursuance of a requirement of the probation order, the probation officer responsible for his supervision shall carry out the supervision to such extent only as may be necessary for the purpose of the revocation or amendment of the order.

(6) Where the person by whom or under whose direction an offender is being treated for dependency on drugs or alcohol in pursuance of a probation order is of the opinion that part of the treatment can be better or more conveniently given in or at an institution or place which -

(a) is not specified in the order; and

(b) is one in or at which the treatment of the offender will be given by or under the direction of a person having the necessary qualifications or experience,

he may, with the consent of the offender, make arrangements for him to be treated accordingly.

(7) Such arrangements as are mentioned in sub-paragraph (6) above may provide for the offender to receive part of his treatment as a resident in an institution or place notwithstanding that the institution or place is not one which could have been specified for that purpose in the probation order.

(8) Where any such arrangements as are mentioned in sub-paragraph (6) above are made for the treatment of an offender -

(a) the person by whom the arrangements are made shall give notice in writing to the probation officer responsible for the supervision of the offender, specifying the institution or place in or at which the treatment is to be carried out; and

(b) the treatment provided for by the arrangements shall be deemed to be treatment to which he is required to submit in pursuance of the probation order.

(9) In this paragraph the reference to the offender being dependent on drugs or alcohol includes a reference to his having a propensity towards the misuse of drugs or alcohol, and references to his dependency on drugs or alcohol shall be construed accordingly.

[Schedule 1A Powers of Criminal Courts Act 1973]

Criminal Justice Act 1991

Restrictions on imposing community sentences

6.- (1) A court shall not pass a community sentence, that is to say, a sentence which consists of one or more community orders, unless it is of opinion that the offence, or the combination of the offence and one other offence associated with it, was serious enough to warrant such a sentence.

(2) Subject to subsection (3) below, where a court passes a community sentence -

(a) the particular order or orders comprising or forming part of the sentence shall be such as in the opinion of the court is, or taken together, are, the most suitable for the offender; and

(b) the restrictions on liberty imposed by the order or orders shall be such as in the opinion of the court are commensurate with the seriousness of the offence, or the combination of the offence and other offences associated with it.

(3) In consequence of the provisions made by section 11 below with respect to combination orders, a community sentence shall not consist of or include both a probation order and a community service order.

(4) In this Part "community order" means any of the following orders, namely -

(a) a probation order;

(b) a community service order;

(c) a combination order;

(d) a curfew order;

(e) a supervision order;

(f) an attendance centre order.

[Section 6 Criminal Justice Act 1991]

Procedural requirements for community sentences.

7.- (1) In forming any such opinion as is mentioned in subsection (1) or (2)(b) of section 6 above, a court shall take into account all such information about the circumstances of the offence (including any aggravating or mitigating factors) as is available to it.

(2) In forming any such opinion as is mentioned in subsection (2) (a) of that section, a court may take into account any information about the offender which is before it.

(3) A court shall obtain and consider a pre-sentence report before forming any such opinion as to the suitability for the offender of one or more of the following orders, namely -

(a) a probation order which includes additional requirements authorised by Schedule 1A to the 1973 Act;

(b) a community service order;

(c) a combination order; and

(d) a supervision order which includes requirements imposed under section 12, 12A, 12AA, 12B or 12C of the Children and Young Persons Act 1969 ("the 1969 Act").

(4) No community sentence which consists of or includes such an order as is mentioned in subsection (3) above shall be invalidated by the failure of a court to comply with that subsection, but any court on an appeal against such a sentence -

(a) shall obtain a pre-sentence report if none was obtained by the court below; and

(b) shall consider any such report obtained by it or by that court.

[Section 7 Criminal Justice Act 1991]

Probation and community service orders 8. - [Section 8 amends section 2 PCCA 73, printed as amended, *supra*]. **Additional requirements which may be included in such orders 9.**- [Section 9 substitutes new s3 to s4B PCCA 73, printed as amended, *supra*]. **Community service orders 10.**- [Section 10 makes various amendments to s14 and s15 Powers of Criminal Courts Act 1973, printed as amended, *supra*].

Orders combining probation and community service

11.- (1) Where a court by or before which a person of or over the age of sixteen years is convicted of an offence punishable with imprisonment (not being an offence for which the sentence is fixed by law) is of the opinion mentioned in subsection (2) below, the court may make a combination order, that is to say, an order requiring him both -

(a) to be under the supervision of a probation officer for a period specified in the order, being not less than twelve months nor more than three years; and

(b) to perform unpaid work for the number of hours so specified, being in the aggregate not less than 40 nor more than 100.

(2) The opinion referred to in subsection (1) above is that the making of a combination order is desirable in the interests of -

(a) securing the rehabilitation of the offender; or

(b) protecting the public from harm from him or preventing the commission by him of further offences.

(3) Subject to subsection (1) above, Part I of the 1973 Act shall apply in relation to combination orders -

(a) in so far as they impose such a requirement as is mentioned in paragraph (a) of that subsection, as if they were probation orders; and

(b) in so far as they impose such a requirement as is mentioned in paragraph (b) of that subsection, as if they were community service orders.

Curfew orders

12.- (1) Where a person of or over the age of sixteen years is convicted of an offence (not being an offence for which the sentence is fixed by law), the court by or before which he is convicted may make a curfew order, that is to say, an order requiring him to remain, for periods specified in the order, at a place so specified.

(2) A curfew order may specify different places or different periods for different days, but shall not specify -

(a) periods which fall outside the period of six months beginning with the day on which it is made; or

(b) periods which amount to less than 2 hours or more than 12 hours in any one day.

(4) A curfew order shall include provision for making a person responsible for monitoring the offenders's whereabouts during the periods specified in the order; and a person who is made so responsible shall be of a description specified in an order made by the Secretary of State.

(5) Before making a curfew order, the court shall explain to the offender in ordinary language -

(a) the effect of the order (including any additional requirements proposed to be included in the order in accordance with section 13 below);

(b) the consequences which follow under Schedule 2 to this Act if he fails to comply with any of the requirements of the order; and

(c) that the court has under that Schedule power to review the order on the application either of the offender or of the supervising officer,

and the court shall not make the order unless he expresses his willingness to comply with its requirements.

(6) Before making a curfew order, the court shall obtain and consider information about the place proposed to be specified in the order (including information as to the attitude of persons likely to be affected by the enforced presence there of the offender).

(7) The Secretary of State may by order direct -

(a) that subsection (2) above shall have effect with the substitution, for any period there specified, of such period as may be specified in the order; or

(b) that subsection (3) above shall have effect with such additional restrictions as may be so specified.

Electronic monitoring of curfew orders

13.- (1) Subject to subsection (2) below, a curfew order may in addition include requirements for securing the electronic monitoring of the offender's whereabouts during the curfew periods specified in the order.

(2) A court shall not make a curfew order which includes such requirements unless the court -

(a) has been notified by the Secretary of State that electronic monitoring arrangements are available in the area in which the place proposed to be specified in the order is situated; and

(b) is satisfied that the necessary provisions can be made under those arrangements.

(3) Electronic monitoring arrangements made by the Secretary of State under this section may include entering into contract with other persons for the electronic monitoring by them of the offender's whereabouts.

Enforcement etc. of community orders

14.- (1) Schedule 2 to this Act (which makes provision for dealing with failures to comply with the requirements of certain community orders, for amending such orders and for revoking them with or without the substitution of other sentences) shall have effect.

(2) Sections 5, 6, 16 and 17 of, and Schedule 1 to, the 1973 Act (which are superseded by Schedule 2 to this Act) shall cease to have effect.

Regulation of community orders

15.- (1) The Secretary of State may make rules for regulating -

(a) the supervision of persons who are subject to probation orders;

(b) the arrangements to be made under Schedule 3 to the 1973 Act for persons who are subject to community service orders to perform work under those orders and the performance by such persons of such work;

(c) the monitoring of the whereabouts of persons who are subject to curfew orders (including electronic monitoring in cases where arrangements for such monitoring are available); and

(d) without prejudice to the generality of paragraphs (a) to (c) above, the functions of the responsible officers of such persons as are mentioned in those paragraphs.

(2) Rules under subsection (1)(b) above may in particular -

(a) limit the number of hours work to be done by a person on any one day;

(b) make provision as to the reckoning of hours worked and the keeping of work records;

(c) make provision for the payment of travelling and work expenses in connection with the performance of work.

(3) In this Part "responsible officer" means -

(a) in relation to an offender who is subject to a probation order, the probation officer responsible for his supervision;

(b) in relation to an offender who is subject to a community service order, the relevant officer within the meaning of section 14(4) of the 1973 Act; and

(c) in relation to an offender who is subject to curfew order, the person responsible for monitoring his whereabouts during the curfew periods specified in the order.

(4) This section shall apply in relation to combination orders -

(a) in so far as they impose such a requirement as is mentioned in paragraph (a) of subsection (1) of section 11 above, as if they were probation orders; and

(b) in so far as they impose such a requirement as is mentioned in paragraph (b) of that subsection, as if they were community service orders.

[Section 15 Criminal Justice Act 1991]

Reciprocal enforcement of certain orders

16.- (1) Schedule 3 to this Act shall have effect for making provision for and in connection with -

(a) the making and amendment in England and Wales of community orders relating to persons residing in Scotland and Northern Ireland; and

(b) the making and amendment in Scotland or Northern Ireland of corresponding orders relating to persons residing in England and Wales.

Interpretation of Part I

31.- [Relevant extracts only] In this Part -

"attendance centre order" means an order under section 17 of the [Criminal Justice Act] 1982;

"combination order" means an order under section 11 above;

"community order" has the meaning given by section 6(4) above;

"community sentence" has the meaning given by section 6(1) above;

"curfew order" means an order under section 12 above;

"custodial sentence" means -

(a) in relation to an offender over the age of twenty-one years, a sentence of imprisonment; and

(b) in relation to an offender under that age, a sentence of detention in a young offender institution or under section 53 of the Children and Young

Persons Act 1933 ("the 1933 Act"), or a sentence of custody for life under section 8(2) of the 1982 Act;

"mentally disordered", in relation to any person, means suffering from a mental disorder within the meaning of the 1983 Act;

"pre-sentence report" has the meaning given by section 3(5) above;

"responsible officer" has the meaning given by section 15(3) above;

"sentence of imprisonment" does not include a committal or attachment for contempt of court;

"sexual offence" means an offence under the Sexual Offences Act 1956, the Indecency with Children Act 1960, the Sexual Offences Act 1967, section 54 of the Criminal Law Act 1977 or the Protection of Children Act 1978, other than -

(a) an offence under section 12 or 13 of the Sexual Offences Act 1956 which would not be an offence but for section 2 of the Sexual Offences Act 1967;

(b) an offence under section 30, 31 or 33 to 36 of the said Act of 1956; and

(c) an offence under section 4 or 5 of the said Act of 1967;

"supervision order" means a supervision order under the 1969 Act;

(2) For the purposes of this Part, an offence is associated with another if -

(a) the offender is convicted of it in the proceedings in which he is convicted of the other offence, or (although convicted of it in earlier proceedings) is sentenced for it at the same time as he is sentenced for that offence; or

(b) the offender admits the commission of it in the proceedings in which he is sentenced for the other offence and requests the court to take it into consideration in sentencing him for that offence.

(3) -

[Section 31 Criminal Justice Act 1991: Relevant extracts only]

73.- [Power to appoint H M Inspectors of Probation. Not reproduced]. **74.-** [Default powers where probation committee fails to discharge its statutory duty. Not reproduced]. **75.-** [Adjustments relating to the inner London probation area. Not reproduced]. **94.-** [Cash limits for probation service. Not reproduced]

Grants by probation committees
97.- In Schedule 3 to the PCCA 1973 (the probation service and its functions), after paragraph 12 there shall be inserted the following paragraph -

"Payment of grants in prescribed cases
12A. A probation committee may, in prescribed cases, make such payments to such persons as may be prescribed."

Schedule 2 Criminal Justice Act 1991 ENFORCEMENT OF
COMMUNITY ORDERS: PART I: PRELIMINARY
1.- (1) In this Schedule "relevant order" means any of the following orders, namely, a probation order, a community service order and a curfew order; and "the petty sessions area concerned" means -

(a) In relation to a probation or community service order, the petty sessions area for the time being specified in the order; and

(b) In relation to a curfew order, the petty sessions area in which the place for the time being specified in the order is situated.

(2) Subject to sub-paragraph (3) below, this Schedule shall apply in relation to combination orders -

(a) in so far as they impose such a requirement as is mentioned in paragraph (a) of subsection (1) of section 11 of this Act, as if they were probation orders; and

(b) in so far as they impose such a requirement as is mentioned in paragraph (b) of that subsection, as if they were community service orders.

(3) In its application to combination orders, paragraph 6(3) below shall have effect as if the reference to section 14(1A) of the 1973 Act were a reference to section 11(1) of this Act.

PART II: BREACH OF REQUIREMENT OF ORDER

Issue of summons or warrant

2.- (1) If at any time while a relevant order is in force in respect of an offender it appears on information to a justice of the peace acting for the petty sessions area concerned that the offender has failed to comply with any of the requirements of the order, the justice may -

(a) issue a summons requiring the offender to appear at the place and time specified in it; or

(b) if the information is in writing and on oath, issue a warrant for his arrest.

(2) Any summons or warrant issued under this paragraph shall direct the offender to appear or be brought before a magistrates' court acting for the petty sessions area concerned.

Powers of magistrates' court

3.- (1) If it is proved to the satisfaction of the magistrates' court before which an offender appears or is brought under paragraph 2 above that he has failed without reasonable excuse to comply with any of the requirements of the relevant order, the court may deal with him in respect of the failure in any one of the following ways, namely -

(a) it may impose on him a fine not exceeding £1,000;

(b) subject to paragraph 6(3) to (5) below, it may make a community service order in respect of him;

(c) where the relevant order is a probation order and the case is one to which section 17 of the 1982 Act applies, it may make an order under that section requiring him to attend at an attendance centre; or

(d) where the relevant order was made by a magistrates' court, it may revoke the order and deal with him, for the offence in respect of which the order was made, in any manner in which it could deal with him if he had just been convicted by the court of the offence.

(2) In dealing with an offender under sub-paragraph (1)(d) above, a magistrates' court -

(a) shall take into account the extent to which the offender has complied with the requirements of the relevant order; and

(b) may assume, in the case of an offender who has wilfully and persistently failed to comply with those requirements, that he has refused to consent to a community sentence which has been proposed by the court and requires that consent.

(3) Where a relevant order was made by the Crown Court and a magistrates' court has power to deal with the offender under sub-paragraph (1)(a), (b) or (c) above, it may instead commit him to custody or release him on bail until he can be brought or appear before the Crown Court.

(4) A magistrates' court which deals with an offender's case under sub-paragraph (3) above shall send to the Crown Court -

(a) a certificate signed by a justice of the peace certifying that the offender has failed to comply with the requirements of the relevant order in the respect certified in the certificate; and

(b) such other particulars of the case as may be desirable;

and a certificate purporting to be so signed shall be admissible as evidence of the failure before the Crown Court.

(5) A person sentenced under sub-paragraph (1)(d) above for an offence may appeal to the Crown Court against the sentence.

Powers of Crown Court

4.- (1) Where by virtue of paragraph 3(3) above an offender is brought or appears before the Crown Court and it is proved to the satisfaction of the court that he has failed to comply with any of the requirements of the relevant order, that court may deal with him in respect of the failure in any one of the following ways, namely -

(a) it may impose on him a fine not exceeding £1,000;

(b) subject to paragraph 6(3) to (5) below, it may make a community service order in respect of him;

(c) where the relevant order is a probation order and the case is one to which section 17 of the 1982 Act applies, it may make an order under that section requiring him to attend at an attendance centre; or

(d) it may revoke the order and deal with him, for the offence in respect of which the order was made, in any manner in which it could deal with him if he had just been convicted before the court of the offence.

(2) In dealing with an offender under sub-paragraph (1)(d) above, the Crown Court -

(a) shall take into account the extent to which the offender has complied with the requirements of the relevant order; and

(b) may assume, in the case of an offender who has wilfully and persistently failed to comply with those requirements, that he has refused to consent to a community sentence which has been proposed by the court and requires that consent.

(3) In proceedings before the Crown Court under this paragraph any question whether the offender has failed to comply with the requirements of the relevant order shall be determined by the court and not by the verdict of a jury.

Exclusions

5.- (1) Without prejudice to paragraphs 7 and 8 below, an offender who is convicted of a further offence while a relevant order is in force in respect of him shall not on that account be liable to be dealt with under paragraph 3 or 4 above in respect of a failure to comply with any requirement of the order.

(2) An offender who is required by a probation order to submit to treatment for his mental condition, or his dependency on drugs or alcohol, shall not be treated for the purposes of paragraphs 3 or 4 above as having failed to comply with that requirement on the ground only that he has refused to undergo any surgical, electrical or other treatment if, in the opinion of the court, his refusal was reasonable having regard to all the circumstances.

Supplemental

6(1) Any exercise by a court of its powers under paragraph 3(1)(a), (b) or (c) or 4(1)(a) or (b) above shall be without prejudice to the continuance of the relevant order.

(2) Section 18 of the Act shall apply for the purposes of paragraph 3(1)(a) above as if the failure to comply with the requirement were a summary offence punishable by a fine not exceeding level 3 on the standard scale; and a fine imposed under that paragraph or paragraph 4(1)(a) above shall be deemed for the purposes of any enactment to be a sum adjudged to be paid by a conviction.

(3) The number of hours which an offender may be required to work under a community service order made under paragraph 3(1)(b) or 4(1)(b) above -

(a) shall be specified in the order and shall not exceed 60 in the aggregate; and

(b) where the relevant order is a community service order, shall not be such that the total number of hours under both orders exceeds the maximum specified in section 14(1A) of the 1973 Act.

(4) Section 14(2) of the 1973 Act and, so far as applicable -

(a) The following provisions of that Act relating to community service orders; and

(b) the provisions of this Schedule so far as relating,

Shall have effect in relation to a community service order under paragraph 3(1)(b) or 4(1)(b) above as they have effect in relation to a community service order in respect of the offender.

(5) Where the provisions of this Schedule have effect as mentioned in sub-paragraph (4) above, the powers conferred by those provisions to deal with the offender for the offence in respect of which the community service order was made shall be construed as powers to deal with the offender for the failure to comply with the requirements of the relevant order in respect of which the community service order was made.

PART III: REVOCATION OF ORDER

Revocation of order with or without resentencing

7.- (1) This paragraph applies where a relevant order is in force in respect of any offender and, on the application of the offender or the responsible officer, it appears to a magistrates' court acting for the petty sessions area concerned that, having regard to circumstances that have arisen since the order was made, it would be in the interests of justice -

(a) that the order should be revoked; or

(b) that the offender should be dealt with in some other manner for the offence in respect of which the order was made.

(2) The court may -

(a) if the order was made by a magistrates' court -

(i) revoke the order; or

(ii) revoke the order and deal with the offender, for the offence in respect of which the order was made, in any manner in which it could deal with him if he had just been convicted by that court of the offence; or

(b) if the order was made by the Crown Court, commit him to custody or release him on bail until he can be brought or appear before the Crown Court.

(3) The circumstances in which a probation order may be revoked under sub-paragraph (2)(a)(i) above shall include the offender's making good progress or his responding satisfactorily to supervision.

(4) In dealing with an offender under sub-paragraph (2)(a)(ii) above, a magistrates' court shall take into account the extent to which the offender has complied with the relevant order.

(5) An offender sentenced under sub-paragraph 2(a)(ii) above may appeal to the Crown Court against sentence.

(6) Where the court deals with an offender's case under sub-paragraph (2)(b) above, it shall send to the Crown Court such particulars of the case as may be desirable.

(7) Where a magistrates' court proposes to exercise its powers under this paragraph otherwise than on the application of the offender, it shall summon him to appear before the court and, if he does not appear in answer to the summons, may issue a warrant for his arrest.

(8) No application may be made by the offender under sub-paragraph (1) above while an appeal against the relevant order is pending.

8.- (1) This paragraph applies where an offender in respect of whom a relevant order is in force -

(a) is convicted of an offence before the Crown Court; or

(b) is committed by a magistrates' court to the Crown Court for sentence and is brought or appears before the Crown Court; or

(c) by virtue of paragraph 7(2)(b) above is brought or appears before the Crown Court.

(2) If it appears to the Crown Court to be in the interests of justice to do so, having regard to circumstances which have arisen since the order was made, the Crown Court may -

(a) revoke the order; or

(b) revoke the order and deal with the offender, for the offence in respect of which the order was made, in any manner in which it could deal with him if he had just been convicted by or before the court of the offence.

(3) The circumstances in which a probation order may be revoked under sub-paragraph (2)(a) above shall include the offender's making good progress or his responding satisfactorily to supervision.

(4) In dealing with an offender under sub-paragraph (2)(b) above, the Crown Court shall take into account the extent to which the offender has complied with the requirements of the relevant order.

Revocation of order following custodial sentence

9.- (1) This paragraph applies where -

(a) an offender in respect of whom a relevant order is in force is convicted of an offence before a magistrates' court other than a magistrates' court acting for the petty sessions area concerned; and

(b) the court imposes a custodial sentence on the offender.

(2) If it appears to the court, on the application of the offender or the responsible officer, that it would be in the interests of justice to do so having regard to circumstances that have arisen since the order was made, the court may -

(a) if the order was made by a magistrates' court, revoke it; and

(b) if the order was made by the Crown Court, commit the offender in custody or release him on bail until he can be brought or appear before the Crown Court.

(3) Where the court deals with an offender's case under sub-paragraph (2)(b) above, it shall send to the Crown Court such particulars of the case as may be desirable.

10. Where by virtue of paragraph 9(2)(b) above an offender is brought or appears before the Crown Court and it appears to the Crown Court to be in the interests of justice to do so, having regard to circumstances which have arisen since the relevant order was made, the Crown Court may revoke the order.

Supplemental

11.- (1) On the making under this Part of this Schedule of an order revoking a relevant order, the clerk to the court shall forthwith give copies of the revoking order to the responsible officer.

(2) A responsible officer to whom in accordance with sub-paragraph (1) above copies of a revoking order are given shall give a copy to the offender and to the person in charge of any institution in which the offender was required by the order to reside.

PART IV: AMENDMENT OF THE ORDER

Amendments by reason of change of residence

12.- (1) This paragraph applies where, at any time while a relevant order is in force in respect of an offender, a magistrates' court acting for the petty sessions area concerned is satisfied that the offender proposes to change, or has changed, his residence from that petty sessions area to another petty sessions area.

(2) Subject to sub-paragraphs (3) and (4) below, the court may, and on the application of the responsible officer shall, amend the relevant order by substituting the other petty sessions area for the area specified in the order or, in the case of a curfew order, a place in that other area for the place so specified.

(3) The court shall not amend under this paragraph a probation or curfew order which contains requirements which, in the opinion of the court, cannot be complied with unless the offender continues to reside in the petty sessions area concerned unless, in accordance with paragraph 13 below, it either -

(a) cancels those requirements; or

(b) substitutes for those requirements other requirements which can be complied with if the offender ceases to reside in that area.

(4) The court shall not amend a community service order under this paragraph unless it appears to the court that provision can be made for the offender to perform work under the order under the arrangements which exist for persons who reside in the other petty sessions area to perform work under such orders.

Amendment of requirements of probation or curfew order

13.- (1) Without prejudice to the provisions of paragraph 12 above, but subject to sub-paragraph (2) below, a magistrates' court for the petty sessions area concerned may, on the application of the offender or the responsible officer, by order amend a probation or curfew order -

(a) by cancelling any requirement of the order; or

(b) by inserting in the order (either in addition to or in substitution for any such requirement) any requirement which the court could include if it were then making the order.

(2) The power of a magistrates' court under sub-paragraph (1) above shall be subject to the following restrictions, namely -

(a) The court shall not amend a probation order -

(i) by reducing the probation period, or by extending that period beyond the end of three years from the making of the original order; or

(ii) by inserting in it a requirement that the offender shall submit to treatment for his mental condition, or his dependency on drugs or alcohol, unless the amending order is made within three months after the date of the original order; and

(b) the court shall not amend a curfew order by extending the curfew periods beyond the end of six months from the date of the original order.

(3) In this paragraph and paragraph 14 below, references to the offender's dependency on drugs or alcohol include references to his propensity towards the misuse of drugs or alcohol.

Amendment of certain requirements of probation order

14.- (1) Where the medical practitioner or other person by whom or under whose direction an offender is being treated for his mental condition, or his dependency on drugs or alcohol, in pursuance of any requirement of a probation order -

(a) is of the opinion mentioned in sub-paragraph (2) below; or

(b) is for any reason unwilling to continue to treat or direct the treatment of the offender,

he shall make a report in writing to that effect to the responsible officer and that officer shall apply under paragraph 13 above to a magistrates' court for the petty sessions area concerned for the variation or cancellation of the requirement.

(2) The opinion referred to in sub-paragraph (1) above is -

(a) that the treatment of the offender should be continued beyond the period specified in that behalf in the order;

(b) that the offender needs different treatment, being treatment of a kind to which he could be required to submit in pursuance of a probation order;

(c) that the offender is not susceptible to treatment; or

(d) that the offender does not require further treatment.

Extension of community service order

15.- Where -

(a) a community service order is in force in respect of any offender; and

(b) on the application of the offender or the responsible officer, it appears to a magistrates' court acting for the petty sessions area concerned that it would be in the interests of justice to do so having regard to circumstances which have arisen since the order was made,

the court may, in relation to the order, extend the period of twelve months specified in section 15(2) of the 1973 Act.

Supplemental

16.- No order may be made under paragraph 12 above, and no application may be made under paragraph 13 or 15 above, while an appeal against the relevant order is pending.

17.- (1) Subject to sub-paragraph (2) below, where the court proposes to exercise its powers under this Part of this Schedule, otherwise than on the application of the offender, the court -

(a) shall summon him to appear before the court; and

(b) if he does not appear in answer to the summons, may issue a warrant for his arrest;

and the court shall not amend a relevant order under this Part of this Schedule unless the offender expresses his willingness to comply with the requirements of the order as amended.

(2) This paragraph shall not apply to an order cancelling a requirement of a relevant order or reducing the period of any requirement, or substituting a new petty sessions area or a new place for the one specified in the relevant order.

18.- (1) On the making under this Part of this Schedule of an order amending a relevant order, the clerk to the court shall forthwith -

(a) if the order amends the relevant order otherwise than by substituting a new petty sessions area or a new place for the one specified in the relevant order, give copies of the amending order to the responsible officer;

(b) if the order amends the relevant order in the manner excepted by paragraph (a) above, send to the clerk to the justices for the new petty sessions area or, as the case may be, for the petty sessions area in which the new place is situated -

    (i) copies of the amending order; and

    (ii) such documents and information relating to the case as he considers likely to be of assistance to a court acting for that area in exercising its functions in relation to the order;

and in a case falling within paragraph (b) above the clerk to the justices for that area shall give copies of the amending order to the responsible officer.

(2) A responsible officer to whom in accordance with sub-paragraph (1) above copies of an order are given shall give a copy to the offender and to the person in charge of any institution in which the offender is or was required by the order to reside.

[Schedule 2 Criminal Justice Act 1991]

NOTE Schedule 3 to the Act (not reproduced) contains provisions concerning reciprocal enforcement and transfer of certain orders relating to community sentences, ie probation orders, community service orders and combination orders, as between England, Scotland and Northern Ireland. Readers are referred to the statute for this detailed information.

Chapter 6

Unit Fines

Unit fines began by way of experiment in magistrates' courts at Basingstoke, Bradford, Swansea and Teesside in 1988/9. Under the method, the *seriousness* of an offence is assessed in units on a scale from one to 50. This number is then multiplied by the offender's own *disposable weekly income* to create the unit fine. The formula is thus:

Units of seriousness

x

Disposable weekly income

The principle is 'equal sacrifice', or 'equal impact'. The general aim is improved fairness through fines linked directly to means. Unit fines are a clear example of proportionality in sentencing. This is achieved primarily via the units. It becomes easier for a fine to reflect seriousness if considerations affecting the gravity of the offence are separated from those concerning the means of the offender. The method also represents straightforward punishment, untouched by more complex sentencing considerations.

Information about the experiments

Information about the experiments and the experiences of the four pilot courts is contained in *Unit Fines* (Gibson, Waterside Press, 1990) and Home Office Research and Planning Paper No 59 *Unit Fines: Experiments in Four Courts* (Moxon, Sutton and Hedderman, HMSO, 1990). The background is summarised in *Chapter 8* of *Introduction to the Criminal Justice Act 1991*. This particular chapter concentrates on the legal framework for unit fines contained in s18 to s23 CJA 91. In large measure, the framework mirrors the experimental schemes. The essential features of the statutory scheme are:

Application to individuals before the magistrates' court
Unit fines are mandatory in the case of *individuals* (as opposed to *corporations*): s18(1). However, the method does not apply, even to individuals, in relation to certain offences where the maximum fine exceeds the normal statutory maximum on summary conviction (for example the £20,000 under s9 or s10 Video Recordings Act 1984): an effect of s18(1)(a) and (b) CJA 91; or, generally speaking, in the Crown Court: s18(1). [There is an anomalous exception to the principle that unit fines do not apply in the Crown Court, *semble*. Section 18(1) CJA 91 states that unit fines apply 'where a magistrates'

court imposes a fine ...'. In two limited situations the Crown Court can deal with summary offences, when it must deal with the offender '... only in a manner in which a magistrates' court could have dealt with him': see s40(2) and s41(7) CJA 1988. To avoid the Crown Court having to use unit fines in relation to s41 (ie where a summary offence is committed to the Crown Court for trial alongside an offence triable either way), s18(9) CJA 91 specifically provides that s41(7) of the 1988 Act shall have effect as if s18 CJA 91 (ie the unit fines provisions) had not been enacted. However, no comparable exception is made in relation to s40 CJA 1988, which contains a further route by which the Crown Court can come to use magistrates' court powers (ie where a count charging a person with one of certain specified summary offences - common assault, taking etc a vehicle without consent, driving whilst disqualified, summary criminal damage - founded on the same facts as a count charging an indictable offence is joined in the same indictment pursuant to s40). The powers of the Crown Court in relation to s40 are set out in s40(2) CJA 88 in equivalent terms to those in s41(7) CJA 1988, *supra*. But the CJA 1991 contains *no* savings provision in relation to s40. The effect is that the Crown Court must impose a unit fine. This appears to be unintended. There are other analogous situations: see, eg s24 Road Traffic Act 1991 (alternative verdicts). The position might be temporarily rectified via the relevant commencement order. This could 'defer' implementation of s18 to s23 'to the extent that they might apply to the Crown Court'. However, there is a cogent argument that unit fines should be extended to the Crown Court, *a fortiori* where that court imposes fines for summary matters.]

The basic formula
Unit fines are the 'product' of units of seriousness and individual weekly disposable income: s 18(2)(a) and (b). These key provisions read:

'... the amount of the fine shall be the product of - (a) the number of units which is determined by the court to be *commensurate* with the seriousness of the offence, or the combination of the offence and other offences associated with it; and (b) the value to be given to each of those units, that is to say, the amount which, at the same or any later time, is determined by the court in accordance with rules made by the Lord Chancellor to be the offender's disposable weekly income' (italics supplied).

Commensurate sentences
The words 'commensurate with the seriousness of the offence' in s18(2)(a) link unit fines to the principle of proportionality; but given the nature of the fine there is no additional or alternative 'protection of the public' criterion. It is the number of units which must be commensurate. Magistrates' courts can be expected to create their own unit sentencing guidelines, ranking common offences in order of seriousness against the one to 50 scale. It is implicit in the scheme that only whole units can be given. The Magistrates' Association has published draft unit sentencing guidelines, examples of which appear in *Chapter 8* of *Introduction to the Criminal Justice Act 1991*.

Aggravating and mitigating factors
The level of the fine, ie the number of units, must take account of '... all ... the circumstances of the offence', including any *aggravating* or *mitigating* factors: s18(3). Section 28 CJA 91 (the general mitigation provision) applies equally to unit fines as it does to custody and community sentences. Critically for the unit method, s 28(3) provides: '... Any mitigation of a fine the amount of which falls to be fixed under s 18 above [unit fines] shall be effected by determining under [s18(2)(a)] ... a smaller number of units than would otherwise have been determined.'

Similarly, previous convictions, cannot make an offence more serious so as to increase the number of units: s29(1) CJA 91; but if aggravating factors are disclosed by the circumstances of other offences these can be taken into account in forming an opinion about the seriousness of the present offence:s29(2), *ibid*. Under s18(1) there is *no* limit on the number of offences which can be viewed, in combination, in order to determine seriousness for the purposes of unit fines (ct both custody: s1(2) CJA 91; and community sentences: s6(1)). 'Associated offence' is defined in s 31 CJA 91: see *Statutory Provisions* in *Chapter 4*.

Maximum fines
The maximum overall cash ceilings of fines for level 1 to 5 offences are increased to £200, £500, £1,000, £2,500 and £5,000, respectively: s37 CJA 1982 as substituted by s17(1) CJA 91. Unit fines are also linked to unit maxima by s 18(4) CJA 91 as follows:

Level 1	**2 units**
Level 2	**5 units**
Level 3	**10 units**
Level 4	**25 units**
Level 5	**50 units**

Multiple offences
Fifty units of disposable weekly income approximate to the amount which can be afforded in a year. This acts as a benchmark for sentencing under pre-existing principle, ie it is generally recognized that fines should normally be payable within a year, whether they relate to a single offence or multiple offences: see under the heading *Application of existing law, post*. When adding units together for several offences the court should thus hesitate before going beyond the 50 unit mark. The 'totality principle' is preserved by s28(2)(b) CJA 91.

No separate penalty
Whilst not mentioned by the legislation, the device was used in the unit fines experiments of marking cases 'no separate penalty' when an adequate sentence had already been imposed for other offences dealt with on the same occasion. This remains a vaild approach following the shift to commensurate sentences, as a result of the totality principle being preserved, *supra*.

Disposable weekly income limits
Lower and upper disposable weekly income limits are set by s18(5)(a) and (b). These are based on 1/50th of the cash ceiling for a level 1 and a level 5 fine, *supra*, respectively. Thus, the limits will be £4 to £100 at the commencement of the scheme. The highest unit fine will be for a level 5 offence, ie 50 units at £100 = £5,000. See also under the heading *Individual disposable weekly income, post*.

Special provision for young people
People within the youth court age range who are ordered to pay unit fines are assessed within reduced limits. The adult ceiling and weekly disposable income limits are adjusted downwards. The effect is as follows:

Children 10-13

Cash ceiling: £250

Disposable income limits: 20 pence to £5

Young persons 14-17

Cash ceiling: £1,000

Disposable income limits: 80 pence to £20

The cash ceiling is reduced if this would exceed the maximum penalty for a given offence in the case of an adult. The income limits are based on fractions of one-twentieth and one-fifth of the adult rate, respectively: s18(6). However, where a parent or guardian is required to pay the fine (see *Chapter 9*, post, and *Chapter 6* of *The Youth Court* entitled *Parental Responsibility*) the disposable weekly income is based on the *parent's* or *guardian's* means, not those applicable to the child or young person: s57(3) CJA 91. The effect is that the value of each unit will be on the adult scale of £4 to £100. It follows that the parent or guardian should complete a means form and administrative arrangements by courts should reflect this. However, the Act stops short of invoking the punitive provisions of s20 as against parents who fail to complete means forms, even though they will risk a higher fine than is appropriate if a form is not completed. Where a *local authority* has parental responsibility then the authority becomes liable for financial penalties in place of the parent or guardian, subject to the terms of s55(5) CYPA 1933. In this situation, the unit value is always the maximum amount which would have been payable by an offender of the age of the child in question: s57(4) CJA 91.

Duty to provide information
There is a statutory duty on offenders to provide information to the court about

means: s20(1) CJA 91. But this duty arises only following an order made *on conviction*. Home Office administrative advice, currently in draft, states that there is no reason why courts should not request information ahead of court hearings (with safeguards where there is a not guilty plea). Indeed, it is essential, for all practical purposes, that a significant proportion of defendants who are intending to plead guilty complete means forms and send these to the court in advance of the hearing (but despite representations by the Magistrates' Association and Justices' Clerks' Society, there was government resistance to allowing the law itself to require them to). Rule 3 of the Magistrates' Courts (Unit Fines) Rules 1992, again in draft, places a duty on clerks to justices to make arrangements to secure the service of a means enquiry form on defendants or parents or guardians of defendants. The Rules (reproduced in *Statutory Provisions*) deal with associated matters, including prescribed means forms. The prescribed form asks the defendant or parent or guardian to complete the form and either to send it to the court in advance of the hearing or to bring it when he or she attends court.

Penalties for failure to furnish information
Section 20(2) CJA 91 makes failure, without reasonable excuse, to comply with a *court order* to furnish information an offence. The maximum penalty is a level 3 fine, ie 10 units. A person who '... in furnishing any statement in pursuance of an order under subsection [20(1)] ... (a) makes a statement which he knows to be false in a material particular; (b) recklessly furnishes a statement which is false in a material particular; or (c) knowingly fails to disclose any material fact' is liable to a level 4 fine, ie 25 units and/or 3 months imprisonment: s20(3) CJA 91. The offence under s20(3) is subject to a special time limit: s20(4) - see *Statutory Provisions, post.*

It is suggested that a good procedure for commencement, prosecution and trial of such offences (which is not laid down expressly by statute) should be one analogous to that for failure to surrender to court bail, ie the court should initiate the proceedings at the invitation of the Crown Prosecutor, who should then conduct the case at the instance of the magistrates: cf *Practice Note (Bail:Failure to Surrender)* 1987 1 All ER 128, [1987] 1WLR 79. If so, then it also follows that proceedings should not be brought once magistrates have indicated that they are overlooking matters: cf *France v Dewsbury Magistrates' Court* (1987) 152 JP 301, [1988] Crim LR 295.

Individual disposable weekly income
The effect of the scheme is to deprive an individual offender of his or her spare weekly income (after allowing for essential living expenses: see next section) for the number of weeks indicated by the units of seriousness. The Act gives power to the Lord Chancellor to create statutory assessment rules concerning how disposable weekly income should be calculated by courts (within the limits of £4 to £100 a week: s 18(5)(a) and (b), or the special lower limits for young people: s18(6)). The Magistrates' Courts (Unit Fines) Rules 1992 are appended in draft

in the *Statutory Provisions*. The Rules govern the procedure to be followed and the financial assessments to be made in operating of the new system.

Means form and assessment
The pilot courts adopted a broad brush approach to the assessment of means (see *Unit Fines*, Gibson, p 54). No change to this is intended under the statutory scheme. The Home Office *Guide to Fines and Other Financial Penalties* states:

'It should be emphasised that ... determination (of disposable weekly income) will not be based on a detailed examination of all the offender's income, outgoings, savings and liabilities. The court is not expected to carry out an intricate assessment of the offender's financial position. All the court is, in essence, required to do is make a judgement, on the basis of information supplied by the offender, about how much of his weekly income the offender could afford to give up in order to pay his or her fine without suffering undue hardship'.

The Unit Fines Rules place a duty on justices' clerks to make arrangements for the service of a prescribed means inquiry form on defendants and, where appropriate, the parent or guardian of a juvenile defendant: r3. Means enquiry forms are set out in *Schedule 1* to the Rules. These forms must be used, or forms 'to like effect': r 2(1)(b). Rule 4 provides the formula whereby the court is to determine the 'value of a unit', ie the offender's disposable weekly income. This is:

$$\frac{I - E}{3}$$

where I is the amount of weekly income and E the amount of the appropriate expenditure determined under the Rules. The effect is to introduce a 'divider' so that only one third of spare is taken into account. [For most people, spending tends to rise with income, and broadly in proportion. Some expenses are unexpected or difficult to avoid in the short term. To maintain fairness and slow down the rate at which people progress towards the upper spare income limit, not every extra pound disclosed by a broad brush assessment should be treated as 'spare income'. An innovation first tried at Swansea and later used in North Oxfordshire and other courts is a divider of disposable weekly income. A divider of three is adopted by the draft Rules, viz the above formula].

Rule 4 also provides that the magistrates' court is to *take into account* the information provided on the means enquiry form 'and any other relevant information': r4(3); thus allowing the court to draw inferences generally, *semble*. It is submitted that r4(3) is wide enough to allow the court to reject a particular piece of information in the form in favour of other contradictory information, which arguably extends to matters of which judicial notice can be taken, eg the state of the local economy. Where the offender consents, the maximum unit value (ie £100) can be applied without the defendant completing details of means: r4(2).

Schedule 2 to the Rules requires the magistrates for each petty sessions area to set local expenditure levels which they are to take into account when determining an offender's disposable weekly income. The Rules state what items are to be taken into account in doing this: Schedule 2, para 3. The effect is to create notional expenditure levels which are then applied in working out the expenditure ('E') part of the equation, *supra*. This is subject to any adjustments to take account of certain items set out in para 4 of sch 2, including 'exceptional expenditure' to the extent that the court thinks fit.

Rule 5 provides that an offender ordered to submit a statement of means under section 20(1) CJA 91, is to do so in a prescribed means enquiry form. Rule 6 amends the form on which defendants plead guilty by post under s12 MCA 1980 to request that they fill in a means enquiry form. It will be necessary for the Rules to come into force alongside the general unit fines provisions of the Act itself (or marginally ahead of this to allow a lead-in period for the sending out of means forms with summonses).

Lack of information
Where the court has insufficient information to make a proper determination it may make such determination as it thinks fit within the £4 to £100 range. In the experiments, a rule of practice was developed to the effect that offenders who failed to provide information should forfeit the right to any reduction on the standard top limit, generally £25 per unit in the pilot areas. This becomes a somewhat harsher rule when applied in the context of the new £100 maximum unit value. Within the terms of s18(8) (see *Statutory Provisions*) courts may use estimates. There should be some basis for this, *semble*, eg items revealed by the case papers or evidence: occupation, address, make of car, circumstances disclosed in evidence, responses made in answer to a charge ('We could not afford it'; 'I was made redundant last week'). The best basis, of course, is to work from a means form (however difficult to obtain), so that the aim of courts should always be to keep estimate situations to a minimum, *semble*.

Adjustment of certain fines
Notwithstanding the unit method, s18(7) CJA 91 permits the adjustment of certain fines despite the unit basis of s18(2)(a). Section 18(7) states that: 'Nothing in [s18(2)] shall prevent any of the following, namely - (a) in the case of an offence in relation to which a compensation order is made, the *reduction* of the amount of the fine in pursuance of section 35(4A) [Powers of Criminal Courts Act 1973, ie to give priority to *Compensation, post*]; (b) in the case of a fixed penalty offence within the (meaning of Part III of the Road Traffic Offenders Act 1988), the *increase* of the amount of the fine to the level of the fixed penalty; and (c) in the case of an offence of installing or using apparatus for wireless telegraphy except under a licence granted under section 1 of the Wireless Telegraphy Act 1949, the *increase* of the amount of the fine by an amount not exceeding the sum which would have been payable on the issue of such a

licence' (italics supplied).

A general 'no profit' provision which appeared in early drafts of the Criminal Justice Bill, and which would have allowed courts to increase fines generally to eliminate gain was removed by Parliament. Profit, gain or benefit is, in fact, often difficult to assess with certainty and such a provision could have led to endless argument in court and on appeal. Profit may sometimes be reflected in the seriousness of the offence and hence the number of units (see s18(2)(a) CJA 91), eg the value of stolen goods. In many cases, compensation is the correct route to the elimination of profit etc; in other instances, eg no vehicle insurance, the gain to the offender from uninsured use of a vehicle on one occasion is hardly the whole of the annual premium. If a person commits an offence repeatedly, he or she is at risk of conviction and punishment several times over. The penalty points and disqualification system, including the 'totting up' provisions (all unaffected by the switch to proportionate sentences in the CJA 91, the purpose being road safety not punishment) caters for people who commit relevant traffic offences repeatedly. In relation to the particular offence of no vehicle insurance (which tends to cause concern with magistrates) the maximum fine is increased from 25 to 50 units by s26 of and sched 2 to the Road Traffic Act 1991.

Enforcement
To compensate for the broad brush approach of the method (and the risk that some offenders may find that the disposable income has been set higher than is appropriate to their case, particularly if no, or insufficient, financial information was available at the original hearing) courts are given more flexible powers of remission in enforcement proceedings: see s20 CJA 91 in the *Statutory Provisions*. This includes power in circumstances set out in s21(1) to '... remit the whole or part of the fine if the court considers that its payment by the offender within twelve months of the imposition of the fine would cause the offender undue hardship': s21(2). 'Undue hardship' is a question of fact.

Custody in default is linked to units (as opposed to cash) by s22(2) as follows:

Not more than 2 units **7 days**
More than 2 units but not more than 5 units **14 days**
More than 5 units but not more than 10 units **28 days**
More than 10 units but not more than 25 units **45 days**
More than 25 units **3 months**

On part payment, the maximum period of imprisonment is reduced *pro rata* according to the proportion of the fine which the offender has paid: s22(3); subject to the rule that the maximum period must not fall below 7 days: s22(4). The existing table for 'cash fines', *post*, in s31(3A) PCCA 1973 is amended by s23 CJA 91 by increasing the cash amounts (up to £5,000) which attract a given maximum level of custody in default (up to 3 months). Subject to the CJA 91, the court is bound by existing procedures and restrictions on enforcement and the use of custody in default of paying fines, contained principally in s75 to s91 MCA 1980. Default periods for *'Cash fines', post*, are altered by a substituted para 1 of Sch 4 MCA 1980: see *Statutory Provisions*.

Existing law

The unit method is superimposed on existing legal principle except where this is altered, explicitly or by implication. Existing law also continues to regulate 'cash fines', *post*, subject to any express provisions of the Act, eg fines can be *increased* on account of means: s 19(2).

Fifty units - payment within a year
The long held view is that fines should normally be payable within 'around a year'. This view is supported by *The Structure of a Decision* (Judicial Studies Board, 1987) and the *Sentencing Guide for Criminal Offences* (Magistrates' Association, 1989). There is ample case law to the effect that '... Save in exceptional circumstances a fine should be capable of being paid within 12 months or thereabouts': eg *Hewitt* (1971) 55 Cr App R 433; *Knight* (1980) 2 Cr App R (S) 82; *Owen* [1984] Crim LR 436; *Nunn* (1984) Cr App R (S) 203. Fifty units represents approximately one year's disposable weekly income.

The ruling in *Olliver* (1989) 11 Cr App R (S) 10 cast doubt on the 12 months principle, although commentators have suggested that, in extending the limit to three years, that case, so far as it affects fines (as opposed to compensation) did no more than reflect the existing rule that the 12 months' limit can be exceeded in exceptional circumstances, eg to 'mop up' the proceeds of crime. In the Preface to *Stone's Justices Manual* (1990 Edn) the learned editors state '... We think it would be unwise for magistrates to venture into longer orders for payment in most cases on the strength of (the *Olliver*) case alone'. The editors suggest '... that if the period is much beyond one year, one should think carefully before making such an order'.

Increasing fines for the better off
The provisions of s18 and s19 translate into statutory form the rule that fines can be reduced on account of limited means: see *Fairbairn* (1980) 2 Cr App R (S) 315 and s35 MCA 1980 (repealed by sch 13 CJA 91). The provisions also settle the debate about whether fines can be increased for the better off (as to which see *Unit Fines*, p93).

Punishment is personal to the offender
An offender can only be fined to the extent of his or her *own* means. Earnings by others cannot found a basis for increasing a fine beyond the offender's own affordability: *Baxter* [1974] Crim LR 611 (spouse); *Charalambous* [1985] Crim LR 328 (family). In asking whether anyone else contributes towards the offender's household expenses, the statutory means form (see *Statutory Provisions*) is merely seeking to establish whether or not allowances against income need to be given to the offender in respect of such people.

Potential income

An offender should not be allowed to reduce his or her responsibility for a fine by deliberately avoiding the opportunity to earn. This is supported by *Lewis* [1985] Crim LR 121. The approach is unaffected by the statutory scheme, but *quaere* the need of a sound basis for the inference about potential income: cf Williams v Williams [1974] 3 All ER 377, a family case on a similar point.

'Cash fines'

Fines on corporations (the effect of s 18(1), which applies the unit method only to *individuals*), or fines for offences which are subject to unusually high maxima (the effect of s18(1) (a) and (b) CJA 91), must be imposed subject to s19 CJA 91, which requires the court to take into account, *inter alia*, the means of the offender, whether this '... has the effect of *increasing* or *reducing* the amount of the fine': s19(2). This clarifies the former grey area of law, *supra*. Under the unit method, the necessary adjustment is automatic, within the limits set by s 17(2) and 18(5): the effect of s18(2)(a) and (b) CJA 91. The Crown Court will also continue to use cash fines, save in anomalous situations identified under the heading *Application to individuals, supra*. Section 19 will apply to those fines. Default periods relating to the enforcement of 'cash fines' are contained in a substituted para 1 of Schedule 4 MCA 1980. Section 20 CJA 91 (statements as to offenders' means; duty to provide information etc) is of general application, including to unit fines *or* cash fines. Default periods relating to the enforcement of cash fines are contained in a substituted para 1 of Schedule 4 MCA 1980: see under s17 CJA 91 in *Statutory Provisions, post*.

Attachment of income support

Under s24 CJA 91, a new system is introduced for recovering fines, other penalties and compensation by means of attachment of state benefits. The method applies where magistrates enforce their own fines etc, or where they enforce fines imposed by the Crown Court under s32 PCCA 1973 and s41 Administration of Justice Act 1970. The benefits which may be attached are income support under the Social Security Act 1986, whether standing alone or together with unemployment, sickness or invalidity benefit, retirement pension, or severe disablement allowance *paid at the same time*.

The court may apply to the Secretary of State under s24(1) CJA 91 for sums payable to be deducted from the offender's entitlements. The Fines (Deductions from Income Support) Regulations 1992 are currently in draft and a model form of application to the Secretary of State is in the process of being designed. It is anticipated that the regulations will provide for a means enquiry before a request is made and that they will contain a formula for determining the level at which deductions can be made (predictably at somewhat less than the rate of £2 a week at the time of going to press). Present Department of Social Security regulations provide that deductions for housing, fuel or water debts may not exceed five per cent of the personal allowance for a single claimant aged 25 or over and deductions for a combination of such debts may not exceed 15 per cent.

Deductions for fines will be subject to the same overall maximum. If the defaulter does not receive enough benefit to cover all deductions, other debts rank ahead of those for fines and other financial penalties. The power to apply for attachment extends to certain other penalties and costs: s24(4) CJA 91: see *Statutory Provisions*.

Compensation
Under s35 PCCA 1973, compensation of up to £5,000 (sched 4 CJA 91) per offence may be awarded by magistrates for 'personal injury, loss or damage', whether resulting from the offence charged, or any offences taken into consideration. Compensation can stand alone as a penalty in its own right. Under s35(4A) PCCA 1973, the court is required to give preference to the payment of compensation in cases where both a fine and a compensation order would be appropriate, where the offender does not have the resources for both. In this event, s18(7) CJA 91 allows the amount of the fine determined under the unit fine system to be reduced to a level which would enable the offender to pay the compensation order.

Compensation cannot be valued in units, but the regular availability of financial information should lead to an increased use of such orders. The *Olliver* decision, *supra*, as it applies to compensation, suggests that this can be ordered to be paid over a period of *two years*, or even over *three years* in an appropriate, if exceptional, case. Maximum affordability may thus be 100 to 150 times the disposable weekly income figure, subject to the new legal maximum for magistrates of £5,000 (sched 4 CJA 91) .

Statutory Provisions

Criminal Justice Act 1991
Increase in certain maxima
17.- (1) In section 37 (standard scale of fines) of the Criminal Justice Act 1982 ("the 1982 Act") and section 289G of the Criminal Procedure (Scotland) Act 1975 (corresponding Scottish provision), for subsection (2) there shall be substituted the following subsection -
"(2) The standard scale is shown below -

Level on the scale	Amount of Fine
1	£200
2	£500
3	£1,000
4	£2,500
5	£5,000".

(2) Part I of the Magistrates' Courts Act 1980 ("the 1980 Act") shall be amended as follows -
(a) in section 24(3) and (4) (maximum fine on summary conviction of

young person for indictable offence) and section 36(1) and (2) (maximum fine on conviction of young person by magistrates' court), for "£400" there shall be substituted "£1,000";

(b) in section 24(4) (maximum fine on summary conviction of child for indictable offence) and section 36(2) (maximum fine on conviction of child by magistrates' court), for "£100" there shall be substituted "£250"; and

(c) in section 32(9) (maximum fine on summary conviction of offence triable either way), for "£2,000" there shall be substituted "£5,000";

and in section 289B(6) of the Criminal Procedure (Scotland) Act 1975 (interpretation), in the definition of "prescribed sum", for "£2,000" there shall be substituted "£5,000".

(3) Schedule 4 to this Act shall have effect as follows -

(a) in each of the provisions mentioned in column 1 of Part I (the general description of which is given in column 2), for the amount specified in column 3 there shall be substituted the amount specified in column 4;

(b) in each of the provisions mentioned in column 1 of Part II (the general description of which is given in column 2), for the amount specified in column 3 there shall be substituted the level on the standard scale specified in column 4;

(c) in each of the provisions mentioned in column 1 of Part III (the general description of which is given in column 2), for the amount specified in column 3 there shall be substituted a reference to the statutory maximum;

(d) the provisions set out in Part IV shall be substituted for Schedule 6A to the 1980 Act (fines that may be altered under section 143); and

(e) the provisions mentioned in Part V shall have effect subject to the amendments specified in that Part, being amendments for treating certain failures as if they were summary offences punishable by fines not exceeding levels on the standard scale.

[Section 17 Criminal Justice Act 1991]

NOTE Section 17(3) and **Schedule 4** The effect of these provisions is to alter the maximum fines for various offences.

Fixing of certain fines by reference to units

18. - (1) This section applies where a magistrates' court imposes a fine on an individual -

(a) for a summary offence which is punishable by a fine not exceeding a level on the standard scale; or

(b) for a statutory maximum offence, that is to say, an offence which is triable either way and which, on summary conviction, is punishable by a fine not exceeding the statutory maximum.

(2) Subject to the following provisions of this section, the amount of the fine shall be the product of -

(a) the number of units which is determined by the court to be commensurate with the seriousness of the offence, or the combination of the offence and other offences associated with it; and

(b) the value to be given to each of those units, that is to say, the amount which, at the same or any later time, is determined by the court in accordance with rules made by the Lord Chancellor to be the offender's weekly disposable income.

(3) In making any such determination as is mentioned in subsection (2)(a) above, a court shall take into account all such information about the circumstances of the offence (including any aggravating or mitigating factors) as is available to it.

(4) The number of units determined under subsection 2(a) above shall not exceed -

(a) 2 units in the case of a level 1 offence;

(b) 5 units in the case of a level 2 offence;

(c) 10 units in the case of a level 3 offence;

(d) 25 units in the case of a level 4 offence; and

(e) 50 units in the case of a level 5 offence or a statutory maximum offence;

and in this subsection "level 1 offence" means a summary offence which is punishable by a fine not exceeding level 1 on the standard scale, and corresponding expressions shall be construed accordingly.

(5) Subject to subsection (6) below, the amount determined under subsection (2)(b) above in the case of any offender shall not be -

(a) less than 1/50th of level 1 on the standard scale (£4 at the commencement of section 17 above); or

(b) more than 1/50th of level 5 on that scale (£100 at that commencement).

(6) Where a fine is payable by a person who is under the age of 18 years, subsection (5) above shall have effect as if for the reference to a fraction or amount there were substituted -

(a) a reference to 1/20th of that fraction or amount in the case of a fine payable by a person who is under the age of 14 years; and

(b) a reference to 1/5th of that fraction or amount in the case of a fine payable by a person who has attained that age.

(7) Nothing in subsection (2) above shall prevent any of the following, namely -

(a) in the case of an offence in relation to which a compensation order is made, the reduction of the amount of the fine in pursuance of section 35(4A) of the 1973 Act;

(b) in the case of a fixed penalty offence (within the meaning of Part III of the Road Traffic Offenders Act 1988), the increase of the amount of the fine to the level of the fixed penalty; and

(c) in the case of an offence of installing or using any apparatus for wireless telegraphy except under a licence under section 1 of the Wireless Telegraphy Act 1949, the increase of the amount of the fine by an amount not exceeding the sum which would have been payable on the issue of such a licence.

(8) Where the offender -

(a) has been convicted in his absence in pursuance of section 11 or 12 of the 1980 Act (non-appearance of the accused); or

(b) has failed to comply with an order under section 20(1) below,

and (in either case) the court has insufficient information to make a proper determination under subsection (2)(b) above, it may, within the limits set by subsection (5) above, make such determination as it thinks fit.

(9) In section 41 of the Criminal Justice Act 1988 ("the 1988 Act"), subsection (7) (Crown Court sentencing powers in relation to summary offence dealt with together with either way offence) shall have effect as if this section had not been enacted.

[Section 18 Criminal Justice Act 1991]

NOTES Section 18(1) '**... on an individual**' Unit fines do not apply, eg to corporations. **S18(1)(a)** and **(b)** Unit fines cannot be used for certain offences punishable with unusually high maximum fines: s18(1) CJA 91, and see s 19, *ibid*. **S18(2)** ie the formula for a unit fine is: Number of units of seriousness x Disposable weekly income. **S18(2)(a)** '**... associated with it**' Note that there is *no limit* on the number of associated offences which may be taken into account in order to assess the appropriate number of units. 'An offence is associated with another if - (a) the offender is convicted of it in the proceedings in which he is convicted of the other offence, or (although convicted of it in earlier proceedings) is sentenced for it at the same time as he is sentenced for that offence; or (b) the offender admits the commission of it in the proceedings in which he is sentenced for the other offence and requests the court to take it into consideration in sentencing him for that offence.': section 31(2) CJA 91. **S18(2)(b)** The draft rules are set out in this chapter, *post*. **S18(3)** 'aggravating or mitigating factors' See also s28 CJA 91 (general mitigation provision) and s29(1) and (2) CJA 91 (effect of previous convictions: these cannot be taken into account, but nothing prevents factors disclosed by the circumstances of other offences and which serve to aggravate the seriousness of the present offence being taken into account). **S18(5)** Weekly disposable income determines the value of each unit. It does not necessarily set the rate of payment. Orders can still be made, eg for 'payment forthwith' (by drawing on savings, for example), 'within 28 days' or, at the opposite extreme, at '... £2 a week'. **S18(5)(a)** and **(b)** Fractions The use of fractions to determine spare income limits means that the limits will adjust automatically in line with any future aleteration in the maximum fining levels in s37 CJA 1982. **S18(7)** Under s35(4A) PCCA 1973, the court is required to give preference to the payment of compensation in cases where both a fine and a compensation order would be appropriate, but the offender does not have the resources for both. In this case, s18(7) allows the amount of the fine determined under the unit fine system to be reduced to a level which would enable the offender to pay the compensation order. **S18(8)** This regulates the position where a person does not provide information about his means for either of the reasons set out in subsections (a) and (b). In effect, courts are free to estimate disposable income on the basis of whatever information is available. It is submitted that there must be some basis of inference for this, otherwise the rule applied in the pilot projects whereby persons not responding to requests for information were treated as top income people is the only sensible rule which can be applied. If not, there is an incentive for the better off not to respond to the request for information. See also main text under the heading *Lack of information*. Section 18(8) applies where the offender is convicted in his or her absence in pursuance of s11 or 12 MCA 1980, or has failed to comply with an order under s20(1) CJA 91. **S18(9)** Unit fines do not apply in the Crown Court, even where that Court is dealing with a summary matter under s 41 CJA 1988. But see the note in brackets in the main text under the heading *Application to individuals*.

Fixing of fines in other cases

19.- (1) In fixing the amount of a fine (other than one the amount of which falls to be fixed under section 18 above), a court shall take into account among other things the means of the offender so far as they appear or are known to the court.

(2) Subsection (1) above applies whether taking into account the means of the offender has the effect of increasing or reducing the amount of the fine.

[Section 19 Criminal Justice Act 1991]

NOTES Section 19(2) This clarifies the former grey area of law concerning whether magistrates' courts can increase fines for the better off (cash fines, like unit fines, are subject to the overall statutory maxima in s37 CJA 82: see s17 CJA 91, *supra*). Under the unit method in s18, such adjustment is automatic within the parameters of s17(2) and s18(5), ie from £4 to £100 per unit.

Statements as to offenders' means

20.- (1) Where a person has been convicted of an offence by a magistrates' court, the court may, before sentencing him, order him to furnish to the court within a period specified in the order such a statement of his means as the court may require.

(2) A person who without reasonable excuse fails to comply with an order under subsection (1) above shall be liable on summary conviction to a fine not exceeding level 3 on the standard scale.

(3) If a person in furnishing any statement in pursance of an order under subsection (1) above -

    (a) makes a statement which he knows to be false in a material particular;

    (b) recklessly furnishes a statement which is false in a material particular; or

    (c) knowingly fails to disclose any material fact,

he shall be liable on summary conviction to imprisonment for a term not exceeding three months or a fine not exceeding level 4 on the standard scale or both.

(4) Proceedings in respect of an offence under subsection (3) above may, notwithstanding anything in section 127(1) of the 1980 Act (limitation of time), be commenced at any time within two years of the date of the commission of the offence or within six months from its first discovery by the prosecutor, whichever period expires earlier.

(5) Without prejudice to the generality of subsection (1) of -

    (a) section 84 of the Supreme Court Act 1981; and

    (b) section 144 of the 1980 Act,

the power to make rules under each of those sections shall include power to prescribe the form in which statements are to be furnished in pursuance of orders under subsection (1) above; and rules made by virtue of this subsection may make different provision for different cases or classes of case.

[Section 20 Criminal Justice Act 1991]

NOTES Section 20(1) This power arises only *on conviction*. However, there is nothing to prevent courts seeking information in advance and this is positively encouraged by Home Office administrative advice to courts and by Rule 3 Magistrates' Courts (Unit Fines) Rules 1992 (*post*, currently in draft). See also Home Office letter to courts dated 16 April 1991. The Rules prescribe a means form, or one 'to like effect'. **S20(2)** and **(3)** A suggestion is made in the main text concerning the practical means whereby proceedings might be brought: see under the heading *Penalties for failure to furnish information.* Note also that parents or guardians cannot commit this offence in respect of fines on their children.

Remission of fines fixed under section 18

21.- (1) This section applies where, in the case of a fine the amount of which has been fixed by a magistrates' court under section 18 above, the determination of the offender's disposable weekly income -

(a) would have been of a lesser amount but for subsection (5)(a) of that section; or

(b) was made by virtue of subsection (8) of that section.

(2) In a case falling within subsection (1)(a) above, the court may, on inquiring into an offender's means or at a hearing under section 82(5) of the 1980 Act (issue of warrant of commitment for default), remit the whole or any part of the fine if the court considers that its payment by the offender within twelve months of the imposition of the fine would cause the offender undue hardship.

(3) In a case falling within subsection (1)(b) above, the court may, on inquiring into the offender's disposable weekly income or at such a hearing as is mentioned in subsection (2) above, remit the whole or any part of the fine if the court thinks it just to do so having regard -

(a) to the amount of that income as determined by the court under this subsection in accordance with rules made by the Lord Chancellor; and

(b) if applicable, to the provisions of subsection (2) above.

(4) Where the court remits the whole or part of a fine under subsection (2) or (3) above after a term of imprisonment has been fixed under the said section 82(5), it shall also reduce the term by an amount which bears the same proportion to the whole term as the amount remitted bears to the whole fine or, as the case may be, shall remit the whole term.

(5) In calculating the reduction in a term of imprisonment required by subsection (4) above, any fraction of a day shall be left out of account.

[Section 21 Criminal Justice Act 1991]

NOTES Section 21(1) **'undue hardship'** Note that although this is a basis for remission it is not a basis for setting the fine at a level below £4 per unit in the first instance under s18, *ibid.* Only in enforcement proceedings, ie 'on inquiring into the offender's means or at a hearing under section 82(5) [MCA 1980]' can a court reduce the fine below that produced by application of the statutory £4 bottom weekly limit. But the bottom limit does not necessarily determine the *rate* of payment, even at the time of sentence: see main text under the heading *Disposable weekly income.*

Default in paying fines fixed under section 18

22.- (1) Where default is made in paying a fine the amount of which has been fixed under section 18 above without applying paragraph (b) or (c) of subsection

106

7 of that section, this section shall have effect, in place of Schedule 4 to the 1980 Act, in relation to any committal of the defaulter to prison.

(2) Subject to subsection (3) below, the maximum period of imprisonment applicable in the case of a fine fixed on the basis of a number of units specified in the first column of the following Table shall be the period set out opposite to it in the second column of that Table.

TABLE

Not more than 2 units	7 days
More than 2 units but not more than 5 units	14 days
More than 5 units but not more than 10 units	28 days
More than 10 units but not more than 25 units	45 days
More than 25 units	3 months

(3) Where the amount of a fine due at the time the imprisonment is imposed is so much of the fine as remains due after part payment, then, subject to subsection (4) below, the maximum period given by subsection (2) above shall be reduced by such number of days as bears to the total number of days in it the same proportion as the part of the fine paid bears to the whole fine.

(4) In calculating the reduction required under subsection (3) above, any fraction of a day shall be left out of account and the maximum period shall not be reduced to less than 7 days.

(5) In this section "prison" includes a young offender institution and imprisonment includes detention in such an institution.
[Section 22 Criminal Justice Act 1991]

NOTES Section 22(1) '...in place of Schedule 4' etc Schedule 4 MCA 1980 still applies to 'cash fines' as opposed to unit fines.

Default in other cases
23.- (1) In the Tables in section 31(3A) of the 1973 Act and paragraph 1 of Schedule 4 to the 1980 Act (maximum periods of imprisonment for default in paying fines etc.), for the entries relating to amounts not exceeding £5,000 there shall be substituted the following entries -

"An amount not exceeding £200	7 days
An amount exceeding £200 but not exceeding £500	14 days
An amount exceeding £500 but not exceeding £1,000	28 days
An amount exceeding £1,000 but not exceeding £2,500	45 days
An amount exceeding £2,500 but not exceeding £5,000	3 months"

(2) Table for Scotland.
[Section 23 Criminal Justice Act 1991]

Recovery of fines etc by deduction from income support
24.- The Secretary of State may by regulations provide that where a fine has

been imposed on an offender by a magistrates' court, or a sum is required to be paid by a compensation order which has been made against an offender by such a court, and (in either case) the offender is entitled to income support -

(a) the court may apply to the Secretary of State asking him to deduct sums from any amounts payable to the offender by way of income support, in order to secure the payment of any sum which is or forms part of the fine or compensation; and

(b) the Secretary of State may deduct sums from any such amounts and pay them to the court towards satisfaction of any such sum.

(2) [Power to make regulations]

(3) In subsection (1) above -

(a) the reference to a fine having been imposed by a magistrates' court includes a reference to a fine being treated, by virtue of section 32 of the 1973 Act, as having been so imposed; and

(b) the reference to a sum being required to be paid by a compensation order which has been made by a magistrates' court includes a reference to a sum which is required to be paid by such an order being treated, by virtue of section 41 of the Administration of Justice Act 1970, as having been adjudged to be paid on conviction by such a court.

(4) In this section -

"fine" includes -

(a) a penalty imposed under section 8(1) or 18(4) of the Vehicles (Excise) Act 1971 or section 102(3)(aa) of the Customs and Excise Management Act 1979 (penalties imposed for certain offences in relation to excise licences);

(b) an amount ordered to be paid, in addition to any penalty so imposed, under section 9, 18A or 26A of the said Act of 1971 (liability to additional duty);

(c) an amount ordered to be paid by way of costs which is, by virtue of section 41 of the Administration of Justice Act 1970, treated as having been adjudged to be paid on conviction by a magistrates' court;

"income support" means income support within the meaning of the Social Security Act 1986, either alone or together with any unemployment, sickness or invalidity benefit, retirement pension or severe disablement allowance which is paid by means of the same instrument of payment;

"prescribed" means prescribed by regulations made by the Secretary of State.

(5) [Adjustments relating to Scotland]

[Section 24 Criminal Justice Act 1991]

NOTES Section 24(3) a fine 'being treated ... as having been so imposed' ie a fine imposed by the Crown Court: see s32 PCCA 73. S24(1)(a) '... may apply to the Secretary of State asking him' Attachment of state benefits can only occur following a *request* by the court and subject to the *discretion* of the Secretary of State.

Interpretation

31.- ['Associated offence' see *Statutory Provisions* in *Chapter 4*].

Responsibility of parent or guardian for financial penalties
57.- [This section contains new provisions and amendments (to s55 CYPA 1933, in particular) concerning the liability of parents, guardians and local authorities for financial penalties imposed on young people. The position is noted, in outline, in the main text. A fuller treatment and the statutory provisions themselves are contained in *Chapter 6* of *The Youth Court* entitled *Parental Responsibility*].

Magistrates' Courts (Unit Fines) Rules 1992 **Draft**

The Lord Chancellor, in exercise of the powers conferred on him by section 144 of the Magistrates' Courts Act 1980 [as extended by s145 MCA 1980 and s20(5) CJA 91] and section 18(2)(b) of the Criminal Justice Act 1991, after consultation with the Rule Committee appointed under the said section 144, hereby makes the following rules:

Citation and commencement
1.-- (1) These Rules may be cited as the Magistrates' Courts (Unit Fines) Rules 1992 and shall come into force on   1992.
    (2) Nothing in these Rules shall apply in relation to offences committed before [date of coming into force of Rules].

Interpretation
2 -- (1) In these Rules --
(a) "the Act" means the Criminal Justice Act 1991;
(b) any reference to a "means enquiry form" is a reference to Form A or B set out in Schedule 1 to these Rules or a form to like effect, and "the appropriate means enquiry form" shall be construed accordingly;
(c) any reference to an offender, and an offender's disposable weekly income, shall have effect, in a case to which section 57(3) of the Act applies, as if it were a reference to the parent or guardian against whom the order to pay the fine of the child or young person in question is made, and to the disposable weekly income of the parent or guardian.
    (2) The provisions of these Rules shall have effect subject to subsections (5), (6) and (8) of section 18 of the Act.

Arrangements for service of means enquiry form
3. The clerk to the justices for each petty sessions area shall make arrangements to secure, where a person is to be tried before a magistrates' court for the area for an offence to which section 18 of the Act applies, the provision to him of the appropriate means enquiry form or, where that person is a child or young person, the provision of the appropriate means enquiry form to his parent or guardian.

Determination of disposable weekly income
4. -- (1) Subject to paragraph (2) below, for the purposes of fixing the amount of a fine under section 18 of the Act (fixing of certain fines by reference to units) the amount of an offender's disposable weekly income shall be determined by the court by the application of the formula $\frac{I - E}{3}$, where --
(a) I is the amount of his weekly income,
(b) E the amount of the appropriate expenditure level in his case,

so determined in accordance with these Rules.

(2) Where an offender so consents, the court may determine his disposable weekly income to be an amount equal to 1/50th of level 5 on the standard scale (£100 at the date of the coming into force of these Rules), or, where section 18(6) of the Act applies, the appropriate fraction of that amount.

(3) In determining, in the case of any offender, the amount of his weekly income and of his appropriate expenditure level, the court shall take into account the information contained in any means enquiry form submitted by him and any other relevant information before the court.

Order for statement of means
5. Where, in relation to an offence to which section 18 applies, an offender is ordered to furnish a statement of means under section 20(1) of the Act it shall be furnished on a means enquiry form.

"Guilty by post" form
6. In Form 27 of Schedule 2 to the Magistrates' Courts (Forms) Rules 1981 (notice to defendant: plea of guilty in absence) there shall be added after the words "A form which you can use for writing to the clerk is enclosed" the words "Please also complete the enclosed means enquiry form to enable the court to take your income into account."

SCHEDULE 1 (Rule 2) MEANS ENQUIRY FORMS

MEANS ENQUIRY FORM A: DEFENDANT
(Sections 18 and 20 Criminal Justice Act 1991)

A *[Before Hearing
If you are convicted the court may order you to pay a fine. It will take your weekly income into account in setting the amount of the fine. The court can require you to supply information about your means and failure to comply with that request may be an offence.

You are asked to complete this statement of your means which can either be sent to the court in advance of the hearing or brought with you when you attend court. In the absence of this information, the court may decide that you can pay a fine based on a spare income ** of up to [***] a week.]

B. * [Following Conviction
You have been convicted of an offence and the court is considering ordering you to pay a fine. If it decides to order a fine, it will take your weekly income into account. In the absence of information about your means, the court may decide that you can pay a fine based on a spare income ** of up to [***] a week.

The court requires the following information about your means. Failure to supply this information is an offence carrying a fine of up to [***]. If you supply misleading information you may commit an offence carrying a fine of up to [***] and 3 months' imprisonment.]
* Delete as appropriate   ** "Spare income" means "disposable weekly income" as

110

calculated under rule 4 of these Rules *** Insert appropriate amount.

MEANS ENQUIRY FORM B: PARENT/GUARDIAN
(Sections 18 and 57 Criminal Justice Act 1991 and section 55 Children and Young Persons Act 1933)

A *[Before Hearing
A juvenile of whom you are the parent/guardian has been charged with an offence and is to appear in court. If he/she is convicted the court may impose a fine which you may be ordered to pay. In this case, the court will take your weekly income into account in setting the amount of the fine.

You are asked to complete this statement of your means which can either be sent in advance of the hearing or brought with you when you attend court with the juvenile. In the absence of this information, the court may decide that you can pay a fine based on a spare income ** of up to [***] a week.]

B. * [Following Conviction
A juvenile of whom you are the parent/guardian has been convicted of an offence and the court is considering imposing a fine, which you may be ordered to pay. It will take your weekly income into account. In the absence of information about your means, the court may decide that you can pay a fine based on a spare income ** of up to [***] a week.

The court requires the following information about your means.]

* Delete as appropriate   ** "Spare income" means "disposable weekly income" as calculated under rule 4 of these Rules *** Insert appropriate amount.

MEANS ENQUIRY FORMS A AND B:-

PERSONAL DETAILS
1. Name...
2. Address ....
3. Date of birth ....
4. Occupation ....

FINANCIAL DETAILS Are you willing to pay a fine based on a spare income of [*   ] a week, without further enquiry into your income? YES/NO.
IF YES, go straight to question 12.

<u>Income</u>
5. What is your total income from --

Take home earnings	£	per week
Savings and investments	£	per week
State benefit (after deductions)	£	per week
(Do not include child or one parent benefit)		
Other (including maintenance) - specify	£	per week

<u>Outgoings</u>
6. How many people do you support?   (a) adults .....   (b) children .....

7. Does anyone else pay towards your household expenses?
(ie wife/husband/partner/adult or children)   YES/NO
IF YES, how much do they give?   £   per week
8. What are your housing costs (rent, mortgage etc)?   £   per week
9. If you are paying maintenance to anyone living outside your household state
amount   £   per week
10. Other exceptional outgoings can be listed in Box A at the back of this form.

<u>Payment of Fines Etc</u>
11. If a fine is imposed how much per week could you pay ?   £   per week
12. Do you have any outstanding fines or compensation to pay?
                                    YES/NO
IF YES, how much are you paying each week ?   £   per week
Through which court ? ....
When will payment be completed? ....
If you want to say anything else about your financial position (for example, any
changes in your financial circumstances in the next 12 months) please use Box B at
the back of this form.
If you are to be represented by a solicitor you would be well advised to show the form
to him before returning it to the court office.

I believe the information on this form is true
Date: ....   Signature ....

<u>YOU SHOULD BRING TO COURT DOCUMENTS, SUCH AS PAY SLIPS, TO BACK UP
THE INFORMATION GIVEN IN THIS FORM.</u>

EXCEPTIONAL OUTGOINGS   BOX A

Debts/Loans?
How much?
What for?
Other?
How much?
What for?

CHANGE IN CIRCUMSTANCES   BOX B

Insert appropriate amount

112

SCHEDULE 2 (Rule 4) DETERMINATION OF DISPOSABLE WEEKLY INCOME

1. In determining an offender's disposable weekly income there shall be disregarded --
(a) any child benefit paid to the offender under section 1 of the Child Benefit Act 1975; and
(b) any sum or sums payable by the offender as a result of any fine imposed or compensation order made in proceedings other than those in respect of which the determination is to be made.

2. The magistrates for each petty sessions area shall, from time to time and taking into account local conditions, determine amounts that appear to them to represent the weekly expenditure levels in respect of the items of expenditure specified in column 2 below of notional households in their petty sessions area, in this Schedule referred to as "notional expenditure levels".

| Column 1 | Column 2 |
Member of household	Items of expenditure
OFFENDER	Food
	Heating
	Housing costs
	Community charge
	Water rates
	Clothing
	Travel to work
SPOUSE/COHABITEE	Food
	Community charge
	Clothing
ADULT DEPENDANTS/CHILDREN	Food
	Clothing

3.-- (1) Subject to paragraph (2) below, in these Rules "the appropriate expenditure level" for an offender shall be an amount determined by the court as representing the sum of the amounts determined in accordance with the notional expenditure levels set under paragraph 2 above as they relate to the offender and the other members of his household.

(2) The amount determined by the court under paragraph (1) above shall be --
(a) reduced to take account of expenditure on the other members of the offender's household which is met out of those members' incomes, and of exceptionally low expenditure on housing; and
(b) increased to take account of the offender's expenditure on maintenance and, where the court thinks fit, of the offender's exceptional expenditure.

Magistrates' Association Guidelines

An extract from the Association's *Sentencing Guidelines* is included in Chapter 8 of *Introduction to the Criminal Justice Act 1991*. The complete version can be found in the Association's Annual Report for 1991.

Chapter 7

The Youth Court & Young Offenders

The following introduction to the youth court brings together the main legal and practice issues involved in the new jurisdiction over people aged *10 to 17* charged with criminal offences. Each topic (together with related *Statutory Provisions*) is treated in detail in the companion volume to this work *The Youth Court*. This chapter also includes: a summary of changes affecting young people aged *18 to 20*; and an outline of the new children's evidence provisions of the CJA 91 (again dealt with more fully in *The Youth Court*: see *Chapter 9* of that work). The new remand provisions affecting young people aged 10 to 16 are summarised in *Chapter 9* of this work, *post*.

The youth court
There is no new overall body of law applicable to the youth court. Rather, the 'new jurisdiction' is a mixture of legal and practice changes, the combined effect of which is to create a fresh ethos. The changes all operate subject to the existing welfare principle in s44 CYPA 1933. The principal shifts brought about by the CJA 91 are that it:

- Renames the 'juvenile court' as the 'youth court': s70 CJA 91.
- Extends the jurisdiction so that the youth court and not the magistrates' court will deal with people *under 18* (formerly *under 17*): s68 and sched 8, *ibid*.
- Gives youth court magistrates new sentencing powers (Part III CJA 91) to be exercised within the new overall sentencing framework (*Chapter 1*, *ante*) along with a new scheme of post-custody supervision.
- Follows the principle that sentencing of young people should be governed by individual 'maturity', *post*.
- Re-directs the existing emphasis on parental responsibility
- Creates a fresh impetus by making 17 year olds subject to former juvenile court practices, bringing a new focus for a strategy which will be put into practice via 'action plans' and multi-agency co-operation.

Development of sentencing criteria
The sentencing criteria in Part I CJA 91 apply to offenders of all ages. The criteria for passing a custodial sentence contained in s1(2), *ibid*, are similar (though with important differences) to the criteria governing the use of

custody for offenders under 21 which were contained in s1(4) and (4A) CJA 82 (repealed by sched 13 to the CJA 91). The White Paper, *Crime Justice and Protecting the Public*, proposed the extension of similar criteria to all offenders: 'The Criminal Justice Act 1982 set out the circumstances in which courts could give custodial sentences to offenders under 21. These requirements were refined in the Criminal Justice Act 1988. The provisions reflected the widespread view that, so far as possible, young offenders should not be sentenced to custody, since this is likely to confirm them in a criminal career. Since 1983, the number of offenders under 17 sentenced to custody has been halved and there has been no discernible increase in the number of offences committed by juveniles. In the last year, there has been a significant drop in the number of young adults aged 17 to 20 sentenced to custody ... A more consistent approach to sentencing young offenders has emerged from the Court of Appeal's guidance on interpreting the legislation' (paras 3.6, 3.9).

'Near adults' - 16 and 17 year olds
The White Paper, *supra*, said of offenders aged 16 and 17: 'The Government proposes major changes in arrangements for dealing with young offenders aged 16 and 17. As teenagers approach adulthood, their parents' responsibility for them is reduced. Young people should begin to take more responsibility for the consequences of their own decisions and actions. They are at an intermediate stage between childhood and adulthood. The arrangements for dealing with offenders of this age should reflect this' (para 8.14). The proposal was that 16 and 17 year olds should be dealt with as 'near adults' and that there should be greater flexibility in the overall sentencing arrangements for this age group. As a result, the law governing custodial sentencing of 17 year olds is brought into line with that which applied to 16 year olds. Section 63 of the Act reduces the maximum term of detention in a young offender institution for an offender aged 17 to 12 months, and Schedule 8 to the Act brings 17 year olds within the ambit of s53 CYPA 1933 under which longer terms of detention can be ordered by the Crown Court in respect of certain 'grave crimes'. The full range of community penalties previously available for 16 year olds is retained and extended to 17 year olds.

Maturity of the offender
At the same time, 16 year olds become eligible for community penalties or maxima previously restricted to those aged 17 and over, ie in relation to probation, community service and attendance centre orders. The purpose of these arrangements is to allow courts to select the most suitable sentence according to the maturity and circumstances of the offender and the arrangements available locally. The overall effect of the adjustments is as follows:

- the youth court will be able to give *either* a probation order or a

supervision order to a 16 or 17 year old
- the maximum number of hours of work that can be imposed in a community service order will be 240 hours for offenders aged 16 and 17 (the existing maximum for 16 year olds being 120)
- both 16 and 17 year olds can be ordered to attend an attendance centre for up to 36 hours (the maximum hitherto applicable to 17 to 20 year olds. The maximum re 16 year olds was 24 hours)
- the new combination order introduced by s11 CJA 91 and the new curfew order introduced by s12 will be available for 16 and 17 year olds as well as adults.

Parental responsibility
The White Paper, *supra*, placed considerable emphasis on parental responsibility. Under Part III CJA 91, courts *may* require the parents or guardians of 16 year olds and 17 year olds to attend court or to pay any financial penalties imposed. Similarly, the court *may* bind over the parents or guardians of offenders aged 16 and 17 to take proper care of and to exercise proper control over the offender. However, the court is *not* placed under a duty to consider exercising these powers, in contrast to the position in relation to offenders below the age of 16. With these younger offenders the court *must* exercise its powers to require parents or guardians to attend court or to pay any financial penalty imposed unless the parents or guardians cannot be found or it would be unreasonable; and it *must* bind over the parent or guardian if it is satisfied that this would be desirable in the interests of preventing further offending. Under the new system of unit fines (*Chapter 6*), parents or guardians who are ordered to pay the fines of their children will be assessed on the basis of their own disposable income, not that of the child.

Apart from responsibilities introduced by the Children Act 1989 (as to which see *The Youth Court*), there are new ones under the CJA 91 for local authorities. Where a child is in care or accommodated by a local authority and the authority has parental responsibility, it can be ordered to pay fines and compensation imposed on the child or young person. Under the system of unit fines, all fines ordered to be paid by a local authority are assessed at the top level of disposable income for a child of the age in question (*Chapter 6*).

Guilty plea in the absence of the defendant
Among the new procedures contained in the CJA 91, section 12 MCA 1980 (plea of guilty in the absence of the defendant) is amended by sched 11 CJA 91 so as to enable a person who has reached the age of 16 to enter a plea of guilty in writing, in the youth court, where the procedure envisaged by s12 of the 1980 Act has been adopted by the prosecutor: see new s12(1A),

Evidence
The evidence provisions of the CJA 91 apply in all criminal courts where

children have to give evidence. For convenience, they are set out in full in *The Youth Court* rather than in this work and summarised below. The provisions operate in part by amending changes already made by the CJA 1988 and in part by the introduction of totally new provisions. The changes are as follows:

- *Committal proceedings* The repeal of s103(3)(a) Magistrates' Courts Act 1980 means that a defendant can no longer oblige the prosecution to call a child witness to give evidence at committal proceedings merely by objecting to the use of a statement (which may be a video recording made for the purposes of the trial: s54 CJA 91) made by or taken from a child: s55(1) CJA 91. In order to avoid possible prejudice to the welfare of a child who may be called upon as a witness at the trial the Director of Public Prosecutions is given an unappealable power to order that the trial of an offence (to which s32(2) CJA 1988 applies) be transferred directly to the Crown Court if he is satisfied that a child who is either the victim or a witness of such an offence will be called as a witness and that there is sufficient evidence for the case to be committed to that court for trial. The notice of transfer must be served before committal proceedings have commenced. Detailed regulations relating to transfer procedures are contained in Schedule 6 CJA 91; the schedule also makes provision for bail, witness orders and legal aid.

- *Video recordings* Section 54 CJA 91 adds a new s32A to the CJA 1988 which makes provision for the evidence in chief of a child witness (in a case to which s32(2) CJA 1988 applies) to be given in the form of a video recording of an interview between the child and an adult relating to any matter in issue in the proceedings: s32A(2). Section 32(2) CJA 1988 applies mainly to violent or sexual offences, together with conspiring or attempting to commit such offences, or to being a secondary party to such offences. Leave of the court is required and this will be given unless it appears to the court that the child will not be available for cross-examination, or that the party tendering the evidence has not complied with any rules of court for disclosing the circumstances under which it was made, or that in the interests of justice it should not be admitted: s32A(3). The court may order that a part of the recording should be excluded, but in reaching this decision it should weigh the likely prejudice to the accused by showing those parts against the desirability of showing the whole of the recording: s32A(4). Once such a recording is admitted the child should not be examined in chief on any matters covered in the recording. He or she may give evidence on other matters and may be cross-examined, though this can take place through a video link: s32A(5). It is made clear that any statement (which may include drawings and models) disclosed in such a recording is to be treated as if the child were giving oral evidence in the witness box (ie it is not to be regarded as hearsay simply because it is a recording), but that it should not be regarded as corroborating any other evidence given by him:

s32A(6).

A child is defined as a person who is (i) in the case of a sexual offence, either under 17 at the time of the hearing, or under 18 at the time of the hearing if he was under 17 at the time the recording was made; (ii) in the case of other offences covered by s32(2) CJA 1988, under 14 at the date of the hearing, or under 15 if he was under 14 at the time the recording was made. Section 32A applies to the trial of offences covered by s32 CJA 1988 in the Crown Court or youth court and in appeals therefrom (including a reference by the Attorney-General).

- *Television links* Two major changes are made to the provisions of s32 CJA 1988 which deals with evidence through live television links. By s55(2), (3) CJA 1991, the use of such links is extended to proceedings before the youth court and appeals therefrom. It is also provided that if the particular court does not possess television link facilities, the hearing should be moved to a court which does, even if that involves going outside the petty sessions area for which the court acts: s55(4) CJA 1991. Section 32 CJA 1988 is extended so that it now applies also to (i) a child under the age of 17 at the time of the hearing where the offence is covered by s32(2)(c), (d) (sexual offence) and (ii) a witness who is to be cross-examined following the admission under s32A 1988 of a video recording of his or her evidence in chief.

- *Child witnesses* Section 52 CJA 1991 does away with the need to test children to see whether they can give sworn or unsworn testimony. In future, under a new s33A CJA 1988 children under 14 will give unsworn evidence and children aged 14 years or over will give sworn evidence. The unsworn testimony of children will be treated as though it was given on oath. The Act makes clear that the court may, as it does with any witness, determine that a child witness is not competent to give evidence. It would appear that there is no minimum age below which, as a matter of law, a child will be regarded as incompetent; this is simply a matter for the court of trial. Where the court is trying an offence which falls within s32(2) CJA 1988 and the witness is alleged to be the victim or a witness of the offence and is either (i) a child or (ii) a witness who is to be cross-examined following the reception by that court of his or her evidence in video recorded form, the accused shall not be permitted to cross-examine the witness in person. For this purpose, a 'child' is a person who is under 14 at the time of the hearing unless the offence is a sexual one, in which case he or she must be under 17.

Note of items dealt with in *The Youth Court*
The following subjects are dealt with (insofar as they affect the 10 to 17 years inclusive age group) in the companion volume to this work *The Youth Court*: *Chapter 1* General Introduction; 2 Juvenile Justice - A

Decade of Progress; *3* The New Jurisdiction; *4* Age Ranges; *5* Sentencing; *6* Parental Responsibility; *7* Procedures; *8* Remands; *9* Evidence; *10* Action Plans and Inter-Agency Co-operation; *11* Presentence Reports; *12* Sentencing Options.

Young adult offenders

With the extension of the jurisdiction of the youth court to include 17 year olds, *supra*, it is important to stress that special considerations of age still attach to persons aged 18 to 20. This is underlined by the *Code of Practice for the Crown Prosecution Service* (1986). With respect to sentencing, the government, in noting with approval the general reduction in the level of sentences imposed on juveniles, stated that it was '... reasonable to look to a significant drop in the number of young adults sentenced to custody': *Punishment, Custody and the Community*, 1988, Cm 424, p 7. Later in 1988, the Home Office urged probation areas to establish 'action plans', in collaboration with other criminal justice agencies, to encourage 'punishment in the community' for this age group. There are several distinctive features in the law concerning the sentencing of young adults compared with the sentencing of people aged 21 or over, or in some instances those below the age of 18:

No power to suspend sentences
The power in s22 Powers of Criminal Courts Act 1973 to suspend custodial sentences was removed in relation to people below the age of 21 by the CJA 82. The absence of such a power serves to concentrate the mind of the sentencer on the special character of custody.

Minimum and maximum sentences
In contrast to the one year limit on custodial sentences for offenders below the age of 18 (s1B CJA 82 as amended by s63 CJA 91) the maximum term of a custodial sentence for a young adult offender is the same as that for a person aged 21 or over; but there is a special minimum sentence, applicable to either sex, of 21 days: s1A(4A) CJA 82 as inserted by s63 CJA 91.

Life sentences
A sentence of custody for life under s8(2) CJA 82 can only be imposed on a person aged 18 to 20 following the CJA 91 (formerly 17 to 20): s8(2), *ibid*, as amended by s63(5) CJA 91. Except where a sentence of custody for life is fixed by law, the usual restrictions on custodial sentences in s1(2) CJA 91 apply: s1(1), *ibid*, and see the definition of 'custodial sentence' in s31(1) CJA 91 (*Chapter 4, ante*).

Detention for default or contempt
Detention (as opposed to imprisonment for full adults) for default (eg non-payment of fine) or contempt can only be ordered in the case of a person aged 18 to 20 following the CJA 91. This particular form of detention is

specifically excluded from the definition of 'custodial sentence' in s31(1) CJA 91, so that the restrictions and procedures in s1 to 4, *ibid*, do not apply. Whereas a person below the age of 18 (after the CJA 91; formerly below 17) cannot be sent to custody for non-payment of fine, or eg cannot be detained for refusal to be bound over (*Veater v Glennon* (1981) 72 Cr App R 331, [1981] Crim LR 563), a person aged 18 to 20 can be: s9 CJA 82 and cf *Howley v Oxford* (1985) 81 Cr App R 246, 149 JP 363).

Case law
Restrictions on custodial sentences which, until the CJA 91, applied only to persons aged below 21, now apply, in their new form, to offenders of whatever age. However, historically speaking, statutory approaches to young adults have a greater affinity with those relating to the younger age group than with those which affect full adults of 21 years of age or over. Sections 1(4) and (4A) CJA 1982 (repealed by sched 13 to the CJA 91) applied equally to all those below 21: see the summaries of cases in *Chapters 2* and *3, ante*. (By far the largest proportion of this existing case law concerns appeals by offenders aged 17 to 20. These rulings must remain persuasive in relation to the application of the 'seriousness' and 'protection of the public' criteria in s1(2) CJA 91, *a fortiori*, where young offenders below the age of 21 are concerned).

The nature of custody for young adults
Within the Prison Department, the status of young adults is recognised in their placement in young offender institutions for persons aged 15 to 20: cf s1C CJA 82 which (as amended by s63(4) CJA 91) provides *inter alia* that those under 18 serving sentences of detention in a young offender institution may not be held in a prison or remand centre except for a 'temporary purpose'. When they are not held in a young offender institution, but placed in a prison, every effort is made to ensure that young offenders are kept separate from adults. This principle dates from the Prevention of Crime Act 1908 which established the borstal system.

Attendance centre
Apart from custodial sentencing, the only sentence available for those aged 18 to 20 which is not also available for adults is an attendance centre order, not exceeding 36 hours (the same as for offenders aged 16 to 20 following the CJA 91): s17 CJA 82 as amended by s67 CJA 91.

Mode of trial and committal for sentence
All persons aged 18 or over (formerly 17 or over) are subject to the mode of trial procedures contained in s19 MCA 1980, *et al*. However, persons below the age of 21 cannot be committed to the Crown Court for sentence under the 'protection of the public' limb of s38 MCA 1980 as amended by s25 CJA 91. They can be so committed under the new 'seriousness' limb of s38: see further *Chapter 2, ante* under the heading *Seriousness and Mode of Trial*.

Post-custody supervision

A special scheme of post-custody supervision applies to all offenders under 22 when released from a sentence of detention in a young offender institution or under s53 CYPA 33: *Chapter 10, post.* Such people may be supervised by a social worker or a probation officer: s43(5) CJA 91. Section 65 CJA contains special arrangements for the supervision of all such offenders on release. These preserve the current arrangements under which they receive a minimum of three months' compulsory supervision (subject to this not extending beyond the 22nd birthday). In relation to this age group, the post-custody supervision arrangements apply even in relation to sentences of less than 12 months (cf full adults).

Chapter 8

Pre-sentence Reports

An important feature of the new sentencing framework is the statutory duty placed on courts to take account of all the circumstances of an *offence*. This duty occurs in relation to all types of sentence. The pre-sentence report (PSR) is an integral part of the information gathering and fact-finding process as this relates to the more severe forms of sentence; part of the Act's structured approach to sentencing. The court must obtain and consider a report *before* making certain decisions. The PSR is also the primary means by which the court receives information about the *offender*. Pre-sentence reports will be buttressed by *National Standards* affecting various aspects of probation service work, including report writing and presentation.

The practical implications of the new regime are considerable. A special chapter is devoted to the background and wider issues arising in *Introduction to the Criminal Justice Act 1991*: see *Chapter 11* of that work. The Secretary of State has power to regulate the form and content of pre-sentence reports: s3(5)(b) CJA 91 (albeit, it is understood, at the time of writing, there are no immediate plans to exercise that power, beyond what is necessary to comply with the legalities of the definition of pre-sentence reports in s3(5) CJA 91, *post*). *National Standards* will thus be given the opportunity to show that they can work. The purpose is '... To help in the consistent attainment of good quality, impartial PSRs that are the greatest assistance to courts': *Towards National Standards for Pre-sentence Reports: Discussion Document* CPO 46/1991.

Meaning of 'pre-sentence report'

The term 'pre-sentence' report is defined in s3(5) CJA 91 as a report *in writing* which '... (a) with a view to assisting the court in determining the most suitable method of dealing with an offender, is made or submitted by a probation officer or by a social worker of a local authority social services department; and (b) contains information as to such matters, presented in such manner, as may be prescribed by rules made by the Secretary of State'.

These provisions do not prevent a 'stand down' written report (or even a 'stand down' oral report in situations where a pre-sentence report in writing is not required by law) should the circumstances be appropriate. The Crown Court pilot projects mentioned under the heading *Information, post*, indicate the scope for 'short notice' written reports. *Medical and psychiatric reports* (see under that heading, *post*) are a distinct, though procedurally analogous, form of report.

Custody

Before a decision can be taken whether custody is justified, or concerning the length of custody, the court must obtain and consider a pre-sentence report: s3(1) CJA 91; except where the offence or any other offence associated with it is triable *only* on indictment and provided that, in the circumstances, the Crown Court is of the opinion that a pre-sentence report is unnecessary: s3(2), *ibid*. This exception thus applies only to a restricted category of very serious matters where custody must, by any standard, be a reasonable presumption (albeit open to challenge. A report will often be desirable). This apart, the Crown Court, like the magistrates court, is under a duty to obtain and consider reports before imposing custody (or certain other sentences: see next section).

Community sentences

Pre-sentence reports are required in relation to certain community orders *before* the court decides on sentence. Section 7(3) CJA 91 provides that the court must obtain and consider a pre-sentence report before forming any opinion as to the suitability of the offender for any one or more of the following orders: a probation order which includes additional requirements authorised by Schedule 1A PCCA 73; a community service order; a combination order; or a supervision order which includes requirements imposed under s12, s12A, s12AA, s12B or s12C CYPA 1969.

Information

So far as the facts of cases are concerned, much will depend on what information Crown Prosecutors and police (details of previous offences) make available to probation officers or place before courts. Defence advocates, too, have a role to play. Good communications between the probation service and all the criminal justice agencies is essential to effective report writing. There is considerable scope for liaison, as identified by work by the Vera Institute of Justice in five Crown Court pilot areas which have experimented with producing pre-sentence reports. This is particularly so in relation to what has been termed the 'short-notice' pre-sentence report prepared when a plea changes from 'not guilty' to 'guilty' at a late stage in the proceedings. In the pilots, reports were prepared pre-trial in those cases where it was known that the plea would be guilty. This left around 30 per cent of reports to be prepared post-conviction within timescales ranging from 12 hours to 28 days. The Vera research is due for publication in February 1992.

The offence

The court must obtain and consider a report *before* forming an opinion concerning custody: s3(1) CJA 91; a provision which emphasises that there should be no provisional decision making. It also follows from s3(1) that, in relation to custody, the report should address those matters which the court must consider in relation to s1(2)(a) or (b) CJA 91 ie the *seriousness* of the offence or the *protection of the public*, including, in relation to the latter criterion, information (in relation to violent or sexual offences) about the *offender*: see s3(3)(b), *ibid*. Generally, the court must '... take account of all such information about the circumstances of the offence (including any aggravating or mitigating factors) as is available to it': s3(3)(a), *ibid*; of which the information in a pre-sentence report will form part. The report should thus address any aggravating or mitigating factors relating to the *offence*, as well as any factors within the meaning of s28 CJA 91 (general mitigation provision) or s29, *ibid* (aggravating factors disclosed by other offences): as to both of which see *Chapters 1* and *2*. The report should also include information about any matters which might affect the *length* of a custodial sentence: a further effect of s3(1), *ibid*. It is suggested that none of this should be at a 'legalistic' level; but report writers will need to be familiar with the main themes of, eg guideline rulings of the Court of Appeal.

Similar considerations apply in relation to community sentences and seriousness (*only*: the 'protection of the public' ground does not apply in determining whether the community sentence threshold has been reached). Before making any decision on seriousness in relation to community sentences, as required by s6(1) CJA 91, the court must take into account all the circumstances of the offence: s7(1) CJA 91; similarly, before deciding whether restrictions on liberty are commensurate with seriousness in accordance with s6(2)(b) CJA 91: *ibid*. Strictly speaking, there is no *statutory* obligation on a court to obtain and consider a report before forming these opinions about the *offence* in so far as community sentences are concerned (cf custody, *supra*: s3(1) CJA 91). On the other hand, if a report does contain relevant information the court must take it into account along with any other information: see s7(1).

The offender
The definition of 'pre-sentence report' in s3(5) CJA 91, *supra*, appears to contemplate a wide approach by report writers to matters concerning the *offender*. In addition, apart from the specific provision affecting violent or sexual offences already mentioned in relation to custody, *supra*, matters which concern the *offender* as opposed to the *offence* are mentioned specifically at several points in the Act. Thus, before a community sentence can be used, the court must be of opinion that:

'... the particular order or orders comprising or forming part of the sentence [are] such as in the opinion of the court is, or taken together are, the most suitable for the *offender*': s6(2)(a) CJA 91 (italics supplied).

Section 7(3) CJA 91 (see under the heading *Community sentences, supra*) requires the court to obtain and consider a pre-sentence report *before* forming an opinion as to the suitability of the *offender* for one or more of the community orders mentioned in that subsection. There is also an inescapable need to address specific matters concerning the *offender* in relation to probation orders: see the criteria in s2 PCCA 73 (as substituted by s8 CJA 91); community service orders: s14(2) PCCA 73 (as substituted by s10 CJA 91); and combination orders: an effect of s11(3) CJA 91. All of these *offender* based criteria are set out and discussed in *Chapter 5*.

National standards
The emerging *National Standards* for pre-sentence reports envisage that report writers will target information by '... providing impartial, professional and timely advice relevant to the sentencing decision. The most important components would seem to be: an analysis of the offence (or offences) and of the offender - for example, relevant information about his or her attitude to the offence, circumstances, problems, motivation, etc, and background, and an assessment of the risk of serious harm to the public; advice relevant to sentencing, where appropriate describing a community sentence under which the probation service considers it and/or others could most suitably work with the offender to reduce the risk of his or her re-offending, or a fine or discharge, *if* the court were so to decide.': *Towards National Standards for Pre-sentence Reports: Discussion Document, ibid*, para 6.

It is likely that there will be an emphasis on *describing* community sentences, or other disposals, which might be suitable for the offender as opposed to recommending particular sentences. 'The criticism by some sentencers that current recommendations ... can be 'unrealistic' (ie envisaging a community disposal when the sentencer considers only custody to be a sufficient penalty) would no longer be relevant since the sentencer's exclusive responsibility for deciding what sentence was appropriate would be more clearly identified': para 7, *ibid*. This need not, however, prevent the report writer from indicating which community sentence he or she considers the most *suitable* for the offender.

Failure to obtain a report
No custodial sentence is invalidated by the failure of a court to obtain a pre-sentence report, although any court on appeal against such a sentence must obtain and consider a pre-sentence report if none was obtained by the court below: s3(4) CJA 91; and consider any report which was obtained: *ibid*. The same is true in relation to a community sentence falling within the ambit of s7(3) CJA 91, *supra*: s7(4), *ibid*; and medical reports: s4(4), *ibid*.

Pre-sentence reports and mentally disordered offenders
If the offender *is*, or *appears to be* mentally disordered, section 4 CJA 91 requires a medical report to be obtained on the offender's mental condition before a custodial sentence is passed, other than where the sentence is fixed by law: s4(1); except where, in the circumstances, the court forms the opinion that it is unnecessary to obtain a medical report: s4(2), *ibid*. This exception is of general application (cf that in relation to pre-sentence reports under s3(2),

supra, which is confined to 'indictable *only*' cases). In any event, before passing a custodial sentence (other than one fixed by law) on an offender who is or appears to be mentally disordered, a court must consider: '(a) any information before it which relates to his mental condition (whether given in a medical report, a pre-sentence report or otherwise); and (b) the likely effect of such a sentence on that condition and on any treatment which may be available for it.': s4(3) CJA 91.

A sentence is not invalidated if the court fails to comply with any of these requirements concerning medical reports, but an appellate court must remedy any omission by obtaining and considering comparable information: s4(4), *ibid*.

A medical report means '... a report as to an offender's mental condition made or submitted *orally* or in *writing* by a registered medical practitioner': s4(5), *ibid*; who is 'duly approved' for the purposes of s12 Mental Health Act 1983 as having special experience in the diagnosis or treatment of mental disorder: *ibid*. Whilst compliance with the provisions concerning medical reports is *not* a legal pre-requisite to a community sentence, in practice such a report may prove critical to the correct choice of sentence.

When is a report 'unnecessary'?
Section 3(2) CJA 91, *supra*, empowers the Crown Court to dispense with a pre-sentence report when sentencing for offences triable only on indictment when the court considers a report 'unnecessary'. The provision is similar to (though more restricted than) that in s2(3) CJA 1982 relating to young offenders (repealed by the 1991 Act). Section 2(2), *ibid*, required courts to obtain a social inquiry report before imposing a custodial sentence on a young offender; but s2(3) stated that this did not apply '...if, in the circumstances of the case, the court is of the opinion that it is unnecessary to obtain a social inquiry report'. A similarly worded provision and exception applied to the imposition of a prison sentence on an adult offender who had not already served one: see s20 and s20A PCCA 1973 (again repealed and replaced by the CJA 91).

There has been relatively little judicial guidance on the circumstances making a social inquiry report unnecessary. The unreported case of *Griffiths* (1984), heard in the High Court on February 14, concerned a 19 year old offender who was given a three months' detention centre order without a social inquiry report. Watkins LJ said:

'... It may well be that had the judge taken the precaution which Parliament bids every judge in this sort of circumstance to do, he would still have imposed the sentence which he did upon this appellant. But this court, because of the judge's failure adequately to inform himself, has come to the conclusion that, bearing in mind the contents of the social inquiry report which is before us, we have no alternative but to quash the sentence imposed'.

In *Massheder* (1983) 5 Cr App R (S) 442, a 15 year old defendant admitted being concerned with others in an offence of arson involving criminal damage valued at over £5,000. No social inquiry report had been prepared because of industrial action and the then practice of social services not to prepare reports in circumstances where no finding of guilt had been recorded. The trial judge described this as a 'disgraceful situation' and, despite an offer from the representative of the social services department, refused to adjourn the case. He imposed a term of 18 months' detention under s53 CYPA 1933 and implied that the nature of the offence placed it 'beyond anything in the nature of probation'. On appeal, Macpherson LJ stated that: '... the whole purpose of obtaining a report is to give help and balance to the consideration of all available courses open to the court. In this case, in spite of the difficulty, the matter should have been adjourned to see whether a report was produced'. Varying sentence to a supervision order, he added: '... If the case had been adjourned and a report like the one before us had been obtained, we feel it is likely that the judge would have been affected and perhaps persuaded by it as we have been.'

It is submitted that a pre-sentence report could be regarded as 'unnecessary' only where the court is sure that, whatever it contained, it would, by virtue of the seriousness of the offence or the need to protect the public, make no difference to the sentence imposed (including, now, the length of any custodial sentence or the composition of restrictions on liberty). The circumstances in which it is possible to predict this with certainty must be comparatively few. The same formula is used in s4(2) CJA 91 in relation to medical reports (but applied to a much wider range of cases). Analogous principles would seem to apply, *a fortiori*, perhaps.

Statutory Provisions

Criminal Justice Act 1991
Procedural requirements for custodial sentences.
3.- (1) Subject to subsection (2) below, a court shall obtain and consider a pre-sentence report before forming any such opinion as is mentioned in subsection (2) of section 1 or 2 above.

(2) Where the offence or any other offence associated with it is triable only on indictment, subsection (1) above does not apply if, in the circumstances of the case, the court is of the opinion that it is unnecessary to obtain a pre-sentence report.

(3) In forming any such opinion as is mentioned in subsection (2) of section 1 or 2 above a court -

(a) shall take into account all such information about the circumstances of the offence (including any aggravating or mitigating factors) as is available to it; and

127

(b) in the case of any such opinion as is mentioned in paragraph (b) of that subsection, may take into account any information about the offender which is before it.

(4) No custodial sentence which is passed in a case to which subsection (1) above applies shall be invalidated by the failure of a court to comply with that subsection but any court on an appeal against such a sentence -

(a) shall obtain a pre-sentence report if none was obtained by the court below; and

(b) shall consider any such report obtained by it or by that court.

(5) In this Part "pre-sentence report" means a report in writing which -

(a) with a view to assisting the court in determining the most suitable method of dealing with an offender, is made or submitted by a probation officer or by a social worker of a local authority social services department; and

(b) contains information as to such matters, presented in such manner, as may be prescribed by rules made by the Secretary of State.

[Section 3 Criminal Justice Act 1991]

NOTES

S3(1) pre-sentence report, ie as defined in s3(5). The exception under which courts need not obtain a report applies in the Crown Court in relation to offences triable *only* on indictment. That court *is* under a duty to obtain and consider reports in other cases: s3(1); and on appeal: s3(4) (cf s4(4); s7(4), *post*). **Before forming any such opinion** There should thus be no provisional decision making. However, the court will have to make some assessment of the risk of custody etc in order to know whether to ask for a report. It follows that the report should address those matters affecting the offence which the court will have to consider in relation to s1(2)(a) or (b) CJA 91, ie *seriousness* and *protection of the public*: *Chapter 4, Custody*; as well as the most suitable method of dealing with the *offender*: s3(5)(a) and see main text. **'... subsection (2) of section 1 or 2 above'** ie before deciding on custody or the length of custody. **Associated with it** 'Associated offence' is defined in s31(2) CJA 91: *Chapter 4*. **S3(2) 'unnecessary'** see *When is a report unnecessary?* in main text. **S3(3)(a) aggravating** or *mitigating* **factors** Apart from the facts of the offence under consideration, note also the effect of s28 CJA 91 (general mitigation provision), and s29(2), *ibid* (aggravating factors disclosed by other offences). **S3(3)(b)** Note that under this subsection, courts must address their minds to both the *offence* and the *offender*. **About the offence ... as is available to it** ... Much will also depend on what other information the Crown Prosecutor, the defence and other agencies place before the court. **S3(5) Pre-sentence report** Note that reports must be *in writing*. This does not prevent a 'standdown' written report, or a 'standdown' oral report in situations where a pre-sentence report is not required by law, should the circumstances be appropriate to this. See also the comments concerning 'short-notice' reports in the main text. **S3(5)(b)** ie the content and style of pre-sentence reports can be prescribed by regulation. It is understood, as of the time of writing, that there is no intention to make regulations (beyond what is necessary to give effect to the legal definition of pre-sentence reports in s3(5) CJA 91) whilst *National Standards* are given an opportunity to work.

Additional requirements in the case of mentally disordered offenders.

4.- (1) Subject to subsection (2) below, in any case where section 3(1) above applies and the offender is or appears to be mentally disordered, the court shall obtain and consider a medical report before passing a custodial sentence other than one fixed by law.

(2) Subsection (1) above does not apply if, in the circumstances of the case, the court is of the opinion that it is unnecessary to obtain a medical report.

(3) Before passing a custodial sentence other than one fixed by law on an offender who is or appears to be mentally disordered, a court shall consider -

(a) any information before it which relates to his mental condition (whether given in a medical report, a pre-sentence report or otherwise); and

(b) the likely effect of such a sentence on that condition and on any treatment which may be available for it.

(4) No custodial sentence which is passed in a case to which subsection (1) above applies shall be invalidated by the failure of a court to comply with that subsection, but any court on an appeal against such a sentence -

(a) shall obtain a medical report if none was obtained by the court below; and

(b) shall consider any such report obtained by it or by that court.

(5) In this section -

"duly approved", in relation to a registered medical practitioner, means approved for the purposes of section 12 of the Mental Health Act 1983 ("the 1983 Act") by the Secretary of State as having special experience in the diagnosis or treatment of mental disorder;

"medical report" means a report as to an offender's mental condition made or submitted orally or in writing by a registered medical practitioner who is duly approved.

(6) Nothing in this section shall be taken as prejudicing the generality of section 3 above.

[Section 4 Criminal Justice Act 1991]

NOTES

S4 applies only to custodial sentences. Medical reports may be highly desirable in other situations also. **S4(2) 'unnecessary'** See *When is a report unnecessary?* in the main text.

Restrictions on imposing community sentences

6.- (1) A court shall not pass a community sentence, that is to say, a sentence which consists of one or more community orders, unless it is of opinion that the offence, or the combination of the offence and one other offence associated with it, was serious enough to warrant such a sentence.

(2) Subject to subsection (3) below, where a court passes a community sentence -

(a) the particular order or orders comprising or forming part of the sentence shall be such as in the opinion of the court is, or taken together are, the most suitable for the offender; and

(b) the restrictions on liberty imposed by the order or orders shall be such as in the opinion of the court are commensurate with the seriousness of the offence, or the combination of the offence and other offences associated with it.

(3), (4).

[Section 6 CJA 91: reproduced in full in *Chapter 5*].

Procedural requirements for community sentences.

7.- (1) In forming any such opinion as is mentioned in subsection (1) or (2)(b) of section 6 above, a court shall take into account all such information about the circumstances of the offence (including any aggravating or mitigating factors) as is available to it.

(2) In forming any such opinion as is mentioned in subsection (2)(a) of that section, a court may take into account any information about the offender which is before it.

(3) A court shall obtain and consider a pre-sentence report before forming any such opinion as to the suitability for the offender of one or more of the following orders, namely -

(a) a probation order which includes additional requirements authorised by Schedule 1A to the 1973 Act;

(b) a community service order;

(c) a combination order; and

(d) a supervision order which includes requirements imposed under section 12, 12A, 12AA, 12B or 12C of the Children and Young Persons Act 1969 ("the 1969 Act").

(4) No community sentence which consists of or includes such an order as is mentioned in subsection (3) above shall be invalidated by the failure of a court to comply with that subsection, but any court on any appeal against such a sentence -

(a) shall obtain a pre-sentence report if none was obtained by the court below; and

(b) shall consider any such report obtained by it or by that court.

[Section 7 Criminal Justice Act 1991]

Interpretation of Part I

31.- In this Part -

"pre-sentence report" has the meaning given by section 3(5) above.

Chapter 9

Remands of Children and Young Persons

This chapter deals with the remand of persons below 18 years of age, an issue which is looked at more fully in the companion volume to this work *The Youth Court* where the relevant *Statutory Provisions* are also reproduced. The remand of defendants below the age of 18 is affected by both the Children Act 1989 and the CJA 91, although the full effects will not be seen for several years. The legislation includes a 'transitory stage'. During this stage it will be important to read the provisions subject to the 'transitory amendments'.

Age limits
Remand is the one major area of court's powers where, following the CJA 91, 17 year olds are *not* treated in the same manner, and subject to the same provisions, as 16 year olds.

Bail
The CJA 1991 makes no substantive changes to the law governing the granting of bail to children and young persons.

Remands to local authority accommodation
Under s23 CYPA 1969, as amended by the Children Act 1989 and the CJA 91, defendants under 17 who are refused bail are normally remanded 'to local authority accommodation'. As such, they become children 'looked after by a local authority' within the meaning of s22 Children Act 1989.

The local authority may place such a juvenile in secure accommodation for up to 72 hours within any 28 day period. If they wish to detain the young person in secure accommodation for longer than this, they must apply to a youth court or other magistrates' court for authorisation: Reg 10 Children (Secure Accommodation) Regulations 1991 SI 1505; s60(3) CJA 91. In the case of a remanded juvenile, the maximum period of the authorisation is the period of the remand; but, where the child is committed to the Crown Court for trial, the order may be for a maximum of 28 days. Section 25 Children Act 1989 provides that the court may make a secure accommodation order in respect of the child if it appears:

'(a) that - (i) he has a history of absconding and is likely to abscond from any other description of accommodation; and (ii) if he absconds, he is likely to suffer significant harm; or (b) that if he is kept in any other description of accommodation he is likely to injure himself or other persons.'

However, where a remanded juvenile is charged with or convicted of an offence punishable with 14 years' imprisonment or more in the case of an adult or a violent offence, or has previously been convicted of a violent offence, different criteria are laid down by Regulation 6 Children (Secure Accommodation) Regulations 1991 SI 1505. These criteria are that -

(a) the child is likely to abscond from non-secure accommodation; or
(b) the child is likely to injure himself or other people if he is kept in non-secure accommodation.

A court *cannot* make a secure accommodation order unless the child is legally represented or has been offered legal aid but has refused or failed to apply for it. Section 31(9) Children Act 1989 defines 'harm' for the above purposes as 'ill-treatment or the impairment of health or development'; 'development' as 'physical, intellectual, emotional, social or behavioural development'; 'health' as 'physical or mental health'; and states that ill-treatment 'includes sexual abuse and forms of ill-treatment which are not physical'. Section 31(10) states that:

'... where the question of whether harm suffered by a child is significant turns on the child's health or development, his health or development shall be compared with that which could reasonably be expected of a similar child'.

Schedule 11 to the CJA 91 amends s22(11) Prosecution of Offences Act 1985 to make it clear that the time limits on bringing a case to trial when a defendant is remanded in custody apply to juveniles remanded or committed to local authority accommodation.

Remands in custody
Defendants aged 17 or over who are refused bail are remanded in custody and held in a remand centre or prison: s128 MCA 1980. Defendants under 17 refused bail are remanded to local authority accommodation unless the case falls within s23 CYPA 1969. Before its amendment by the CJA 91, s23 provided that a court could remand a defendant under 17 to a prison or remand centre, if it considered that the young person was 'of so unruly a character that he cannot safely be committed to the care of a local authority'. Since 1977 the scope of unruliness certificates has been progressively restricted by a series of statutory instruments and now applies only to boys aged 15 and 16.

Changes made by the CJA 1991
Section 60 of the CJA 91 contains provisions, to be implemented in full at a future and so far unspecified date, which would end completely the remanding in custody, or the committal in custody for trial or sentence, of juveniles, ie those below the age of 17. Section 62 contains 'transitory provisions', whereby the provisions of s60 will initially be implemented in a modified form; these transitory provisions are scheduled to come into force in October 1992 (as at the time of writing).

Certificates of unruliness
The CJA 91 abolishes the existing unruliness certification procedure and allows courts to remand a boy aged 15 or 16 to a remand centre or prison only if he is legally represented (or has been offered legal representation but has refused or failed to apply for it) *and*, after consultation with a probation officer or a local authority social worker, the court declares that -

'(a) he is charged with or has been convicted of a violent or sexual offence, or an offence punishable in the case of an adult with imprisonment for fourteen years or more; or (b) he has a recent history of absconding while remanded to local authority accommodation, and is charged with or has been convicted of an imprisonable offence alleged or found to have been committed while he was so remanded, and (in either case) the court is of the opinion that only remanding him to a remand centre or prison would be adequate to protect the public from serious harm from him'.

'Violent offence' is defined in s31 CJA 91 as an offence which '... leads, or is intended to lead, to a person's death or to physical injury to a person' including offences of arson (ie criminal damage by fire: see s1(3) Criminal Damage Act 1971), whether or not they would otherwise fall within this definition. Section 31 CJA 91 defines 'sexual offences' by reference to a list of statutory provisions. These include most statutory sexual offences with the exception of those concerned with prostitution and certain consenting acts between homosexuals. The definition of 'serious harm' is *not* limited in this context to violent or sexual offences (contrast s1 CJA 91). However, s60, *ibid*, specifies that, where the alleged offence *is* a violent or sexual one, the definition of 'serious harm' to be applied is 'death or serious personal injury, whether physical or psychological'. In judging whether there is a risk of 'serious harm' in relation to offences of any kind, courts should be aware of Court of Appeal decisions interpreting the phrase 'adequate to protect the public from serious harm from him' in s1(4) CJA 1982 (as amended). More extensive information can be found in *Chapter 3*.

Conditions on remand to local authority accommodation
The new s23 CYPA 69 sustituted by s60 CJA 91 gives new powers to courts which are remanding juveniles to local authority accommodation. Section 23(7), *ibid*, empowers courts making such remands, after consultation with the local authority, to impose any condition which could be imposed when granting bail. Section 23(8), *ibid*, states that a court imposing any such condition shall explain in ordinary language and in open court why it is imposing those conditions and a magistrates' court shall cause the reason to be specified in the warrant of commitment and entered in the court register. Section 23(9), *ibid*, empowers the court, after consulting the local authority, to impose on the authority requirements for securing compliance with any such conditions imposed on the juvenile; and empowers the court to require the authority to place the juvenile with a named person.

Security requirement
Section 23(4) CYPA 1969 as substituted by s60(4) CJA 91 empowers a court

remanding a juvenile to local authority accommodation, after consultation with the authority, to impose a 'security requirement' which requires that the juvenile be held in secure accommodation. *This particular provision will not come into force until remands in prison custody of those aged under 17 are completely abolished.* The court will then be able to impose security requirements on a juvenile aged 15 or over if he or she -

(a) is charged with or has been convicted of a violent or sexual offence, or an offence punishable in the case of an adult with 14 years' imprisonment or more, or

(b) has a recent history of absconding while remanded to local authority accommodation, and is charged with or has been convicted of an imprisonable offence alleged or found to have been committed while he or she was so remanded,

and (in either case) 'the court is of the opinion that only such a requirement would be adequate to protect the public from serious harm from him'.

Section 61 places a duty on local authorities to provide secure accommodation for juveniles remanded with a security requirement. An authority may discharge this duty either by providing secure accommodation itself or by arranging to use other authorities' secure accommodation.

Police detention of juveniles
The CJA 91 also contains new rules governing the holding of juveniles under 17 in police detention before they are brought to court. Section 59 provides that juveniles shall not be held in police detention unless a custody officer certifies -

(a) that it is 'impracticable' to transfer the juvenile to local authority accommodation, or

(b) where the juvenile is aged 15 or over, that no secure accommodation is available and that 'keeping him in other local authority accommodation would not be adequate to protect the public from serious harm from him'.

This juxtaposition of (a) and (b) means that it is not possible for a custody officer to take into account the type of local authority accommodation which is available in deciding whether transferring the juvenile to the local authority would be impracticable under paragraph (a). The interpretation of 'impracticable' must therefore be a narrow one: it might, for example, be met if a transfer to local authority accommodation were prevented by particularly adverse weather conditions late at night or by industrial action within the social services department. The definition of 'serious harm' in criterion (b) is not limited to violent or sexual offences; but s59 CJA 91 provides that in relation to violent or sexual offences 'serious harm' means 'death or serious personal injury, whether physical or psychological'.

Statutory Provisions are set out in full in *Chapter 8* of *The Youth Court.*

Chapter 10

Parole and Early Release of Prisoners

Part II of the Criminal Justice Act 1991 (s32 to s51) introduces new arrangements for the early release of prisoners sentenced by the courts. This replaces the existing system of parole and remission. Prison inmates sentenced before the provisions come into force will retain any present entitlements.

The changes are based on the recommendations of the Carlisle Committee (*The Parole System in England and Wales: Report of the Review Committee*, 1988, Cm 532). The committee was concerned with determinate sentence prisoners only. The CJA 91 makes new provision *inter alia* for prisoners serving *discretionary* life sentences (ie those imposed otherwise than for murder). There are no changes to the statutory provisions concerning the review and release of *mandatory* life sentence prisoners. Relevant provisions from the CJA 1967 are consolidated in the new Act.

Fairness, consistency and re-appraisal

The changes are designed to provide fairer and more consistent arrangements for the early release of prisoners, and to restore meaning to the sentence passed by the court. The Carlisle Committee believed that this greater meaning should be reflected in a *reduction* of sentence lengths. The report stated that its proposed scheme

'... should provide the springboard for a thorough re-assessment of present sentencing levels. We therefore recommend that the implementation of our proposals should be accompanied by a determined attempt on the part of the government and the judiciary to secure a corresponding reduction in sentencing at all levels ... [We] are quite clear that it would be an unbalanced approach and add undesirably to the overall quantum of punishment to enhance the meaning of sentences in the way we propose without at the same time working for a reduction in present tariffs, which have evolved within a quite different framework': *Report of the Review Committee, supra*, pp 72-73.

At present, determinate sentence prisoners are released on parole, or under the arrangements for remission of sentence. Prisoners serving terms of 12 months or less are not eligible for parole, and young offenders sentenced under s53 CYPA 1933 are not formally entitled to parole and do not qualify for remission. Prisoners who *are* eligible for parole may be released on licence during the middle third of their sentences. Otherwise, where prisoners qualify for remission, and provided they do not lose remission because of bad behaviour in prison, release takes place either after half of the sentence for those serving 12 months or less, or after two-thirds for those serving over 12 months. Adult offenders released on remission are free from any restriction or obligation during the remainder of their sentence.

The changes
The CJA 91 abolishes remission and makes substantial changes to the parole arrangements. In particular, it changes the current situation where, in many cases, serious offenders who fail to obtain parole are released into the community without the benefit of supervision or the possibility of recall. Under the new system *all* prisoners will be 'at risk' of having their original sentences re-activated if convicted of further imprisonable offences before the end of their original sentence.

Two schemes
There will be two schemes for the early release of determinate sentence prisoners, including section 53(2) CYPA 1933 offenders, based on sentence length: prisoners serving sentences of *under four years* will be released automatically at the half way point of their sentences provided they do not misbehave in prison; and those serving terms of *four years or more* will become eligible for parole at the half way point of their sentence. The Parole Board will consider the cases of inmates serving four years and over, as well as life sentence prisoners. It is estimated that the number of determinate cases falling for discretionary release will be much reduced: about 4,200 cases per annum instead of the current 23,000. There will, under the new scheme, no longer be a role for Local Review Committees (LRCs), which are to be phased out over two years.

Under the new scheme, a period of compulsory supervision is regarded as an integral part of the sentence. All prisoners serving terms of a year or more will be released on licence and will be supervised by the probation service up to the three-quarters point of their sentence. Some sex offenders will be supervised until the 100 per cent point at the direction of the sentencing judge. They may be recalled to prison if they breach the conditions of their licences. The supervision arrangements will be supported by new National Standards for supervision by the probation service.

The new scheme in outline
There are three main heads under the new scheme: 'automatic unconditional release', 'automatic conditional release' (ACR), and 'discretionary conditional realease' (DCR).

Automatic release
Under s33(1)(a) CJA 91, short-term prisoners aged 18 and over serving less than 12 months will be released automatically, as now, after serving half of

their sentence. Under s43(4), *ibid* similar release arrangements will apply to young offenders under 18 serving 12 months or less: there will be no supervision requirements other than those for *young offenders, post*. All released offenders will be 'at risk' if they commit another imprisonable offence.

Automatic conditional release
Those short-term prisoners serving sentences of one year to under four years will be released automatically on licence at the 50 per cent point of their sentence. There will be no selection process as there is now. This will be known as the 'Automatic Conditional Release' or 'ACR' scheme. Section 49(1) CJA 91 gives the Secretary of State a power to lower or raise this four year threshold (subject to Parliamentary approval). The release date can only be delayed by 'additional days' being imposed for breaches of prison discipline.

'At risk'
Section 40 CJA 91 introduces the 'at risk' concept, whereby anyone committing an imprisonable offence between release and the 100 per cent point of their sentence will be at risk of being returned to custody. Section 40(2), *ibid*, empowers the court dealing with the new offence to order the offender to be returned to custody to serve all or part of the balance of the original sentence outstanding at the time the fresh offence was committed, and s40(4), *ibid*, allows courts to order this period to be served consecutively to, or concurrently with, any fresh sentence.

Supervision
Section 33(1)(b) CJA 91 provides for such inmates to be released on licence and to be subject to compulsory supervision. This will expire at the 75 per cent point of the sentence, subject to a minimum of three months' supervision for young offenders. A power introduced in s44, *ibid*, allows for certain sex offenders to be ordered by the judge at the time of their sentence to receive extended supervision to the end of their sentence.

Since the ACR scheme is *not* discretionary, the arrangements are that it will be administered entirely by prison establishments locally. There will be no Prison Service Headquarters involvement in the release of any inmate serving less than four years, with the exception of those to be deported or released early on compassionate grounds. It will be the responsibility of establishments to issue the appropriate licences, which will be signed by the Governor on behalf of the Home Secretary. Given the automatic nature of the ACR scheme, nearly all inmates will be released on a standard form of licence. But there will be provision for the Governor to approve special, additional conditions in exceptional cases when recommended to do so by the supervising officer in the interests of devising an effective programme of supervision.

Discretionary Conditional Release
Under s35(1) CJA 91 long-term inmates, ie those serving sentences of 4 years

or more, will become eligible for parole after having served 50 per cent of their sentence. This is the 'discretionary conditional release' scheme, or 'DCR'. All cases will be considered by the Parole Board, which will continue to have four statutory categories of members on it, as set out in schedule 5, para 2 CJA 91: see *Statutory Provisions, post.*

Criteria for release
The CJA 91 makes clear for the first time what the criteria for release should be. Section 32(6), *ibid* empowers the Secretary of State to give directions to the Parole Board as to matters to be taken into account when making a recommendation. These should be based on the need to *protect the public from serious harm*, the *prevention of further offending* and the *rehabilitation of the offender*. The parole decision should not be a form of resentencing and the onus will be on offenders to show that they meet the criteria for release. Section 33(2) CJA 91 requires those inmates who fall under the DCR scheme, but are refused parole, to be automatically released on licence at the two-thirds point of their sentence. The portion of the sentence during which a prisoner may be under parole supervision when he would otherwise have been in custody is therefore reduced from the present one third of the sentence to one-sixth (ie the difference between one-half and two-thirds). Section 37(1), *ibid* provides that, regardless of whether released on parole or not, everyone will be subject to supervision and be under licence until the 75 per cent point of sentence (or 100 per cent for some sex offenders, *supra*). They will also be subject to the same 'at risk' provisions as those serving shorter sentences.

The Home Secretary will retain formal responsibility for all parole decisions. But he will delegate that responsibility to the Board for sentences under seven years. This goes some way towards meeting the recommendation of the Carlisle Committee that the Board should be an executive body responsible for making all parole decisions. Section 49 CJA 91 gives the Home Secretary leeway to raise or lower the seven year threshold for delegated decision making, subject to Parliamentary approval.

Implementation
Although it will apply to prisoners sentenced on or after 1 October 1992, the new discretionary parole scheme will probably not start up until at least a year after the general implementation date for most of the CJA 91 provisions. The scheme only applies to inmates serving four years and over and they will have to spend a minimum of two years in custody before reaching their parole eligibility date ('PED'). Remand time and the need to start reviews a few months before PED will mean that the first new style parole review will probably begin sometime late in 1993.

Life sentence prisoners
The review procedures for *discretionary* lifers only are to be changed when Part II CJA 91 comes into force. This is to comply with the judgement of the

European Court of Human Rights in *Thynne, Wilson and Gunnell* (1990). The Court found in each case a breach of Article 5(4) of the European Convention on Human Rights, and held that after the expiry of the period set to meet the requirements of retribution and deterrence, discretionary life sentence prisoners are entitled to have the lawfulness of their continued detention decided by a court at reasonable intervals.

Under the new procedures, a court sentencing a person to life imprisonment for an offence other than murder will be able to specify a term (related to the seriousness of the offence and called the 'relevant part') after which the prisoner should be eligible for the new release procedures. This will also apply to those sentenced to custody for life under s8 CJA 82, and to detention for life under s53(2) CYPA 1933. The period specified by the court must take into account the seriousness of the offence (or the combination of the offence and other associated offences) and the effect of the rules relating to parole and early release on the proportion of a determinate sentence which is actually served in custody. The period should therefore presumably be between one-half and two-thirds of the length of the determinate sentence which, if it had not passed a life sentence, the court would have considered commensurate with the seriousness of the offence. The prisoner will be entitled to require the Secretary of State to refer his or her case to the Parole Board when the relevant part has been served, and the Board will have the power to direct the Secretary of State to release the prisoner on licence if satisfied that it is no longer necessary for the protection of the public that the prisoner should be confined. The Secretary of State will have no residual power as in the case of murderers to reject a recommendation by the Parole Board. The Parole Board procedures will need to be adapted for the purpose of dealing with these cases to give them the characteristics of a court in order to comply with the requirements of Article 5(4), *supra*. The procedures will need to provide for the disclosure of reports, and the prisoner's right to be present and be represented at the proceedings.

Existing discretionary lifers
The position of existing discretionary life sentence prisoners who are being detained solely on the grounds of risk to the public are dealt with in Sched 2 CJA 91, para 9. In these cases, the Secretary of State will certify his opinion that if s34 CJA 91 had been in force at the time when the prisoner was sentenced by the court by which he or she was sentenced it would have ordered that that section should apply to him or her as soon as he or she had served the part of his or her sentence specified in the certificate ('the relevant part').

Breach of licence
At present, failure to comply with the conditions of a licence is not in itself an offence; it is dealt with by the Parole Board rather than the courts. Section 38(1) CJA 91 makes such a failure an offence for *short-term offenders* only. Magistrates' courts will deal with licence breaches for this category of offender. Section 38(2) empowers the courts to impose a fine of up to £1,000, order a

return to custody for a maximum of six months (or the outstanding period of the licence if that is less) or both. The recalled period is not treated as a fresh sentence and does not attract any early release entitlement in itself. Recall for breaches of licence conditions for long-term and life prisoners would be dealt with by the Parole Board rather than by the courts.

Openness and the giving of reasons

The White Paper *Crime, Justice and Protecting the Public* indicated that the government favoured moving towards greater openness in the parole decision making process. Ministers have now given a firm commitment to give inmates meaningful reasons for parole decisions and to let them have access to the information on which the reasons are based. Open reporting will extend to ACR inmates as far as is practicable. Going hand-in-hand with openness will be an expansion of sentence planning, concentrating initially on those falling within the discretionary arrangements.

Induction regimes and 'sentence planning'

According to the White Paper, *Care, Custody and Justice: The Way Ahead for the Prison Service in England and Wales* (1991, Cm 1647), the Prison Service aims to provide more effective induction arrangements and a greater assurance of adequate and predictable regimes. Sentence plans will become increasingly important with the implementation of the CJA 91. The proposals include: a review of reception and induction arrangements; comprehensive guidance on regimes for women prisoners; preparing a 'model regime' for local prisons and remand centres; *National Standards* for probation service supervision before and after release; and sentence plans to be provided progressively for all prisoners serving 'substantial' sentences.

'ADAs'

The Act abolishes remission. The present sanction of loss of remission is replaced by 'additional days awarded' spent in prison for misconduct: s42 CJA 91. ADAs will automatically postpone the release date under the ACR scheme, the parole eligibility date and two-thirds point under the DCR scheme, and the expiry date of any licence. ADAs may be retrospective (for remand prisoners), suspended or restored, similar to losses of remission now. It will not be possible for ADAs to extend the original sentence date.

Compassionate release

The Secretary of State is given a new power under s36 CJA 91 to grant release on licence on compassionate grounds to any inmate before the half-way point of his or her sentence. This provision is designed to avoid a problem in the use of the Royal Prerogative of Mercy. The Royal Prerogative, which is currently the only way to arrange compassionate release before an inmate's parole eligibility date, effectively wipes out the remainder of the sentence. Under s36(2), the Parole Board will normally be consulted about the compassionate release of inmates serving four years and over and of life sentence prisoners. The decision will be guided by statutory criteria to be laid down by the Home

Secretary.

Deportees

Inmates liable to deportation or removal will be dealt with slightly differently from other prisoners. Deportees serving less than four years will be released automatically (to be deported) at the half-way point of the sentence. Section 46(1) CJA 91 gives the Secretary of State the power to release those serving four years and over at any time between the half-way and two-thirds point without consulting the Parole Board. Deportees, like other inmates, will be released on licence, but s46(2), *ibid*, exempts them from having a condition of supervision by a probation officer in their licence.

Young offenders

Section 65 CJA 91 contains special arrangements for the supervision of *all* young offenders on release. These preserve the current arrangements under which young offenders receive a minimum three months' compulsory supervision on release by the probation service or social services (subject to this not going beyond the 22nd birthday). If they are serving more than 12 months but less than four years, young offenders will be released on a standard ACR licence, but if this is less than three months in length, for example because of remand time, supervision will continue to a point three months from release. If they are not released on licence, in other words if they are serving sentences of 12 months or less, young offenders will still be subject to three months' supervision and a notice setting out supervision requirements will be issued by the Governor on behalf of the Home Secretary. Failure to comply with the requirements of supervision is a summary offence punishable with a fine not exceeding level 3 (ie 10 units) or a custodial sentence not exceeding 30 days.

Section 43(1) CJA 91 brings those sentenced under s53 CYPA 1933 in line with other inmates. Currently, such detainees serving determinate sentences have no formal entitlement to parole (although the Home Secretary may refer their cases to the Parole Board at any time if he sees fit) and any time spent on remand is not counted towards the sentence. Under the Act, those sentenced under s53(2) will have identical entitlements to other young offenders. See, generally, in relation to young offenders, *Chapters 8* and *9* of *Introduction to the Criminal Justice Act 1991*.

Fine defaulters and contemnors

Section 45 provides that inmates in prison for fine default or contempt of court will be released automatically at the half-way point of sentences if they are serving less than 12 months and at the two-thirds point if they are serving 12 months or more. They will not be on licence and will not be subject to the 'at risk' liability.

Remand time

Section 41 CJA 91 requires that remand time will count in full towards the calculation of an inmate's parole eligibility date (or 50 per cent release point for ACR inmates). However, remand time will not be able to reduce the amount of time that is available for compulsory supervision. All ACR inmates will be supervised for one-quarter of their sentence, even if this goes beyond the three-quarters point and those falling within the discretionary scheme will still receive a minimum of one-twelfth of their sentence under supervision (from two-thirds to three-quarters).

Extradited offenders

Section 47 CJA 91 provides that, where an offender has spent time in custody abroad awaiting extradition to the United Kingdom, a court passing a custodial sentence may order that a specified period of time (not exceeding the time spent in custody abroad) shall be deducted from the length of time which the prisoner will spend in custody. The specified period will operate to reduce time spent in custody in the same way as does a period spent on remand in custody. (The position hitherto has been that the sentencer could make allowance in the sentence itself for the fact that time spent in custody abroad did not count towards the sentence).

Transitional arrangements

These are set out in schedule 12 CJA 91 (not reproduced). Their broad effect is that the new provisions will apply only in relation to sentences passed after the commencement of the provisions of Part II.

Statutory Provisions

Criminal Justice Act 1991

The Parole Board

32.- (1) There shall continue to be a body to be known as the Parole Board ("the Board") which shall discharge the functions conferred on it by this Part.

(2) It shall be the duty of the Board to advise the Secretary of State with respect to any matter referred to it by him which is connected with the early release of prisoners.

(3) The Board shall deal with cases as respects which it makes recommendations under this Part on consideration of -

(a) any documents given to it by the Secretary of State; and

(b) any other oral or written information obtained by it,

and if in any particular case the Board thinks it necessary to interview the person to whom the case relates before reaching a decision, the Board may authorise one of its members to interview him and shall consider the report of the interview made by that member.

(4) The Board shall deal with cases as respects which it gives directions under this Part on consideration of all such evidence as may be adduced before it.

(5) Without prejudice to subsections (3) and (4) above, the Secretary of State may make rules with respect to the proceedings of the Board, including provision authorising cases to be dealt with by a prescribed number of its members or requiring cases to be dealt with at prescribed times.

(6) The Secretary of State may also give to the Board directions as to the matters to be taken into account by it in discharging any functions under this Part; and in giving any such directions the Secretary of State shall in particular have regard to -

(a) the need to protect the public from serious harm from offenders; and

(b) the desirability of preventing the commission by them of further offences and of securing their rehabilitation.

(7) Schedule 5 to this Act shall have effect with respect to the Board.

[Section 32 Criminal Justice Act 1991]

Duty to release short-term and long-term prisoners

33.- (1) As soon as a short-term prisoner has served one-half of his sentence, it shall be the duty of the Secretary of State -

(a) to release him unconditionally if that sentence is for a term of less than twelve months; and

(b) to release him on licence if that sentence is for a term of twelve months or more.

(2) As soon as a long-term prisoner has served two-thirds of his sentence, it shall be the duty of the Secretary of State to release him on licence.

(3) As soon as a short-term or long-term prisoner who -

(a) has been released on licence under subsection (1)(b) or (2) above or section 35 or 36(1) below; and

(b) has been recalled to prison under section 38(2) or 39(1) below,

would (but for his release) have served three-quarters of his sentence, it shall be the duty of the Secretary of State to release him unconditionally.

(4) Where a prisoner whose sentence is for a term of less than twelve months has been released on licence under section 36(1) below and recalled to prison under section 38(2) below, subsection (3) above shall have effect as if for the reference to three-quarters of his sentence there were substituted a reference to one-half of that sentence.

(5) In this Part -

"long-term prisoner" means a person serving a sentence of imprisonment for a term of four years or more;

"short-term prisoner" means a person serving a sentence of imprisonment for a term of less than four years.

[Section 33 Criminal Justice Act 1991]

NOTE S33(1) to (4) Other provisions are substituted re young offenders committed or detained for contempt under s9 CJA 82: see s45 CJA 91, *post*.

Duty to release discretionary life prisoners

34. - (1) A life prisoner is a discretionary life prisoner for the purposes of this

Part if -

(a) his sentence was imposed for a violent or sexual offence the sentence for which is not fixed by law; and

(b) the court by which he was sentenced for that offence ordered that this section should apply to him as soon as he had served a part of his sentence specified in the order.

(2) A part of a sentence so specified shall be such part as the court considers appropriate taking into account -

(a) the seriousness of the offence, or the combination of the offence and other offences associated with it; and

(b) the provisions of this section as compared with those of section 33(2) above and section 25(1) below.

(3) As soon as, in the case of a discretionary life prisoner -

(a) he has served the part of his sentence specified in the order ("the relevant part"); and

(b) the Board has directed his release under this section,

it shall be the duty of the Secretary of State to release him on licence.

(4) The Board shall not give a direction under subsection (3) above with respect to a discretionary life prisoner unless -

(a) the Secretary of State has referred the prisoner's case to the Board; and

(b) the Board is satisfied that it is no longer necessary for the protection of the public that the prisoner should be confined.

(5) A discretionary life prisoner may require the Secretary of State to refer his case to the Board at any time -

(a) after he has served the relevant part of his sentence; and

(b) where there has been a previous reference to the Board, after the end of the period of two years beginning with the disposal of that reference; and

(c) where he is also serving a sentence of imprisonment for a term, after he has served one-half of that sentence;

and in this subsection "previous reference" means a reference under subsection (4) above or section 39(4) below made after the prisoner had served the relevant part of his sentence.

(6) In determining for the purpose of subsection (3) or (5) above whether a discretionary life prisoner has served the relevant part of his sentence, no account shall be taken of any time during which he was unlawfully at large within the meaning of section 49 of the Prison Act 1952 ("the 1952 Act").

(7) In this Part "life prisoner" means a person serving one or more sentences of life imprisonment; but -

(a) a person serving two or more such sentences shall not be treated as a discretionary life prisoner for the purposes of this Part unless the requirements of subsection (1) above are satisfied as respects each of those sentences; and

(b) subsections (3) and (5) above shall not apply in relation to such a person until after he has served the relevant part of each of those sentences.

[Section 34 Criminal Justice Act 1991]

144

Power to release long-term and life prisoners

35.- (1) After a long-term prisoner has served one-half of his sentence, the Secretary of State may, if recommended to do so by the Board, release him on licence.

(2) If recommended to do so by the Board, the Secretary of State may, after consultation with the Lord Chief Justice together with the trial judge if available, release on licence a life prisoner who is not a discretionary life prisoner.

(3) The Board shall not make a recommendation under subsection (2) above unless the Secretary of State has referred the particular case, or the class of case to which that case belongs, to the Board for its advice.

[Section 35 Criminal Justice Act 1991]

Power to release prisoners on compassionate grounds

36.- (1) The Secretary of State may at any time release a prisoner on licence if he is satisfied that exceptional circumstances exist which justify the prisoner's release on compassionate grounds.

(2) Before releasing a long-term or life prisoner under subsection (1) above, the Secretary of State shall consult the Board, unless the circumstances are such as to render such consultation impracticable.

[Section 36 Criminal Justice Act 1991]

Duration and condition of licence

37.- (1) Subject to subsection (2) below, where a short-term prisoner is released on licence, the licence shall, subject to any suspension under section 38(2) below or, as the case may be, any revocation under section 39(1) or (2) below, remain in force until the date on which he would (but for his release) have served three-quarters of his sentence.

(2) Where a prisoner whose sentence is for a term of less than twelve months is released on licence under section 36(1) above, subsection (1) above shall have effect as if for the reference to three-quarters of his sentence there were substituted a reference to one-half of that sentence.

(3) Where a life prisoner is released on licence, the licence shall, unless previously revoked under section 39(1) or (2) below, remain in force until his death.

(4) A person subject to a licence shall comply with such conditions (which shall include on his release conditions as to his supervision by a probation officer) as may for the time being be specified in the licence; and the Secretary of State may make rules for regulating the supervision of any description of such persons.

(5) The Secretary of State shall not include on release, or subsequently insert, a condition in the licence of a long-term or life prisoner, or vary or cancel any such condition, except -

(a) in the case of the inclusion of a condition in the licence of a discretionary life prisoner, in accordance with recommendations of the Board; and

(b) in any other case, after consultation with the Board.

(6) For the purposes of subsection (5) above, the Secretary of State shall be treated as having consulted the Board about a proposal to include, insert, vary or cancel a condition in any case if he has consulted the Board about the implementation of proposals of that description generally or in that class of case.

(7) The power to make rules under this section shall be exercisable by statutory instrument which shall be subject to annulment in pursuance of a resolution of either House of Parliament.

[Section 37 Criminal Justice Act 1991]

NOTE S37(1) to (3) Other provisions are substituted in the case of young offenders committed or detained under s9 CJA 82: see s45 CJA 91, *post*.

Breach of licence conditions by short-term prisoners
38.- (1) A short-term prisoner -

(a) who is released on licence under this Part; and

(b) who fails to comply with such conditions as may for the time being be specified in the licence,

shall be liable on summary conviction to a fine not exceeding level 3 on the standard scale.

(2) The magistrates' court by which a person is convicted of an offence under subsection (1) above may, whether or not it passes any other sentence on him -

(a) suspend the licence for a period not exceeding six months; and

(b) order him to be recalled to prison for the period during which the licence is so suspended.

(3) On the suspension of the licence of any person under this section, he shall be liable to be detained in pursuance of his sentence and, if at large, shall be deemed to be unlawfully at large.

[Section 38 Criminal Justice Act 1991]

NOTE S38(1) and (2) These provisions have considerable implications for courts (including the posssibly of co-ordinated approaches to recall as between courts and the Parole Board) and in relation to information generally. There is scope for multi-agency liaison.

Recall of long-term and life prisoners while on licence.
39.- (1) If recommended to do so by the Board in the case of a long-term or life prisoner who has been released on licence under this Part, the Secretary of State may revoke his licence and recall him to prison.

(2) The Secretary of State may revoke the licence of any such person and recall him to prison without a recommendation by the Board, where it appears to him that it is expedient in the public interest to recall that person before such a recommendation is practicable.

(3) A person recalled to prison under subsection (1) or (2) above -

(a) may make representations in writing with respect to his recall; and

(b) on his return to prison, shall be informed of the reasons for his recall and the right to make representations.

(4) The Secretary of State shall refer to the Board -

(a) the case of a person recalled under subsection (1) above who makes representations under subsection (3) above; and

(b) the case of a person recalled under subsection (2) above.

(5) Where on a reference under subsection (4) above the Board -

(a) directs in the case of a discretionary life prisoner; or

(b) recommends in the case of any other person,

his immediate release on licence under this section, the Secretary of State shall give effect to the direction or recommendation.

(6) On the revocation of the licence of any person under this section, he shall be liable to be detained in pursuance of his sentence and, if at large, shall be deemed to be unlawfully at large.

[Section 39 Criminal Justice Act 1991]

Convictions during currency of original sentences

40.- (1) This section applies to a short-term or long-term prisoner who is released under this Part if -

(a) before the date on which he would (but for his release) have served his sentence in full, he commits an offence punishable with imprisonment; and

(b) whether before or after that date, he is convicted of that offence ("the new offence").

(2) Subject to subsection (3) below, the court by or before which a person to whom this section applies is convicted of the new offence may, whether or not it passes any other sentence on him, order him to be returned to prison for the whole or any part of the period which -

(a) begins with the date of the order; and

(b) is equal in length to the period between the date on which the new offence was committed and the date mentioned in subsection (1) above.

(3) A magistrates' court -

(a) shall not have power to order a person to whom this section applies to be returned to prison for a period of more than six months; but

(b) may commit him in custody or on bail to the Crown Court for sentence in accordance with section 42 of the 1973 Act (power of the Crown Court to sentence persons convicted by magistrates' courts of indictable offences).

(4) The period for which a person to whom this section applies is ordered under subsection (2) above to be returned to prison -

(a) shall be taken to be a sentence of imprisonment for the purposes of this Part;

(b) shall, as the court may direct, either be served before and be followed by, or be served concurrently with, the sentence imposed for the new offence; and

(c) in either case, shall be disregarded in determining the appropriate length of that sentence.

[Section 40 Criminal Justice Act 1991]

NOTES Section **40** introduces the 'at risk' concept, whereby anyone committing an imprisonable offence between release and the 100 per cent point of their sentence can be returned to custody by the court. **S40(2)** empowers the court dealing with the new offence to order the offender to be returned to custody to serve all or part of the balance of the original sentence outstanding at the time the fresh offence *was committed*. **S40(4)** allows courts to order this period to be served consecutively to, or concurrently with, any fresh sentence.

Remand time to count towards time served

41.- (1) This section applies to any person whose sentence falls to be reduced under section 67 of the Criminal Justice Act 1967 ("the 1967 Act") by any relevant period within the meaning of that section ("the relevant period").

(2) For the purpose of determining for the purposes of this Part -

(a) whether a person to whom this section applies has served one-half or two-thirds of his sentence; or

(b) whether such person would (but for his release) have served three-quarters of that sentence,

the relevant period shall, subject to subsection (3) below, be treated as having been served by him as part of that sentence.

(3) Nothing in subsection (2) above shall have the effect of reducing the period for which a licence granted under this Part to a short-term or long-term prisoner remains in force to a period which is less than -

(a) one-quarter of his sentence in the case of a short-term prisoner; or

(b) one-twelfth of his sentence in the case of a long-term prisoner.

[Section 41 Criminal Justice Act 1991]

NOTE S41(1) 'reduced under s67 of the Criminal Justice Act 1967'
S67 CJA 1967 sets out 'relevant periods' by which custodial sentences must be reduced, eg time spent in police detention or in custody on remand.

Additional days for disciplinary offences

42.- (1) Prison rules, that is to say rules made under section 47 of the 1952 Act, may include provision for the award of additional days -

(a) to short-term or long-term prisoners; or

(b) conditionally on their subsequently becoming such prisoners, to prisoners on remand,

who (in either case) are guilty of disciplinary offences.

(2) Where additional days are awarded to a short-term or long-term prisoner, or to a person on remand who subsequently becomes such a prisoner, and are not remitted in accordance with prison rules -

(a) any period which he must serve before becoming entitled to or eligible for release under this Part; and

(b) any period for which a licence granted to him under this Part remains in force,

shall be extended by the aggregate of those additional days.

[Section 42 Criminal Justice Act 1991]

Young offenders

43.- (1) Subject to subsections (4) and (5) below, this Part applies to persons

148

serving sentences of detention in a young offender institution, or determinate sentences of detention under section 53 of the 1933 Act, as it applies to persons serving equivalent sentences of imprisonment.

(2) Subject to subsection (5) below, this Part applies to persons serving -

(a) sentences of detention during Her Majesty's pleasure for life under section 53 of the 1933 Act; or

(b) sentences of custody for life under section 8 of the 1982 Act,

as it applies to persons serving sentences of imprisonment for life.

(3) References in this Part to prisoners (whether short-term, long-term or life prisoners), or to prison or imprisonment, shall be construed in accordance with subsections (1) and (2) above.

(4) In relation to a short-term prisoner under the age of 18 years to whom subsection (1) of section 33 above applies, that subsection shall have effect as if it required the Secretary of State -

(a) to release him unconditionally if his sentence is for a term of twelve months or less; and

(b) to release him on licence if that sentence is for a term of more than twelve months.

(5) In relation to a person under 22 years who is released on licence under this Part, section 37(4) above shall have effect as if the reference to supervision by a probation officer included a reference to supervision by a social worker of a local authority social services department.

[Section 43 Criminal Justice Act 1991]

Sexual Offenders

44.- (1) Where, in the case of a long-term or short-term prisoner -

(a) the whole or any part of his sentence was imposed for a sexual offence; and

(b) the court by which he was sentenced for that offence, having had regard to the matters mentioned in section 32(6)(a) and (b) above, ordered that this section should apply,

sections 33(3) and 37(1) above shall each have effect as if for the reference to three-quarters of his sentence there were substituted a reference to the whole of that sentence.

[Section 44 Criminal Justice Act 1991]

Fine defaulters and contemnors

45. - (1) Subject to subsection (2) below, this Part (except sections 35 and 40 above) applies to persons committed to prison or to be detained under section 9 of the 1982 Act -

(a) in default of payment of a sum adjudged to be paid by a conviction; or

(b) for contempt of court or any kindred offence,

as it applies to persons serving equivalent sentences of imprisonment; and references in this Part to short-term or long-term prisoners, or to prison or imprisonment, shall be construed accordingly.

(2) In relation to persons committed as mentioned in subsection (1) above, the

provisions specified in subsections (3) and (4) below shall have effect subject to the modifications so specified.

(3) In section 33 above, for subsections (1) to (4) there shall be substituted the following subsections -

"(1) As soon as a person committed as mentioned in section 45(1) below has served the appropriate proportion of his term, that is to say -

(a) one-half, in the case of a person committed for a term of less than twelve months;

(b) two-thirds, in the case of a person committed for a term of twelve months or more,

it shall be the duty of the Secretary of State to release him unconditionally.

(2) As soon as a person so committed who -

(a) has been released on licence under section 36(1) below; and

(b) has been recalled under section 38(2) or 39(1) below,

would (but for his release) have served the appropriate proportion of his term, it shall be the duty of the Secretary of State to release him unconditionally."

(4) In section 37 above, for subsections (1) to (3) there shall be substituted the following subsection -

"(1) Where a person committed as mentioned in section 45(1) below is released on licence under section 36(1) above, the licence shall, subject to -

(a) any suspension under section 38(2) below; or

(b) any revocation under section 39(1) below,

continue in force until the date on which he would (but for his release) have served the appropriate proportion of his term; and in this subsection 'appropriate proportion' has the meaning given by section 33(1) above."

[Section 45 Criminal Justice Act 1991]

[**Persons liable to removal from the United Kingdom 46.-** Not reproduced. **Persons extradited to the United Kingdom 47.-** Not reproduced (but see outline in main text). **Life prisoners transferred to England and Wales 48.-** Not reproduced.]

Alteration by order of relevant proportion of sentences

49.- (1) The Secretary of State may by order made by statutory instrument provide -

(a) that references in section 33(5) above to four years shall be construed as references to such other period as may be specified in the order;

(b) that any reference in this Part to a particular proportion of a prisoner's sentence shall be construed as a reference to such other proportion of a prisoner's sentence as shall be so specified.

(2) An order under this section may make such transitional provisions as appear to the Secretary of State necessary or expedient in connection with any provision made by the order.

(3) No order shall be made under this section unless a draft of the order has been laid before and approved by resolution of each House of Parliament.

[Section 49 Criminal Justice Act 1991]

Interpretation of Part II

51.- (1) In this Part -

"the Board" means the Parole Board;

"discretionary life prisoner" has the meaning given by section 34 above (as extended by section 43(2) above);

"life prisoner" has the meaning given by section 34(7) above (as extended by section 43(2) above);

"long-term prisoner" and "short-term prisoner" have the meanings given by section 33(5) above (as extended by sections 43(1) and 45(1) above);

"sentence of imprisonment" does not include a committal in default of payment of any sum of money, or for want of sufficient distress to satisfy any sum of money, or for failure to do or abstain from doing anything required to be done or left undone.

"sexual offence" and "violent offence" have the same meanings as in Part I of this Act.

(2) For the purposes of any reference in [Part II CJA 91], however expressed, to the term of imprisonment to which a person has been sentenced or which, or part of which, he has served, consecutive terms and terms which are wholly or partly concurrent shall be treated as a single term.

(3) Nothing in [Part II CJA 91] shall require the Secretary of State to release a person who is serving -

(a) a sentence of imprisonment for a term; and

(b) one or more sentences of imprisonment for life,

unless and until he is entitled under this Part to be released in respect of each of those sentences.

(4) Subsections (2) and (3) of section 31 above shall apply for the purposes of this Part as they apply for the purposes of Part I of this Act.

[Section 51 Criminal Justice Act 1991]

NOTE S51(1) 'sexual offence' and 'violent offence' see s31(1) CJA 91 reproduced in *Chapter 4*.

Schedule 5 [Extracts]

1. The Board shall consist of a chairman and not less than four other members appointed by the Secretary of State.

2. The Board shall include among its members -

(a) a person who holds or has held judicial office;

(b) a registered medical practitioner who is a psychiatrist;

(c) a person appearing to the Secretary of State to have knowledge and experience of the supervision and after-care of discharged prisoners; and

(d) a person appearing to the Secretary of State to have made a study of the causes of delinquency or the treatment of offenders.

[3, 4, 5]

6. The Board shall as soon as practicable after the end of each year make to the Secretary of State a report on the performance of its functions during that year; and the Secretary of State shall lay a copy of the report before Parliament.

[Schedule 5 to the Criminal Justice Act 1991: invoked by s32(7) (extracts)]

Chapter 11

Justice Without Discrimination

Section 95 CJA 91 (which came into force on 31 October 1991) provides that the Secretary of State shall publish in each year such information 'as he considers expedient' for the two following purposes: first to enable those engaged in administering criminal justice to become aware of 'the financial implications of their decisions':s95(1)(a); and second to facilitate the performance by those people of 'their duty to avoid discriminating against any persons on the ground of race or sex, or any other improper ground'. The background to and need for s95(1)(b) ('non-discrimination') is discussed in *Chapter 5* of *Introduction to the Criminal Justice Act 1991*. The intention would seem to be that this section be interpreted widely, ie as applying to *all* those engaged in the criminal justice process, whether as judges, magistrates, administrators, police, Crown Prosecutors, probation officers, social workers and so on. The judicial oath (taken on appointment by all members of the judiciary) and the rules of natural justice (which require courts to deal with people impartially and without bias: see the extended commentary in *Criminal Jurisdiction of Magistrates*, 11th Edn, Harris, edited Gibson, at p9 *et al*) underpin the 'duty' referred to in s95(1)(b).

Extending the information base
Section 95(1)(b) is a shadow of the provision argued for by various lobbies during early stages of the legislation. There was pressure to place a duty on courts and others 'to treat all defendants fairly' irrespective of race, nationality or other potential ground for discrimination. An amendment to this affect was withdrawn when the government gave a commitment to consider how such principles could be enshrined in the legislation. Section 95 is the somewhat diluted outcome. However, the government has also indicated that it will look to ways of extending and improving the data collected on the subject. A recent paper entitled *Race Issues* prepared for the Home Office Special Conference on the Act in November 1991 contained information of a type which will form the essential backdrop to the collection and monitoring of specific discrimination issues. That paper also notes, eg that only two per cent of magistrates are from the ethnic minorities, one per cent of police officers, two per cent of probation officers and one per cent of solicitors; and confirms that people from ethnic minorities are disproportionately over-represented in the prison population. Section 95 goes beyond race: it explicitly includes sex discrimination and it is submitted that 'any other improper ground' would include religion, disability and sexual orientation. It will be instructive to watch developments.

Financial implications

Section 95(1)(a) obliges the Secretary of State to circulate certain financial information. The unit costs of sentencing options already appear in the *Digest of Criminal Justice Information* (1991, Home Office Research and Statistics Department, see p 75: also reproduced in *Chapter 5* of *Introduction to the Criminal Justice Act 1991*) as does the cost of crime prevention (*ibid*, p76-77), public expenditure on criminal services (*ibid*, p72-74) and costs incurred by victims of crime (*ibid*, p78-79). More than 30,000 copies of the *Digest* were circulated in 1991 and it can be anticipated that this publication will be a vehicle for disseminating information under both limbs of s95. Another convenient method of publishing such information would be by appending cost and discrimination data to the *Sentencing Profile* discussion exercise developed jointly by the Magistrates' Association, Justices' Clerks' Society and Home Office and circulated to courts and others for the first time in 1991.

Statutory Provisions

Criminal Justice Act 1991

95.- (1) The Secretary of State shall in each year publish such information as he considers expedient for the purpose of -
    (a) enabling persons engaged in the administration of criminal justice to become aware of the financial implications of their decisions; or
    (b) facilitating the performance by such persons of their duty to avoid discriminating against any persons on the ground of race or sex or any other improper ground.
(2) Publication under subsection (1) above shall be effected in such manner as the Secretary of State considers appropriate for the purpose of bringing the information to the attention of the persons concerned.
[Section 95 Criminal Justice Act 1991]

NOTES   S95(1) **'persons engaged in the administration of criminal justice'** These words are not further explained, but can be taken to apply widely to judges, magistrates, police, Crown Prosecutors, probation officers, social workers and so on. **'... their duty to avoid discrimination'** ie under the general law or the rules of natural justice, as applicable, *semble*.

Further reading *Black People and the Criminal Justice System* (NACRO, 1986), *Towards An Anti-racist Intermediate Treatment* (National Intermediate Treatment Federation, 1985), *Dealing With Disadvantage* (Justices' Clerks' Society, 1989), *Race and Criminal Justice* (NACRO, 1991), *Women Offenders and Probation Service Provision* (HM Inspectorate of Probation, 1991).

Chapter 12

Miscellaneous Items

The nature of the CJA 91 means that some items do not belong to any other chapter of this book. A selection of these items, some of which deal with matters other than the sentencing of offenders or court procedures, is set out below.

Discharges
Absolute and conditional discharges are not subject to any substantive changes under the CJA 91. Neither do they form part of the new sentencing framework, albeit that the possibility of a discharge must be eliminated in all cases before some other form of sentence is used. Section 1A to s1C PCCA 73 (as substituted by sched 1 CJA 91) is reproduced in *Statutory Provisions, post*.

Definitions
A list of definitions affecting Part I of the Act is contained in s31 CJA 91. The most significant of these are the definitions of 'associated offence', 'sexual offence, 'violent offence' and 'protecting the public from serious harm'. All relevant definitions have been incorporated into the preceding chapters, including extracts from s31 in the *Statutory Provisions* in those chapters. Definitions affecting the parole and early release provisions of Part II CJA 91 are contained in s51 of the Act and appear in the Statutory Provisions in *Chapter 10* .

Maximum penalties
Section 26 CJA 91: reduces the maximum penalty for theft in s7 Theft Act 1968 from ten to seven years; and that for 'non-domestic' burglary (ie burglary under s9 Theft Act 1968 in cases other than where '... the offence is committed in respect of a building which is a dwelling') from 14 to ten years. The maximum penalty for burglary in respect of a dwelling remains at 14 years. The White Paper, *Crime, Justice and Protecting the Public* observed that '... the Court of Appeal has discouraged excessive use of imprisonment for theft' and said of the maximum penalty of 14 years' imprisonment for burglary that '... No distinction is made [by statute at present] ... between burglary of a dwelling and other burglaries and the maximum penalty is the same for both offences. However, the courts already make such a distinction in practice, reflecting the public's view that burglaries of homes are much more serious. So burglars of houses and flats are usually sentenced much more severely for invading people's homes'

(para 3.14). However, it is clear from the White Paper that the government expects the reduction in the maxima for theft and 'non-domestic' burglary to do more than confirm existing sentencing levels and practices. Every ten per cent reduction in sentences for these offences lowers the prison population by around 700 people. The changes are consistent with the principle that a clearer distinction should be drawn between penalties for offences against the person and those for property offences.

Section 26 CJA 91 increases certain maximum penalties under the Badgers Act 1973 and in respect of bomb hoaxes under the Criminal Law Act 1977, and reduces the maximum fine which may be imposed on a person 'sleeping rough'. Also, section 17(3) and sched 4 CJA 91 alter the maximum penalties or amounts across a range of offences and situations, including for:

Compensation in magistrates' courts
Part I of sched 4 to the CJA 91 increases *inter alia* the maximum amount of a compensation order made by a magistrates' court from £2,000 to £5,000: see s40(1) MCA 1980.

Summary criminal damage
There is an increase in the maximum fine for 'summary criminal damage' under s1 Criminal Damage Act 1971, ie where the value of the damage does not exceed £2,000 and the case is tried by magistrates pursuant to s22 MCA 1980: see s33(1)(a), *ibid*, and Part II of sched 4 CJA 91. This is increased from £1,000 to 'level 4', or £2,500 (25 units) as at the commencement of the CJA 91. However, it should be noted that the CJA 91 *does not* increase the *value* above which such an offence becomes triable 'either way'. This remains at £2,000 (having been raised to that figure by the CJA 88).

Criminal justice services
The CJA 91 contains several provisions designed to enable criminal justice services to operate more efficiently and effectively. The most significant of these changes are:

- placing H M Inspectorate of Probation on a statutory footing: s73;
- enabling the Home Secretary to hold a probation service to be in default of its duty if it fails to provide a proper service: s74;
- providing for the cash limiting of magistrates' courts: s93; and probation services: s94;
- enabling probation services to make grants to outside bodies in prescribed cases: s95;
- providing for the appointment of court security officers in magistrates' courts: s77, et al;
- enabling prisons (s84, *ibid*) and prisoner escort services (s80, *ibid*) to be contracted out to the private sector. The provisions also deal with associated matters including the certification and protection of prisoner

custody officers: s89, *et al.*

Commencement of the Act
At the time of going to press, the main body of the Act is scheduled for implementation in October 1992. There have been two commencement orders, the Criminal Justice Act 1991 (Commencement No 1) Order 1991 SI 2208 and the Criminal Justice Act 1991 (Commencement No 2 and Transitional Provisions) Order 1991 SI 2706.

Transitional provisions
The Act's transitional provisions are contained in sched 12 which is reproduced in *Statutory Provisions, post.*

Statutory Provisions

Powers of Criminal Courts Act 1973
Absolute and conditional discharge
1A.- (1) Where a court by or before which a person is convicted of an offence (not being an offence the sentence for which is fixed by law) is of opinion, having regard to the circumstances including the nature of the offence and the character of the offender, that is is inexpedient to inflict punishment, the court may make an order either -
   (a) discharging him absolutely; or
   (b) if the court thinks fit, discharging him subject to the condition that he commits no offence during such period, not exceeding three years from the date of the order, as may be specified in the order.
   (2) An order discharging a person subject to such a condition is in this Act referred to as 'an order for conditional discharge', and the period specified in any such order as 'the period of the conditional discharge'.
   (3) Before making an order for conditional discharge the court shall explain to the offender in ordinary language that if he commits another offence during the period of conditional discharge he will be liable to be sentenced again for the original offence.
   (4) Where, under the following provisions of this Part of this Act, a person conditionally discharged under this section is sentenced for the offence in respect of which the order for conditional discharge was made, that order shall cease to have effect.
   (5) The Secretary of State may by order direct that subsection (1) above shall be amended by substituting, for the maximum period specified in that subsection as originally enacted or previously amended under this subsection, such period as may be specified in the order.
[Section 1A PCCA 1973 as inserted by s8(3) and Schedule 1 CJA 1991]

Commission of further offence by person conditionally discharged
1B.- (1) If it appears to the Crown Court, where that court has jurisdiction in accordance with subsection (2) below, or to a justice of the peace having jurisdiction in accordance with that subsection, that a person in whose case

an order for conditional discharge has been made -

(a) has been convicted by a court in any part of Great Britain of an offence committed during the period of conditional discharge; and

(b) has been dealt with in respect of that offence,

that court or justice may, subject to subsection (3) below, issue a summons requiring that person to appear at the place and time specified therein or a warrant for his arrest.

(2) Jurisdiction for the purposes of subsection (1) above may be exercised -

(a) if the order for conditional discharge was made by the Crown Court, by that court;

(b) if the order was made by a magistrates' court, by a justice acting for the petty sessions area for which that court acts.

(3) A justice of the peace shall not issue a summons under this section except on information and shall not issue a warrant under this section except on information in writing and on oath.

(4) A summons or warrant issued under this section shall direct the person to whom it relates to appear or to be brought before the court by which the order for conditional discharge was made.

(5) If a person in whose case an order for conditional discharge has been made by the Crown Court is convicted by a magistrates' court of an offence committed during the period of conditional discharge, the magistrates' court -

(a) may commit him to custody or release him on bail until he can be brought or appear before the Crown Court; and

(b) if it does so, shall send to the Crown Court a copy of the minute or memorandum of the conviction entered in the court register, signed by the clerk of the court by whom the register is kept.

(6) Where it is proved to the satisfaction of the court by which an order for conditional discharge was made that the person in whose case the order was made has been convicted of an offence committed during the period of conditional discharge, the court may deal with him, for the offence for which the order was made, in any manner in which it could deal with him if he had just been convicted by or before that court of that offence.

(7) If a person in whose case an order for conditional discharge has been made by a magistrates' court -

(a) is convicted before the Crown Court of an offence committed during the period of conditional discharge; or

(b) is dealt with by the Crown Court for any such offence in respect of which he was committed for sentence to the Crown Court,

the Crown Court may deal with him, for the offence for which the order was made, in any manner in which the magistrates' court could deal with him if it had just convicted him of that offence.

(8) If a person in whose case an order for conditional discharge has been made by a magistrates' court is convicted by another magistrates' court of any offence committed during the period of conditional discharge, that other court may, with the consent of the court which made the order, deal with him, for the offence for which the order was made, in any manner in which the court could deal with him if it had just convicted him of that offence.

(9) Where an order for conditional discharge has been made by a

magistrates' court in the case of an offender under eighteen years of age in respect of an offence triable only on indictment in the case of an adult, any powers exercisable under subsection (6), (7) or (8) above by that or any other court in respect of the offender after he has attained the age of eighteen years shall be those which would be exercisable if that offence were an offence triable either way and had been tried summarily.

(10) For the purposes of this section the age of an offender at a particular time shall be deemed to be or to have been that it appears to the court after considering any available evidence to be or to have been his age at that time.

[Section 1B PCCA 1973 as inserted by s8(3) and Schedule 1 CJA 1991]

Effect of discharge

1C.- (1) Subject to subsection (2) below and to section 50(1A) of the Criminal Appeal Act 1968 and section 108(1A) of the Magistrates' Courts Act 1980, a conviction of an offence for which the order is made under this Part of this Act discharging the offender absolutely or conditionally shall be deemed not to be a conviction for any purpose other than -

(a) the purposes of the proceedings in which the order is made and of any subsequent proceedings which may be taken against the offender under the following provisions of this Act; and

(b) the purposes of section 1(2)(bb) Children and Young Persons Act 1969.

(2) Where the offender was of or over eighteen years of age at the time of his conviction of the offence in question and is subsequently sentenced under this Part of this Act for that offence, subsection (1) above shall cease to apply to the conviction.

(3) Without prejudice to the preceding provisions of this section, the conviction of an offender who is discharged absolutely or conditionally under this Part of this Act shall in any event be disregarded for the purposes of any enactment or instrument which -

(a) imposes any disqualification or disability upon convicted persons; or

(b) authorises or requires the imposition of any such disqualification or disability.

(4) The preceding provisions of this section shall not affect -

(a) any right of any offender discharged absolutely or conditionally under this Part of this Act to rely on his conviction in bar of any subsequent proceedings for the same offence; or

(b) the restoration of any property in consequence of the conviction of any such offender; or

(c) the operation, in relation to any such offender, of any enactment or instrument in force at the commencement of this Act which is expressed to extend to persons dealt with under section 1(1) of the Probation of Offenders Act 1907 as well as to convicted persons.

(5) In this section 'enactment' includes an enactment contained in a local Act and 'instrument' means an instrument having effect by virtue of an Act.

[Section 1C PCCA 1973 as amended by s8(3) and Schedule 1 CJA 1991]

Schedule 12 TRANSITIONAL PROVISIONS AND SAVINGS

Custodial and community sentences

1. Each of sections 1 to 13 of this Act shall apply in relation to offenders convicted (but not sentenced) before the commencement of that section as it applies in relation to offenders convicted after that commencement.

2. Neither subsection (2) of section 8 of this Act, nor the repeal by this Act of section 13 of the 1973 Act, shall affect the operation of section 13 in relation to persons placed on probation before the commencement of that subsection or, as the case may be, that repeal.

3. An establishment which immediately before the commencement of Part II of Schedule 1 to this Act is a day centre within the meaning of section 4B of the 1973 Act shall be treated as if, immediately after the commencement, it had been approved by the Secretary of State as a probation centre within the meaning of paragraph 3(7) of Schedule 1A to that Act.

4. Paragraph 6 of Schedule 11 to this Act shall apply in relation to offenders convicted (but not sentenced) before the commencement of that paragraph as it applies to offenders convicted after that commencement.

Community orders: supplemental

5.- (1) Paragraphs 3 and 4 of Schedule 2 to this Act shall apply in relation to pre-existing failures to comply with the requirements of probation orders or community service orders as if, in sub-paragraph (1)(a), for "£1,000" there were substituted "£400".

(2) In this paragraph "pre-existing", in relation to either of those paragraphs, means occuring before the commencement of that paragraph.

Financial penalties

6. None of sections 17 to 20 of this Act shall apply in relation to offences committed before the commencement of that section.

Increase in certain penalties

7. Neither of subsections (3) and (4) of section 26 of this Act shall apply in relation to offences committed before the commencement of that subsection.

Early release: general

8.-(1) In this paragraph and paragraphs 9 to 11 below -
"existing licensee" means any person who, before the commencement of Part II of this Act, has been released on licence under section 60 of the 1967 Act and whose licence under that section is in force at that commencement;
"existing prisoner" means any person who, at that commencement, is serving a custodial sentence;
and sub-paragraphs (2) to (7) below shall have effect subject to those paragraphs.

(2) Subject to sub-paragraphs (3) to (7) below, Part II of this Act shall apply in relation to an existing licensee as it applies in relation to a person who is released on licence under this Part; and in its application to an existing prisoner, or to an existing licensee who is recalled under section 39 of this Act, that Part shall apply with the modifications made by those sub-paragraphs.

(3) Section 40 of this Act shall not apply in relation to an existing prisoner or licensee.

(4) In relation to an existing prisoner whose sentence is for a term of twelve

months, section 33(1) of this Act shall apply as if that sentence were for a term of less than twelve months.

(5) In relation to an existing prisoner or licensee whose sentence is for a term of -

(a) more than twelve months; and

(b) less than four years or, as the case may require, such other period as may for the time being be referred to in s33(5) of the Act,

Part II of this Act shall apply as if he were or had been a long-term rather than a short-term prisoner.

(6) In relation to an existing prisoner or licensee whose sentence is for a term of more than 12 months -

(a) section 35(1) of this Act shall apply as if the reference to one half of his sentence were a reference to one-third of that sentence or six months, whichever is the longer; and

(b) sections 33(3) and 37(1) of this Act shall apply as if the reference to three-quarters of his sentence were a reference to two-thirds of that sentence.

(7) In relation to an existing prisoner or licensee -

(a) whose sentence is for a term of more than twelve months; and

(b) whose case falls within such class of cases as the Secretary of State may determine after consultation with the Parole Board,

section 35(1) of this Act shall apply as if the reference to a recommendation by the Board included a reference to a recommendation by a local review committee established under section 59(6) of the 1967 Act.

(8) In this paragraph "custodial sentence" means -

(a) a sentence of imprisonment;

(b) a sentence of detention in a young offender institution;

(c) a sentence of detention (whether during Her Majesty's pleasure, for life or for a determinate term) under section 53 of the 1933 Act; or

(d) a sentence of custody for life under section 8 of the 1982 Act.

9. - (1) This paragraph applies where, in the case of an existing life prisoner, the Secretary of State certifies his opinion that, if -

(a) section 34 of this Act had been in force at the time when he was sentenced; and

(b) the reference in subsection (1)(a) of that section to a violent or sexual offence the sentence for which is not fixed by law were a reference to any offence the sentence for which is not so fixed,

the court by which he was sentenced would have ordered that that section should apply to him as soon as he had served a part of his sentence specified in the certificate.

(2) In a case to which this paragraph applies, Part II of this Act except section 35(2) shall apply as if -

(a) the existing life prisoner were a discretionary life prisoner for the purposes of that Part; and

(b) the relevant part of his sentence within the meaning of section 34 of this Act were the part specified in the certificate.

(3) In this paragraph "existing life prisoner" means a person who, at the commencement of Part II of this Act, is serving one or more of the following sentences, namely -

(a) a sentence of life imprisonment;

(b) a sentence of detention during Her Majesty's pleasure or for life under section 53 of the 1933 Act; or

(c) a sentence of custody for life under section 8 of the 1982 Act.

(4) A person serving two or more such sentences shall not be treated as a

discretionary life prisoner for the purposes of Part II of this Act unless the requirements of sub-paragraph (1) above are satisfied as respects each of those sentences; and subsections (3) and (5) of section 34 of this Act shall not apply in relation to such a person until after he has served the relevant part of each of those sentences.

10. Prison rules made by virtue of section 42 of this Act may include provision for applying any provisions of Part II of this Act, in relation to any existing prisoner or licensee who has forfeited any remission of his sentence, as if he had been awarded such number of additional days as may be determined by or under the rules.

Early release of young persons detained under 1933 Act

11. In relation to an existing prisoner or licensee whose sentence is a determinate sentence of detention under section 53 of the 1933 Act -

(a) Part II of this Act shall apply as if he were or had been a life rather than a long-term prisoner;

(b) section 35(2) of this Act shall apply as if the requirement as to consultation were omitted; and

(c) section 37(3) of this Act shall apply as if the reference to his death were a reference to the date on which he would (but for his release) have served the whole of his sentence.

Early release of prisoners serving extended sentences

12. - (1) In relation to an existing prisoner or licensee on the passing of whose sentence an extended sentence certificate was issued -

(a) section 33(3) of this Act shall apply as if the duty to release him unconditionally were a duty to release him on licence; and

(b) section 37(1) of this Act shall apply as if the reference to three-quarters of his sentence were a reference to the whole of that sentence.

(2) In this paragraph "extended sentence certificate" means a certificate issued under section 28 of the 1973 Act stating that an extended term of imprisonment was imposed on an offender under that section.

Early release of fine defaulters and contemnors

13. Part II of this Act shall apply in relation to any person who, before the commencement of that Part, has been committed to prison or to be detained under section 9 of the 1982 Act -

(a) in default of payment of a sum adjudged to be paid by a conviction; or

(b) for contempt of court or any kindred offence,

as it applies in relation to any person who is committed after that commencement.

Responsibilities of parent or guardian 14.- [Paragraph 14 is reproduced in *Chapter 6* of *The Youth Court*]. *Remands and committals of children and young persons* 15.- [Paragraphs 15 and 16 are reproduced in *Chapter 8* of *The Youth Court*]. *Custodial sentences for young offenders* 17.- [Paragraphs 17 and 18 are reproduced in *Chapter 5A* of *The Youth Court*]. *Supervision of young offenders after release* 19.- [Paragraph 19 is reproduced in *Chapter 5A* of *The Youth Court*]. *Supervision orders* 20.- [Paragraph 20 is reproduced in *Chapter 5C* of *The Youth Court*].

Attendance centre orders

21.-(1) Subsection (2) of section 67 of this Act shall not apply in relation to attendance centre orders made before the commencement of that section.

(2) Subsection (4) of that section shall not apply in relation to pre-existing failures to attend in accordance with an attendance centre order or pre-existing breaches of rules made under section 16(3) of the 1982 Act.

(3) In this paragraph "pre-existing" means occuring or committed before that commencement.

NOTE Para 21(1) Section 67(2) CJA 91 inserts a new s18(4A) CJA 82 so as to empower courts, on discharging an attendance centre order, to sentence afresh for the original offence.

Provisions for treating persons aged 17 as young persons 22.- [Paragraph 22 is reproduced in *Chapter 4* of *The Youth Court*]. Renaming of juvenile courts etc. 23.- [Paragraph 23 is reproduced in *Chapter 1* of *The Youth Court*].

Supplemental
24.- For the purposes of this Schedule proceedings for an offence shall be regarded as having begun as follows -
(a) in the case of an offence triable only summarily, when a plea is entered;
(b) in the case of an offence triable only on indictment, when the magistrates' court begins to inquire into the offence as examining magistrates;
(c) in the case of an offence triable either way, when the magistrates' court determines to proceed with the summary trial of the offence or, as the case may be, to proceed to inquire into the offence as examining justices.

Criminal Justice Act 1991 (Commencement No.1) Order SI 1991 2208 [Extract - Summarised]

Readers are referred to the above statutory instrument, to which the following information serves as a reminder. Schedule 1: Provisions effective 14 October 1991: s60(3), s99(1) (part), s100 and sched 11 (part), s101(1) and sched 12 (part), s102, para 36 of sched 11, para 23 of sched 12. Schedule 2: Provisions effective 25 October 1991: s26(3) (part), s101(1) and sched 12 (part), para 7 of sched 12. Schedule 3: Provisions effective 31 October 1991: s26(4), (5), s73, s74, s80 to 91, s92(1), s93 to 96, s98, s100 and sched 11 (part), s101(2) and sched 13 (part), sched 10, sched 11 (part), sched 13 (part).

Criminal Justice Act 1991 (Commencement No.2) Order [Scotland] SI 2706 Not reproduced.

Legal Points under the Criminal Justice Act 1991

Index